CONTEMPORARY'S

PRE-GED

SOCIAL STUDIES

McGraw Hill Wright Group

Wright Group

Send all inquiries to:
Wright Group/McGraw-Hill
130 E. Randolph, Suite 400
Chicago, IL 60681

ISBN 0-07-252762-5

6 7 8 9 10 QPD 08 07

The McGraw·Hill Companies

Table of Contents

PART I: CRITICAL THINKING SKILLS IN SOCIAL STUDIES

PART II: UNDERSTANDING SOCIAL STUDIES

CHAPTER 6   World History   151

CHAPTER 7   Civics and Government   199

Acknowledgments

Cartoon on page 6 by Dick Locher. © Tribune Media Services, Inc. All rights reserved. Used with permission.

Cartoon on page 74 by David Hardin Cox. Courtesy the *Morning News of Northwest Arkansas*.

Cartoons on pages 75 and 76 by Jerry Barnett. Reprinted courtesy of the *Indianapolis News*.

Exerpt on page 117 from *The Story of Alice Paul and the National Woman's Party*, originally entitled *Up Hill With Banners Flying*, by Inez Haynes Irwin. Reprinted courtesy of the National Women's Party.

Excerpt on page 128 by Studs Terkel, *Hard Times: An Oral History of the Great Depression*. New York: Random House, 1970.

Cartoon on page 136 by Denny Pritchard. Reprinted by permission of Ms. Margaret Pritchard.

Excerpt on page 145 from "Restoration: New Ideas, New Understanding, New Hope" by Michael Parfit, *National Geographic magazine*, November 1993. Reprinted by permission of the National Geographic Society.

Graphic on page 256, "Colorado River Basin" by Andrew De Vigal and Terry Vopp from the *Chicago Tribune*, July 24, 1994. Reprinted by permission of the Chicago Tribune.

Cartoon on page 298 by Ed Stein. Reprinted by permission of the *Rocky Mountain News*.

Cartoon on page 305 by Mike Smith, *USA Today*. Reprinted by permission.

Cartoon on page 306 by Richard Crowson, *The Jackson Sun*. Reprinted by permission.

To The Student

Congratulations on your decision to use Pre-GED Social Studies to strengthen your critical-thinking skills in comprehending, applying, analyzing, and evaluating social studies materials. You will also learn how to read and understand passages, graphs, charts, and maps in the content areas of U.S. history, world history, civics & government, geography, and economics.

Here is an overview of what you will find in this book, along with some tips on using the book.

Social Studies Pretest—The Pretest, found on pages 1–13, will help you decide which skills you need to work on the most. It will direct you to the parts of the book you may want to spend the most time with.

Chapter 1: Comprehending Social Studies Materials—By working through Chapter 1, you will review how to find the main idea of passages and pictographs, find details in passages and circle graphs, recognize an unstated main idea, and look for context clues.

Chapter 2: Applying Social Studies Ideas—In this chapter you will learn how to apply what you read in passages, maps, and bar graphs to new situations.

Chapter 3: Analyzing Social Studies Materials—This chapter teaches you how to recognize the patterns in which information is presented, such as comparison and contrast, cause and effect, and sequence of events. You will also learn how to interpret ideas in line graphs, how to make inferences, how to draw conclusions, and how to recognize the difference between fact and opinion.

Chapter 4: Evaluating Social Studies Materials—In this chapter you will learn how to judge information presented to you, evaluate a writer's logic, infer tone, and analyze editorial cartoons.

Chapter 5: U.S. History—This chapter presents a brief survey of important events in America from the 1400s through the present. You will learn about foreign and domestic policy, important eras, major trends, and movements for social change.

Chapter 6: World History—This chapter presents a brief overview of important groups and events in world history. The chapter begins by discussing the first river valley civilizations, and continues up until the 21st century

Chapter 7: Civics & Government—This chapter presents an overview of various types of government, the American political process, interest groups and political parties, the U.S. Constitution, branches and duties of federal, state, and local government, and international relations.

Chapter 8: Geography—In this chapter you will learn about the elements of geography, various land regions, population and migration, urban growth, and how to read different types of maps.

Chapter 9: Economics—This chapter introduces you to the topics that economists study, such as early economic systems, how the economy works, how businesses behave, financial institutions, the federal reserve system, the stock market, and the government's role and consumers' role in the economy.

Writing Activities—Every chapter allows you an opportunity to write about various social studies topics and, in this way, improve your writing skills.

Pre-GED Practice—At the end of every chapter, and sometimes more frequently throughout the book, you will find exercises that are formatted as five-item multiple-choice questions to help you prepare for GED-level study. The Pre-GED Practice at the end of each chapter serves as a review of the skills you have learned in that chapter.

Reading Efficiency Activities—This book contains **Reading Efficiency Activities** to help you practice reading speed and accuracy in order to achieve an optimum reading efficiency level. When you take the GED Test, you will be limited to a certain amount of time for each exam and must receive a minimum passing score to obtain your GED certificate. Because of this, it is important that you read at an acceptable rate while comprehending what you read. The Reading Efficiency Activities provide you with the tools to practice those skills and chart your progress.

There are ten Reading Efficiency Activities in this book. For each activity, you should time yourself as you read a 200 to 400-word passage and answer the 5 questions that follow. When you finish, you should record the time it took you to complete the activity and check your answers using the answer key provided in the back of the book.

Efficiency Factor (E-Factor) Chart

Once you complete a Reading Efficiency Activity, you can determine your Efficiency Factor (E-Factor) by using the E-Factor Chart on page 340. This chart provides a quick and easy way for you to determine your level of efficiency for each activity. The E-Factor takes into account an optimum reading rate and score for success on the actual GED Test. By locating your completion time on the vertical axis and your score on the horizontal axis, you can quickly determine your E-Factor. You should aim to achieve an optimum E-Factor of 100 or higher. The optimum range is located in the shaded areas of the chart.

Efficiency Factor Plotting Grid

Once you have located your E-Factor on the chart, you should plot it on the Efficiency Factor Grid on page 341. Possible E-Factor scores are listed on the vertical axis with each activity listed across the horizontal axis. Every point above 100 is shaded so you can instantly see when you have achieved an optimum E-Factor. As each Reading Efficiency Activity is completed and plotted, you can connect the dots to create a graph of your progress.

Social Studies Posttest—The Posttest, found on pages 297–316, will help you to see how well you have learned the critical-thinking and reading skills presented in this book. The Posttest consists of 50 multiple-choice questions.

Answer Key—This feature gives answers and explanations for all the questions in this book. Use the Answer Key only after you have attempted to answer a set of questions in an exercise.

Glossary—Throughout the book, key terms that are important for you to know are printed in boldface and italic type and are defined either in keyword boxes or in the glossary at the back of the book.

Good luck with your studies! Keep in mind that knowing how to read and analyze social studies materials is worth learning for many reasons.

Social Studies

The Social Studies Pretest that follows is a guide to using this book. You should take the Pretest before you begin working on any of the chapters. The test consists of 25 multiple-choice questions that test the social studies reading and reasoning skills covered in this book. All of the questions are based on charts, graphs, diagrams, and reading passages.

Answer each question as carefully as possible. Choose the best of the five answer choices by filling in the corresponding circle on the answer grid. If a question is too difficult, go ahead and come back to that question later. When you have completed the test, check your answers on pages 11–12.

Using the Evaluation Chart on page 13, circle the number of each question that you missed. If you missed many of the questions that correspond to a certain reading skill, you will want to pay special attention to that skill as you work through this book.

Pretest Answer Grid

	①	②	③	④	⑤			①	②	③	④	⑤			①	②	③	④	⑤
1	①	②	③	④	⑤		10	①	②	③	④	⑤		19	①	②	③	④	⑤
2	①	②	③	④	⑤		11	①	②	③	④	⑤		20	①	②	③	④	⑤
3	①	②	③	④	⑤		12	①	②	③	④	⑤		21	①	②	③	④	⑤
4	①	②	③	④	⑤		13	①	②	③	④	⑤		22	①	②	③	④	⑤
5	①	②	③	④	⑤		14	①	②	③	④	⑤		23	①	②	③	④	⑤
6	①	②	③	④	⑤		15	①	②	③	④	⑤		24	①	②	③	④	⑤
7	①	②	③	④	⑤		16	①	②	③	④	⑤		25	①	②	③	④	⑤
8	①	②	③	④	⑤		17	①	②	③	④	⑤							
9	①	②	③	④	⑤		18	①	②	③	④	⑤							

Question 1 refers to the following passage.

1. In 1968, Congress passed the Truth in Lending Act. This act requires that lenders tell people buying on credit the annual percentage rates for interest and the total interest charges over the life of the loan. This act is an example of which of the following?

   (1) consumer protection laws
   (2) Congress following a policy of economic protectionism
   (3) Congress making laws that control profit
   (4) the Federal Reserve trying to control credit
   (5) a government policy that lets lenders do as they please

Questions 2 and 3 refer to the following passage.

The Fall Line is the boundary between the eastern coastal plain and the foothills of the Piedmont. The Fall Line had a great influence on early settlement patterns in the eastern United States. Barge traffic from the coast had to stop at the Fall Line because of steep waterfalls and rapids in the rivers. This forced traders to move larger bulk cargo from riverboats into smaller batches that could be carried overland. Towns grew where such changes were made.

In addition, the water power provided by the falls and rapids along the Fall Line was put to industrial use. As a result, textile and shoe manufacturing plants, lumber mills, and other industries grew. This allowed for further growth of towns and cities.

2. The Fall Line was important to early towns in the eastern United States because of which of the following?

   (1) It provided water for drinking.
   (2) It protected towns from flooding.
   (3) It helped river navigation.
   (4) It provided water power for industry.
   (5) It prohibited all land travel.

3. Based on this passage, which of the following can you conclude?

   (1) Climate determines city location.
   (2) Geographic factors that aid economic activity can influence a town's location.
   (3) Geographic factors do not affect a city's location.
   (4) Westward expansion was blocked by the Fall Line.
   (5) The Fall Line was responsible for new methods of transportation.

PRETEST

Questions 4 and 5 refer to the following passage.

The Articles of Confederation were passed by the Continental Congress in 1781 as the constitutional framework for the new United States. The articles gave a great deal of power to the states and relatively little power to the central, or federal, government. Later developments proved that the new federal government was too weak to deal with securing the country's frontiers, creating a strong military defense, protecting trade, and handling unrest during the troubled 1780s.

Most of the leaders of the revolution were worried about the ineffective federal government. They called for a Constitutional Convention to develop a constitutional framework with a stronger federal government. They hoped to keep the United States from breaking up into separate countries. The convention was held in 1787. A new constitution was then written that established a strong federal government.

4. Why were the Articles of Confederation replaced?

   (1) They gave too much power to the president.
   (2) They gave too much power to the federal government.
   (3) They displeased the states.
   (4) They created an all-powerful national government.
   (5) They created a weak and ineffective federal government.

5. You can infer from this passage that the leaders of the revolution supported a more centralized system. Why is that so?

   (1) They wanted to protect the nation's survival.
   (2) They wanted to have political power for themselves.
   (3) They wanted to establish the president with power like a king's.
   (4) They wanted to have the United States become a world power.
   (5) They wanted to protect their own wealth and investments.

Question 6 is based on the following passage.

The American political system is often described as pluralist. A pluralistic system gets its strength from the large number of interest groups that take part in politics. These groups must share power and make compromises to get things done.

6. Which of the following would be characteristic of decision making in such a system?

   (1) Political decisions are always made quickly.
   (2) One group always tends to dominate the process.
   (3) No single group wins all the time.
   (4) There is little political conflict and argument.
   (5) Political parties play a small role.

Questions 7 and 8 refer to the following chart.

FEDERAL GOVERNMENT EXPENDITURES

Defense	19.6%
Medicare	9.0%
Health Care services and research	7.1%
Social Security	20.7%
Income Security	14.1%
Veterans Benefits	2.4%
Education, Training, and Employment	3.5%
Transportation	2.4%
Science, Space, and Technology	1.2%
Interest on public debt	20.1%

Source: American Almanac: Statistical Abstract of the United States, for 1993

*Includes housing assistance, food and nutrition assistance, unemployment compensation, and federal employees' retirement

7. Many social scientists agree that one important way to determine the real priorities of a society is to examine how it spends its money. Based on the chart, which does the federal government place the highest priority on?

   (1) national defense
   (2) Social Security
   (3) Medicare
   (4) education, training, and employment
   (5) paying interest on the national debt

8. Which of the following can you infer from the chart?

   (1) More Americans are living longer and require old-age benefits.
   (2) Paying off the national debt is the country's top priority.
   (3) The nation's concern for education is reflected in the federal budget.
   (4) A large number of Americans move or travel to different locations.
   (5) The expenditure for the space program has expanded over the past twenty years.

Questions 9 and 10 refer to the following passage.

Today, almost all U.S. citizens, age eighteen and over, have the legal right to vote. However, this was not always the case. The Constitution originally let the states determine qualifications for voting. The right to vote was at first limited to white male property owners.

Property qualifications were gradually eliminated. By 1830 most white males over the age of twenty-one could vote. African Americans gained the legal right to vote from the Fifteenth Amendment in 1870. Women gained the right to vote with the Nineteenth Amendment in 1919.

Some states still tried to deny African Americans the right to vote. Poll taxes, literacy tests, and sometimes scare tactics were used to keep African Americans from voting.

The poll tax on voting in federal elections was finally erased by the Twenty-fourth Amendment in 1962. The Voting Rights Act of 1965 guaranteed the right to vote to all citizens, regardless of race or sex.

PRETEST

9. What provision did the Constitution first make for voter qualifications?

   (1) It gave all white adult males the right to vote.
   (2) It gave all citizens the right to vote.
   (3) It left it up to the Supreme Court to decide.
   (4) It left it to the states to set qualifications.
   (5) It gave all property owners the right to vote.

10. What is the main idea of this passage?

    (1) Equality in voting rights has always been a principle of American democracy.
    (2) Voting rights have been granted to all groups without struggle.
    (3) The right to vote was not won by all citizens at the same time, but over time and with much social conflict.
    (4) The Voting Rights Act was the most important legislation of the 1960s.
    (5) Without the Fifteenth Amendment, women and African Americans would still not have the right to vote.

Question 11 is based on the following passage.

The "golden age" of Greece has several distinguishing characteristics. The Greeks developed a type of government called a democracy where people ruled themselves. Only free men, however were allowed to participate. Ancient Greece was made up of city-states. Not all of these city-states were democracies, and they spent much of their energy fighting each other. Distinctive architecture that is still copied to this day was also characteristic of Greece's "golden age". Greek philosophers asked hard questions about the meaning of life and the role of citizens in a society. Their thinking is still widely read and highly regarded today.

11. What is a possible explanation for why the Greek "golden age" ended?

    (1) Women and slaves were not allowed to participate in the democracy.
    (2) Greece lacked a strong central figure like a pharaoh.
    (3) Greek philosophers' thinking quickly became outdated.
    (4) The city-states' constant fighting weakened them.
    (5) The city-states could not agree on a type of government.

Question 12 refers to the following passage.

Imperialism is the total domination of one country over another. Similarly, colonization is the act of one country taking direct control over another. In the 1800s and 1900s many European nations established colonies in India, Africa, China and South America.

12. Given the fact that the Industrial Revolution was happening in Europe during the 1800s and 1900s, why were European nations able to establish colonies in other parts of the world?

(1) They wanted to learn about other cultures.
(2) They were willing to share their wealth.
(3) They were technologically more advanced.
(4) They feared of the spread of communism.
(5) Foreign governments were willing to be dominated.

Question 13 refers to the following passage.

One of the most important factors affecting home purchases is the interest rate on mortgages. Some economists say that each 1 percent increase in mortgage interest rates makes homes unaffordable to more than 1 million families. The effects of this were clearly seen in 1983. Declining mortgage rates in early 1983 increased home sales very rapidly. The rates dropped in May to around 12 ½ percent. By August they had climbed to almost 14 percent. Economists said that 2.4 million families could no longer afford to buy homes. This slowed home sales by 35 percent.

13. Based on the details in this passage, what can you conclude about a continuing rise in mortgage interest rates?

(1) It would cause an increase in home sales.
(2) It would not affect home sales.

(3) It would not affect the price of homes.
(4) It would cause more homes to be built.
(5) It would cause a decrease in home sales

Questions 14 and 15 refer to the following cartoon.

14. What is the main idea of the cartoon?

(1) The economy needs tinkering with.
(2) Taxes will stay where they are until the economy catches up.
(3) Taxes will get a faster start than the economy.
(4) The economy is large while taxes are small.
(5) The tax-collecting machinery is always ready to work.

15. How would you describe the condition of the U.S. economy as represented by the truck?

(1) large and operating efficiently
(2) small and probably not working well
(3) shrinking in size but working well
(4) large but not working as well as it should
(5) in complete disrepair

Questions 16 and 17 refer to the following chart.

WORLD'S 20 MOST POPULOUS COUNTRIES: 1993 AND 2025

	1993			2025	
Rank	Country	Population	Rank	Country	Population
1.	China	1,178,500,000	1.	China	1,546,300,000
2.	India	897,400,000	2.	India	1,379,600,000
3.	United States	258,300,000	3.	United States	334,700,000
4.	Indonesia	187,600,000	4.	Indonesia	278,200,000
5.	Brazil	152,000,000	5.	Pakistan	275,100,000
6.	Russia	149,000,000	6.	Nigeria	246,000,000
7.	Japan	124,800,000	7.	Bangladesh	211,200,000
8.	Pakistan	122,400,000	8.	Brazil	205,300,000
9.	Bangladesh	113,900,000	9.	Iran	161,900,000
10.	Nigeria	95,100,000	10.	Russia	152,300,000
11.	Mexico	90,000,000	11.	Ethiopia*	140,800,000
12.	Germany	81,100,000	12.	Mexico	137,500,000
13.	Vietnam	71,800,000	13.	Japan	125,800,000
14.	Philippines	64,600,000	14.	Vietnam	107,200,000
15.	Iran	62,800,000	15.	Egypt	104,600,000
16.	Turkey	60,700,000	16.	Zaire	104,500,000
17.	Egypt	58,300,000	17.	Philippines	100,800,000
18.	United Kingdom	58,000,000	18.	Turkey	98,700,000
19.	Italy	57,800,000	19.	Tanzania	73,000,000
20.	France	57,700,000	20.	South Africa	70,000,000

Source: 1993 World Population Data Sheet of the Population Reference Bureau, Inc.
*includes Eritrea

16. Comparing the two lists, which country will no longer be among the top ten most populous countries in the year 2025?

(1) China
(2) United States
(3) Japan
(4) Nigeria
(5) Brazil

17. Which of the following might be a logical explanation for the United Kingdom dropping from the list by the year 2025?

(1) low birthrate in the United Kingdom and higher birthrates in other countries
(2) high birthrate in the United Kingdom and lower birthrates in other countries
(3) low birthrate in the United Kingdom and lower birthrates in other countries
(4) high death rates in the United Kingdom caused by bubonic plague
(5) strict government birth control measures

Questions 18 and 19 refer to the following passage.

James Watt's invention of the steam engine fueled the Industrial Revolution. During the 1800s, steam-driven machines started to do the work that was done by human hands.

18. What was the significance of the invention of the steam engine?

   (1) Without it, the Industrial Revolution would not have occurred.
   (2) Its effects only lasted for a short period of time.
   (3) The Industrial Revolution led to its development.
   (4) It was one of the first technological advancements to spur the Industrial Revolution.
   (5) The steam engine is still used today.

19. What would the reaction of factory workers to the steam engine most likely have been?

   (1) relief that their jobs would become easier
   (2) fear that they would lose their jobs
   (3) confusion about what the steam engine could do
   (4) surprise that it had not been invented sooner
   (5) excitement about its potential

Question 20 is based on the following passage.

During the 1970s and 1980s, there were several federal court decisions concerning the powers of the president and Congress. In the Watergate affair, the courts ruled that the president could not claim executive privilege as a reason to keep certain information from Congress. In 1983, the Supreme Court halted the use of the so-called legislative veto, which had been used by Congress to control and limit many actions of the executive branch.

20. The series of events described in the passage demonstrates that the separation of powers provided for under the Constitution is actually which of the following?

   (1) very dictatorial
   (2) too rigid
   (3) not guiding the government efficiently
   (4) flexible and open to interpretation and change
   (5) the weakest part of the Constitution

PRETEST

Question 21 refers to the following passage.

In the 1880s and 1890s, many American small farmers were driven off the land or forced to become tenants by changing economic conditions. They formed protest organizations and demanded government reforms. They thought reforms would save the small farmers and their way of life, but their efforts were unsuccessful. The small farmers continued to decline in number as agriculture became more mechanized, and larger farms took over the small ones.

21. The American small farmer of the late nineteenth century was a member of which group?

    (1) the upwardly mobile social class
    (2) the rich elite
    (3) the powerful majority
    (4) the social class in decline
    (5) the revolutionary social class

Questions 22 and 23 refer to the map below.

RAILROADS IN THE EASTERN UNITED STATES, 1860

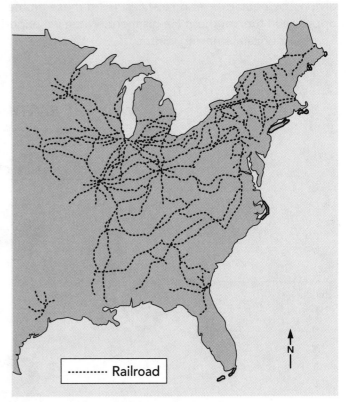

- - - - - - - Railroad

N

22. What does the map show?

    (1) branches of the Mississippi River
    (2) state boundaries in 1860
    (3) the first telegraph lines
    (4) U.S. railroads in the East in 1860
    (5) major highways in 1860

23. What can you infer from this map?

    (1) The Northeast had more commerce and industry than the Southeast.
    (2) River travel was more extensive in the Northeast.
    (3) Communication among cities in the Northeast was not well developed by 1860.
    (4) Few highways had been built in the Southeast.
    (5) Texas was not yet a state in 1860.

Questions 24 and 25 are based on the passage and diagram below.

Most parts of the world experience four seasons—spring, summer, fall, and winter. The seasons are divided by equinoxes and solstices. (Find these on the diagram below.) All four seasons are the opposite in the Southern Hemisphere. When we experience summer in the United States, people in South America are having winter.

WHY THE EARTH HAS SEASONS

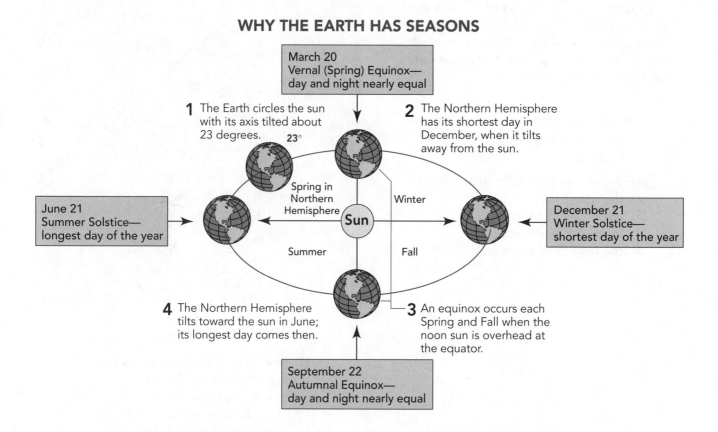

24. Why does the Northern Hemisphere have its shortest day of the year on December 21?

(1) because at that time the Northern Hemisphere is tilted toward, the sun
(2) because at that time the Northern Hemisphere is tilted away from the sun
(3) because at that time an equinox marks the beginning of winter
(4) because at that time a solstice marks the beginning of summer
(5) because at that time the sun's rays are directly over the equator

25. If you were an avid skier, on which date would you find the most snow-covered ski slopes in the Southern Hemisphere?

(1) December 21
(2) January 21
(3) March 20
(4) June 21
(5) September 22

PRETEST

Answer Key

1. (1) People who buy things are consumers. The question tells you that the Truth in Lending Act requires that lenders tell the truth to buyers. Therefore, the people protected by this legislation are consumers.

2. (4) The second paragraph of the passage says that water power along the Fall Line was put to work for industry.

3. (2) The passage shows that towns grew up along the Fall Line because of industry's need for power.

4. (5) The passage refers to the federal government as having "little power" and as being "too weak" and "ineffective."

5. (1) The third sentence lists the problems faced by the new nation. These problems suggest that survival was at stake. There is no evidence in the passage for the other choices.

6. (3) The last sentence says that "These groups must share power and make compromises to get things done." This sentence suggests that all groups get some of what they want but that no single group dominates.

7. (2) The most money is spent on Social Security, so choice (2) is the best answer. The other choices relate to categories with lower percentages of federal spending.

8. (1) With Social Security representing nearly 20.7 percent of the budget, you can infer choice (1).

9. (4) The third sentence says that it left it to the states to decide voting qualifications.

10. (3) The passage tells you how several different groups gained the right to vote, all at different times. It also describes the obstacles that African Americans faced in exercising this right.

11. (4) Although statements (1), (2), and (4) are all characteristics of ancient Greece, the city-states' constant fighting is the most probable cause for the end of the "golden-age." Because Greek philosophers are still studied today, it cannot be said that their thinking became outdated (3). There is nothing in the passage to indicate that the city-states tried to agree on a type of government (5).

12. (3) The fact that the 1800s and 1900s were the time of the Industrial Revolution in Europe implies that Europe was able to dominate other countries because they were technologically more advanced. Europe's domination of other countries does not imply they wanted to learn about other cultures (1) or that they wanted to share their wealth (2). Communism (4) was not yet a factor in world politics at this time, nor is it suggested in the passage. The passage also does not indicate that countries in Africa, South America, China, and Asia were willing to be dominated (5).

13. (5) When mortgage interest rates rise, fewer families can afford to buy homes, and sales fall.

14. (3) The race car symbol shows that taxes are ready to go—very likely upward while the economy lags behind.

15. (4) The driver looking under the hood of the truck shows that the economy may need some work. The large truck, however, is still in one piece, and none of its tires is flat.

16. (3) Japan dropped from a rank of 7 in 1993 to 13 in 2025. The other countries remained in the top ten.

17. (1) Only a low birth rate in the United Kingdom and a higher birth rate in other countries (most of which had larger populations) explain the dropping of the United Kingdom from the list. Choices (4) and (5) cannot be predicted.

18. (4) The passage states that the steam engine began an "explosion of technology" that continues to this day. This indicates that its effects have not been temporary (2). The passage also states that it "fueled the Industrial Revolution," not the other way around (3). While the steam engine was key to the Industrial Revolution (1), it cannot be concluded that without it, the Industrial Revolution would not have occurred. Steam engines are not generally used today (5).

19. (2) Generally, inventions that have replaced workers have not been popular among workers themselves, because it usually means that workers will lose their jobs. Since it was a new invention unlike anything that existed at the time, workers were most likely not surprised it had not been invented sooner (4), and most likely did not realize its potential (5). While they may have been confused by it (3), their most likely reaction would have been fear of losing their jobs.

20. (4) The paragraph describes how the courts reinterpret the constitutional balance of power. The other choices are not supported by the information given.

21. (4) The passage describes American small farmers as being part of a declining social class. American small farmers were forced to change their way of life due to massive economic and technological changes.

22. (4) The title of the map shows that choice (4) is correct.

23. (1) The map shows a greater concentration of railroads in the Northeast than in the Southeast. Railroads made the movement of goods and raw materials in the Northeast easier and enabled this region to develop much faster economically than the Southeast.

24. (2) The diagram shows that the shortest day of the year takes place on December 21 because the Northern Hemisphere is tilted at its greatest point away from the sun.

25. (4) The passage says that winter takes place in the Southern Hemisphere while the Northern Hemisphere has its summer, so choice (4), June 21, is correct.

PRETEST
Evaluation Chart

Use the Answer Key on pages 11–12 to check your answers to the Pretest. Then, on the chart below, circle the numbers of the questions you missed.

If you missed many of the questions that correspond to a particular reading skill, you will want to pay special attention to that skill as you work through this book.

Skill Area/ Content Area	Comprehension (pages 17–32)	Application (pages 33–47)	Analysis (pages 49–66)	Evaluation (pages 67–76)
U.S. History (pages 79–149)	4, 22		5	23
World History (pages 151–197)		19	11	12, 18
Civics & Government (pages 199–236)	9, 10		6	20
Geography (pages 237–262)	2, 16, 24		25	3, 17
Economics (pages 263–296)	7, 14		21	1, 8, 13, 15

Critical Thinking Skills in Social Studies

Chapter 1

Comprehending Social Studies Materials

When you comprehend social studies materials, you understand what they mean. Social studies writers always have a purpose in mind. They present an idea to give you information or to convince you of a certain point of view. First, they communicate their main idea. Then, they use details to support and defend this main idea.

Main Idea of Passages

The main idea of a passage or paragraph is usually found in the first sentence. Sometimes it appears elsewhere. In a longer passage, the main idea usually can be found in an introductory or concluding paragraph.

Follow the steps below to identify the main idea.

- Read the entire passage.

- Find out what the passage is about.

- Look for the main idea in the first or last sentence of a paragraph or a passage.

As you read the following passage, look for the main idea.

Direct Military Action

American military leaders did not want to get involved in direct action in Bosnia-Herzegovina during the early 1990s. They knew the American public would not support direct military action. High-level U.S. Defense Department sources reported that military leaders were well aware of the unpopularity of the Vietnam War. In that war, about 58,000 Americans were killed and some 153,000 were wounded. The war cost more than $140 billion. Because of the lack of public support for the Vietnam War, U.S. military leadership urged the administration to be cautious about direct military involvement in Bosnia-Herzegovina.

What is the main idea of the passage?

_____ 1. Military leaders did not want American soldiers to be killed in Bosnia-Herzegovina.

_____ 2. Military leaders were worried about the high cost of military action.

_____ 3. Military leaders wanted to begin direct military action in Bosnia-Herzegovina.

_____ 4. Military leaders were reluctant to urge military action in Bosnia-Herzegovina.

_____ 5. Military leaders believed that public support justified direct military action in Bosnia-Herzegovina.

You were correct if you chose (4), that military leaders *were reluctant to urge military action in Bosnia-Herzegovina*. The last sentence states the main idea of the passage. The rest of the passage supports this central idea. Details are given about the high cost of the war and the great number of Americans killed or wounded in the Vietnam War. These details tell why the Vietnam War became so unpopular in America.

EXERCISE 1

Directions: Read the passage below and then put a check in front of the correct answer to each question.

Teen Suicide

Suicide is now the third highest cause of death among youths 15 to 19 years old. It ranks just behind accidents and homicide. Youth suicide increased nearly 200 percent between 1970 and 1990. One in every 8,000 adolescents commits suicide. From 1 in 7 to 1 in 15 attempt suicide at least once. While public attention has focused on teenage drug abuse and pregnancy, teenage suicide has been increasing at an alarming rate.

1. What is the main idea of the passage?

_____ (1) The increase in teenage suicide is a disturbing new trend.

_____ (2) Drug abuse is the main problem facing American youth.

_____ (3) Pregnancy is a growing problem among teenagers.

_____ (4) Youth problems are on the decline.

2. The most logical follow-up story would answer the question of why more American teenagers are

_____ (1) on drugs

_____ (2) getting pregnant

_____ (3) committing homicides

_____ (4) committing suicide

Answers are on page 317.

Main Idea of Pictographs

Graphs simplify information. Long passages can be confusing and hard to understand, so graphs are used to show information visually.

When you read a graph, look first at all the important features: the title, how the graph is organized, and the key that shows the meaning of the figures, bars, or lines.

Pictographs

One of the easiest graphs to read is a ***pictograph***. It uses a series of symbols to show an amount or a quantity. The graph below shows you what to look for in a pictograph.

YEARLY WORLD OIL PRODUCTION BY REGION
(in millions of tons)

Region	
Middle East	🛢🛢🛢🛢🛢🛢🛢🛢🛢🛢🛢🛢🛢🛢🛢🛢🛢🛢🛢⸗
United States and Canada	🛢🛢🛢🛢🛢🛢🛢🛢🛢🛢
Former U.S.S.R. and Eastern Europe	🛢🛢🛢🛢🛢🛢🛢🛢
Africa	🛢🛢🛢🛢🛢⸗
Latin America and Caribbean	🛢🛢🛢🛢🛢🛢🛢
Western Europe	🛢🛢🛢🛢⸗
East Asia and Australia	🛢🛢🛢🛢🛢⸗

🛢 = 50 million tons of oil

To understand the main idea of a graph, ask yourself

- **What is the topic (title) of the graph?**
  (yearly world oil production by region)

- **What does each symbol represent?**
  (50 million tons of oil—shown in the key)

- **What does the graph compare?**
  (oil production in different regions)

To read the graph, multiply the value that you are given for a symbol by the number of times it appears on the line. In this graph, you multiply 50 times the number of symbols given after each region. This will show how many million tons of oil each region produces yearly. Note that the last symbol on the line after "Africa" stands for ½ (25 million tons of oil).

Based on the graph, fill in the answers to the questions that follow.

1. How much oil was produced by the nations of Africa?

   _____ tons

2. How much oil was produced by the United States and Canada?

   _____ tons

3. Which region produced more oil—the Middle East or the former Soviet Union and Eastern Europe combined? _____

4. Which region produced the least amount of oil?

   _____

5. Which two pairs of regions each produce 400 million tons of oil?

   _____

   _____

To answer the first question, you count the number of oil wells in Africa (6 ½) and multiply the amount times 50. The correct answer is 325 million tons. For the second question, you count the number of oil wells in the United States and Canada and multiply times 50. The correct answer is 500 million tons. For the third question, compare the amount of oil produced by each region. The Middle East produced about 900 million tons of oil (18 ¼ × 50); the former Soviet Union and Eastern Europe produced 400 million tons (8 × 50). So the Middle East is the correct answer. For the fourth question, you can see that Western Europe has fewer oil wells than any other region and thus has produced the least amount of oil. For the fifth question, both the former U.S.S.R. and Eastern Europe combined and Latin America and the Caribbean combined produce 400 million tons of oil each (8 × 50).

EXERCISE 2

Directions: Study the pictograph below and then answer the questions that follow.

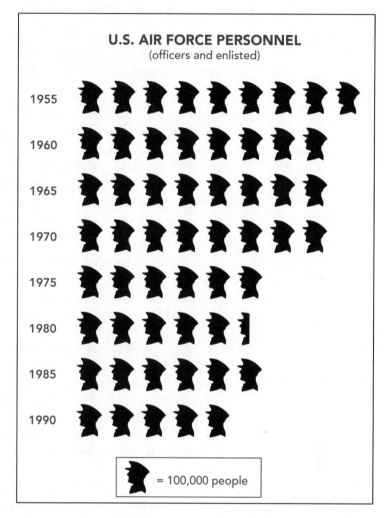

1. How many military personnel were in the U.S. Air Force in 1980?

   _____

2. Which year had the highest number of Air Force personnel?

   _____

3. Which three years showed the number of U.S. Air Force personnel as 800,000?

   _____

4. Which year had the fewest number of U.S. Air Force personnel?

   _____

Answers are on page 317.

Details

Social studies writers support their main idea with *supporting details*. These supporting details expand on the main idea or make it clearer.

For example, if important wars are being presented, the writer might include such details as the dates of each war, the countries involved, the number of casualties suffered, and the causes and outcomes of each war.

Scanning is an important skill to learn. It will help you save time when you are looking for details. *Scanning* is looking over a passage to find a specific detail. Suppose you are reading an article on the history of immigration to the United States. You want to find out quickly from which countries the immigrants came. As you read the following article, focus on the word *immigrant,* and look for references to the countries from which immigrants came to the United States.

A Nation of Immigrants

Scholars believe that the very earliest settlers in what is now the United States crossed over from Asia more than 25,000 years ago. While we think of Native Americans as always having been in the United States, they, too, were immigrants.

The earliest European immigrants came from Spain. They settled in the Southwest and in Florida. In the 1600s, permanent settlers came from northern European countries such as England, the Netherlands, and Germany. Some sought political and religious freedom. Others wanted the opportunity to make a better living for themselves. At the same time, Africans were forcibly carried off from their homeland to work as slaves on large plantations.

After the United States became an independent nation, waves of immigrants came from many different countries. The Chinese and the Irish came for political and economic reasons. In the early twentieth century, many more immigrants came from Italy, Greece, Russia, and other European countries. Recent immigrants have come to the United States from Mexico, Central America, and the countries of Asia looking for better jobs and political freedom.

EXERCISE 3

Directions: Scan the passage on page 22. Circle T for each true statement, or F for each false statement.

T F 1. The earliest immigrants probably came from Asia.

T F 2. The first Spanish immigrants settled in California.

T F 3. Early immigrants from northern Europe sought political and religious freedom and to make a better living.

T F 4. African immigrants were brought to the United States by force to work as slaves.

T F 5. In the early twentieth century, large numbers of immigrants came from France and Spain seeking religious freedom.

T F 6. The largest number of recent immigrants have come from countries outside of Europe.

T F 7. Native Americans were immigrants to the United States.

T F 8. Chinese and Irish people came to the United States before it became an independent country.

T F 9. Recent immigrants from Asia, Mexico, and Central America hoped for better employment opportunities in the United States.

T F 10. Many German, English, and Dutch settlers came to live in the United States in the 1600s.

Answers are on page 317.

EXERCISE 4

Directions: Scan the following passage for important details. Then fill in the blanks with the correct answers from the passage.

The Spread of Slavery in the United States

The Southern slaveowners won many victories from 1820 to the beginning of the Civil War in 1861. In 1820, the Missouri Compromise opened new areas of the country to slavery. The Kansas-Nebraska Act of 1854 cleared more areas for the potential growth of slavery. The greatest victory for the supporters of slavery came in 1857 with the Dred Scott decision. In this case, the Court declared that no slave or free black person could claim U.S. citizenship. Thus, it opened almost all the territories to slavery.

1. The Civil War began in_____.

2. During the 1800s, Southern slaveowners won many_____.

3. The first event to open new areas of the United States to slavery was the_____ in 1820.

4. The _____Act also opened up new areas for the growth of slavery.

5. The _____decision was the greatest victory for the supporters of slavery.

6. The *Dred Scott* decision opened almost all the_____ to slavery.

Answers are on page 317.

Writing Activity 1

Imagine that you are an American living in the 1800s. Write a paragraph convincing someone that slavery should be made illegal. Use several supporting details to expand on your main idea.

Answers will vary.

Main Idea and Details in Circle Graphs

Circle graphs are sometimes called pie graphs because of their shape. Circle graphs show how a total amount of something is divided into parts. The parts of the circle must add up to a whole, or 100 percent. These graphs can be used to show the percentage of groups of people that make up a country. Another use for circle graphs is to show how a budget is divided into different categories. Use the graphs below to practice reading circle graphs.

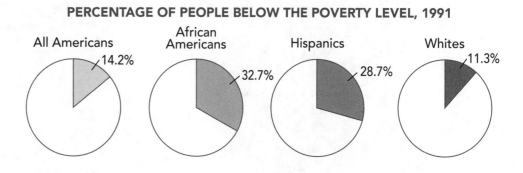

PERCENTAGE OF PEOPLE BELOW THE POVERTY LEVEL, 1991

All Americans — 14.2%

African Americans — 32.7%

Hispanics — 28.7%

Whites — 11.3%

The four circle graphs compare different amounts. You must be able to read each graph by itself. In three of the circle graphs, each whole circle represents 100 percent of a particular group of people—African Americans, Hispanics, or Whites. The first graph represents all the people in the United States. The segments, or parts, of the circle in each graph represent the percent of the whole who fell below the poverty level for 1991.

What is the average number of people in the United States who fell below the poverty level? Look at the graph labeled "All Americans." You can see that category was 14.2 percent. In the graph labeled "Hispanics," you can see that slightly more than one-quarter of the whole is below the poverty level (28.7 percent).

Do the circle graphs show how many people have incomes below the poverty level? No, you would need to have the total population of the United States to find out how many people make up 14.2 percent. You would also need the total number of African Americans, Hispanics, and Whites to find out the number of people for the other graphs.

EXERCISE 5

Questions 1–4 are based on the graphs below.

PERCENTAGE OF TOTAL IMMIGRATION TO THE U.S.

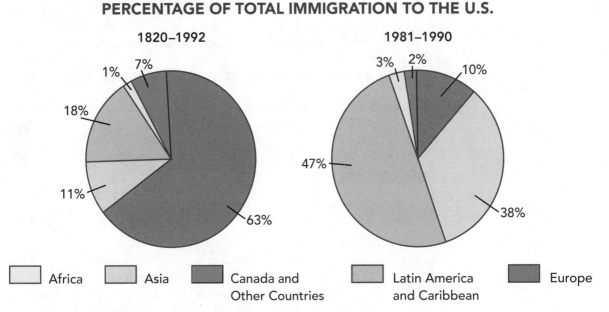

1820–1992

1981–1990

☐ Africa	☐ Asia	■ Canada and Other Countries
☐ Latin America and Caribbean	■ Europe	

Sources: *World Almanac 1994 and American Almanac*

1. Between 1820 and 1992, the largest group of immigrants to the United States came from which of the following?

   (1) Europe
   (2) Asia
   (3) Latin America and the Caribbean
   (4) Africa
   (5) Canada and other countries

2. From 1981 to 1990, which region did the largest group of immigrants come from?

   (1) Europe
   (2) Asia
   (3) Latin America and the Caribbean
   (4) Africa
   (5) Canada and other countries

3. Based on the graphs, which region made the greatest percentage gain in 1981–1990 compared to the period from 1820–1992?

   (1) Europe
   (2) Asia
   (3) Latin America and the Caribbean
   (4) Africa
   (5) Canada and other countries

4. Between 1820 and 1992, what percentage of immigrants to the United States were from Africa?

   (1) 1%
   (2) 7%
   (3) 11%
   (4) 18%
   (5) 63%

Answers are on page 317.

Unstated Main Idea

A key inference skill is understanding an implied or ***unstated main idea***. You have already learned how to locate a main idea when it is stated directly. How would you identify a main idea when it is not stated directly?

An unstated main idea is suggested. To understand it, you must read the passage and study the details. Then you must determine what the writer's main point is. Ask yourself, "What is the passage all about?" Try to express what you think is the unstated main idea in a clear statement.

Practice finding the unstated main idea in the following passage.

> St. Louis, Missouri, and Chicago, Illinois, competed for regional domination throughout the nineteenth century. Both cities were close to rich farming areas. St. Louis had an early lead on Chicago because St. Louis had long been the jumping-off point for westward expansion up the Mississippi River. Chicago took over the lead during the Civil War when the Mississippi River was closed to trade. Chicago's railroads still ran, and access to the Great Lakes remained open. As a result, Chicago flourished as a grain and meat-packing center.

Put a check in front of the unstated main idea of the passage.

_____ **1.** The Civil War caused Chicago and St. Louis to grow rapidly.

_____ **2.** During the Civil War, St. Louis dominated trade because of its better location.

_____ **3.** Chicago became the leading regional city because of its access to trade routes during the Civil War.

_____ **4.** The Civil War caused both St. Louis and Chicago to decline.

_____ **5.** Chicago pushed ahead of St. Louis because it was a more modern city.

The correct answer is choice (3). The third sentence says that "Chicago took over the lead during the Civil War when the Mississippi River was closed to trade." The fourth sentence mentions that "Chicago's railroads still ran, and access to the Great Lakes remained open."

EXERCISE 6

Questions 1–3 are based on the passage below.

Identifying With a Political Party

Political analysts have predicted from time to time that one or both of the major political parties will break up. Increasing numbers of people are calling themselves independents. During the 1970s, the number of people describing themselves as strong Democrats fell from 20 percent to 15 percent. By 1990, the figure was back up to 20 percent. The number of people defining themselves as strong Republicans climbed slowly from 9 percent in the 1970s to a high of 14 percent in 1988. By 1990, the number had dropped to 10 percent. Independents shrank from 15 percent in 1976 to 11 percent in 1990.

1. According to the passage, the number of people describing themselves as strong Democrats from the 1970s to 1990

   (1) remained at 9 percent
   (2) dropped to 10 percent
   (3) remained at 14 percent
   (4) dropped to 15 percent
   (5) rose again to 20 percent

2. According to the passage, the number of people defining themselves as strong Republicans in 1990

   (1) fell from 20 percent to 15 percent
   (2) climbed to 9 percent
   (3) dropped to 10 percent
   (4) shrank to 11 percent
   (5) went back up to 20 percent

3. Which of the following statements best summarizes the main idea of the passage?

   (1) The two-party system appears unlikely to change in the near future.
   (2) The Republicans and Democrats are losing hard-core support.
   (3) More and more people are leaving the Republican party to become Democrats.
   (4) The Democrats can no longer assume the support of union members.
   (5) The growing number of independents will cause the two-party system to break up.

   Answers are on page 317.

Context Clues

While working in this book, you may encounter words you have not seen before. Don't let this stop you from reading the passage. You can get the general meaning of a passage even if you don't know a particular word.

> Rebel city council members held a conclave last month. At the secret meeting, they discussed ways to embarrass the mayor.

If you did not know the meaning of *conclave*, you could guess from the words following it. A conclave is a secret meeting. Here you have used a word's **context**—the words surrounding the unknown word—for clues to its meaning. Sometimes you can get the meaning of a word you don't know by looking at its opposite meaning. Consider the sentence below.

> Unlike the United States, with its official policy of racial integration, South Africa practiced apartheid until the early 1990s.

If you did not know what *apartheid* meant, you could guess that it means "the official policy of racial segregation"—the opposite of a policy of integration. The word *unlike* is a clue to look for an opposite meaning.

Finally, the meaning of a word may not be stated directly. You will have to infer it from the supporting details. This skill is like that of inferring the meaning of an unstated main idea. See if you can determine the meaning of **Gross National Product** from the following passage.

> The U.S. Gross National Product (GNP) doubled from 1980 to 1990, from $2.7 trillion to $5.5 trillion. The rapid growth was determined by adding together the total value of goods and services bought by both consumers and businesses.

From the passage, you can infer that the GNP is the total value of

_____ **1.** consumer goods

_____ **2.** consumer and business goods and services

_____ **3.** business goods and services

_____ **4.** consumer goods and services

The meaning of *Gross National Product* is choice (2), *the goods and services bought by both consumers and businesses.* These are added together to make up the GNP.

EXERCISE 7

Directions: Read the passages below. Then put a check in front of the correct answer to the questions that follow.

Many supporters of school prayer would like to see all schoolchildren recite a standard prayer. They argue that everyone would accept a nondenominational prayer. The prayer would refer to God only in a nonspecific way. It would make no mention of Jesus Christ, the Holy Trinity, Mohammed, or any other religious figure central to the beliefs of a particular religious group.

1. You can infer that *nondenominational* means which of the following?

_____ (1) standardized

_____ (2) not dominant

_____ (3) not connected with any particular religious group

_____ (4) connected with a particular religious group

Historically, Manchuria in China has been the setting for different nomadic peoples who migrated back and forth from Central Asia to the Pacific. It has long been a meeting ground for different peoples and a point of conflict for different national interests.

2. You can infer that *nomadic* refers to peoples who

_____ (1) settle in one region for a long period of time

_____ (2) have many different interests

_____ (3) move from one place to another

_____ (4) thrive on conflict

Answers are on page 317.

EXERCISE 8

Questions 1 and 2 refer to the following pictograph.

CITY TAXES PER PERSON

Key $=$100

New York ———— $ $ $ $ $ $ $ $

San Antonio ———— $

San Francisco ——— $ $ $ $

Washington, D.C. – $ $ $ $ $ $ $ $ $ $
$ $ $

New Orleans ——— $ $

Source: *U.S.: A Statistical Portrait of the American People*

1. Which statement can be supported by the graph?

  (1) San Antonio has the lowest city taxes of all the cities in the United States.
  (2) New York and San Francisco have higher taxes than Washington, D.C.
  (3) San Antonio and San Francisco have lower taxes than New Orleans.
  (4) Of the cities on the graph, Washington, D.C., New York, and San Francisco have the highest city taxes per person.
  (5) Of the cities on the graph, New Orleans and San Francisco have the lowest city taxes per person.

2. What is the main idea of the graph?

  (1) Washington, D.C., is one of the most expensive cities in the country in which to live.
  (2) Washington, D.C., has more public services than New York has.
  (3) San Antonio and New Orleans have very low city taxes.
  (4) City taxes in the United States can range from as little as $100 to as much as $1,300 per person per year.
  (5) City taxes in San Francisco are reasonable, so most people could afford to live there.

Questions 3 and 4 are based on the graph below.

MONTHLY BUDGET

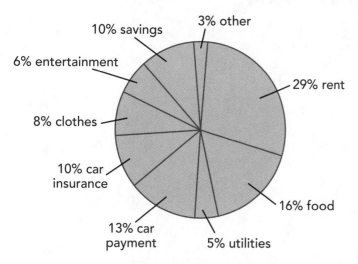

10% savings
3% other
6% entertainment
29% rent
8% clothes
10% car insurance
16% food
13% car payment
5% utilities

3. Which statement is best supported by the graph?

    (1) This person's biggest expense is food.
    (2) This person spends most of her money on necessities.
    (3) More than half of this person's income goes to food and utilities.
    (4) This person saves more of her income than she spends on food.
    (5) This person probably goes to many movies.

4. Which two categories combined account for 18 percent of this person's expenses?

    (1) car insurance and entertainment
    (2) food and car payment
    (3) clothes and rent
    (4) car payment and utilities
    (5) entertainment and other

Questions 5 and 6 are based on the following passage.

The great American megalopolis stretches over four hundred miles from Boston to Washington, D.C. Including such cities as New York, Philadelphia, Newark, and Baltimore, it is the largest urban area in the world.

5. What is a megalopolis?

    (1) a large city and its suburbs
    (2) a state government
    (3) a group of connected cities and suburbs
    (4) a large lottery
    (5) a group of cities in the eastern part of the United States

6. What does the term *urban area* refer to?

    (1) a state
    (2) a country
    (3) a city
    (4) a suburb
    (5) a local government

Answers are on page 318.

Chapter 2

Applying Social Studies Concepts

Have you ever had to read a map to plan a vacation you were taking, to give a friend directions to your home, or to read a chart or graph to find out specific information? If so, you were applying social studies ideas to your everyday life. One of the most important ends of learning is an ability to apply what you have learned.

In this chapter, you will apply ideas you learn in these ways:

- using information

- reading maps

- understanding ideas in bar graphs

Application of Ideas

When you apply an idea, you use information from one situation to explain or understand another. For example, if an airplane flies on a straight course for a long time, you can determine that it will eventually return close to the point where it started. How do you figure this out? Use the idea that Earth is round. Then apply this knowledge to the flight of the airplane.

Practice applying ideas by answering a question about the following passage.

Monroe Doctrine

By 1823, Spain had lost most of its colonies in the Western Hemisphere. Many Americans feared that other European countries might take over these colonies. President James Monroe announced the Monroe Doctrine in a speech to Congress. The Monroe Doctrine warned that any European interference with an independent state in this hemisphere would be regarded by the United States as an unfriendly act.

The Monroe Doctrine would be violated if a European country sent troops to intervene in the affairs of which of the following countries?

_____ **1.** Libya

_____ **2.** New Zealand

_____ **3.** Mexico

_____ **4.** Vietnam

_____ **5.** Turkey

The best choice is (3), Mexico. You need to understand the basic principle of the Monroe Doctrine—that the United States will not tolerate European interference in the Western Hemisphere. You then must remember your geography and apply this intervention to a country in this hemisphere—Mexico.

EXERCISE 1

Directions: Read the passage below and then put a check in front of the correct answer to the questions that follow.

At the heart of economic growth is the growth in labor productivity. One way to measure productivity is by the output of each worker per hour of labor. The more that can be produced per hour, the more productive the economy. The more productive the economy, the faster the economy can grow.

There are several ways to improve productivity. The most important method has been the introduction of modern technology. In the past, the introduction of technology to agriculture produced the greatest surge in farm productivity in European and American history. Today, the introduction of modern technology, such as computers, is leading to increased manufacturing productivity. Other means of increasing productivity include improving management, increasing worker morale, and identifying more efficient ways to speed up the work process.

1. Suppose that Japan had a large lead on the United States in the successful use of modern technology, such as the use of robots in automobile production. Which of the following would be the result for the growth of Japan's economy?

   _____ (1) Its economy would be slower than the U.S. economy because of lower productivity.

   _____ (2) Its economy would decline because robots cannot buy anything.

   _____ (3) Its economy would be about the same as that of the United States.

   _____ (4) Its economy would grow faster than the U.S. economy.

2. If a company wishes to increase productivity, it should focus its efforts on which of the following?

   _____ (1) better marketing

   _____ (2) better supervision of workers

   _____ (3) introducing new technology

   _____ (4) reducing its prices

3. Which of the following factors is *not* mentioned as increasing productivity?

   _____ (1) improving employees' morale

   _____ (2) measuring workers' output

   _____ (3) improving management

   _____ (4) increasing speed and efficiency

Answers are on page 318.

Applying Information in Maps

CALGARY LAND USE

Elbow River

Reservoir

Bow River

■ Central Business

▨ General Business

▨ Industry and Wholesaling

▨ Residences— single family

■ Residences— zone of replacement

▨ Residences— zone of deterioration

▨ Public and quasi-public

▢ Public open spaces

— Municipal boundaries

Maps come in an almost endless variety. Physical maps show different geographic features such as mountains, deserts, lakes, and rivers. Special-purpose maps use different colors, patterns, and symbols to give information.

Most maps also include a key. The *key* (sometimes called a legend) explains the symbols used on the map. Symbols can be route arrows, dots and stars for cities, and different lines for roads, railroads, and canals. Sometimes the key will feature boxes that explain the colors or patterns used on the map.

Practice using the key on the Calgary map by putting a check in front of the correct answer to the questions that follow.

1. What does this map show about Calgary?

_____ (1) its voting districts

_____ (2) its water system

_____ (3) its land uses

_____ (4) its high and low points

2. According to the map, where are the public open spaces?

_____ (1) They are surrounded by the central business district.

_____ (2) They are near the reservoir and outlying areas.

_____ (3) They are beyond the city limits of Calgary.

_____ (4) They are next to the Elbow River.

The answer to the first question is (3), *land uses*. The title of the map also helps you answer this question. The answer to the second question is (2), *near the reservoir and outlying areas*. The key shows markings for "public open space." On the map, you find these dots near the reservoir and the outlying areas.

EXERCISE 2

Directions: Based on the map, circle *T* for each true statement, or *F* for each false statement.

NATURAL RESOURCES OF AUSTRALIA

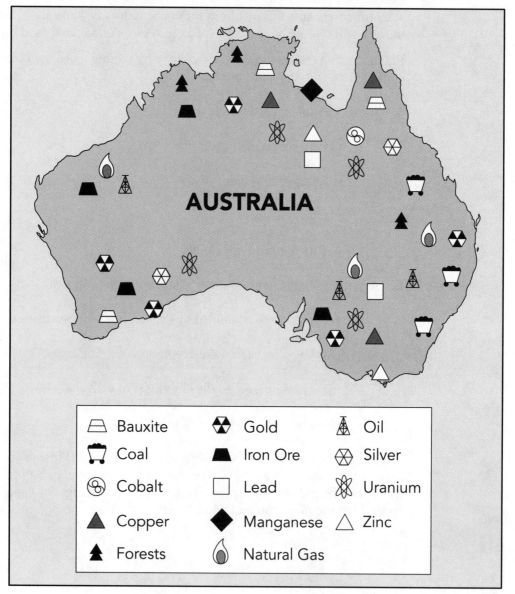

T F **1.** Australia's most abundant natural resource is gold.

T F **2.** Wherever gold mines are located there are also coal mines.

T F **3.** Most of Australia's natural resources are found in the interior of the country.

T F **4.** This map shows that natural gas is a renewable natural resource.

T F **5.** Zinc mines are located only at the southern tip of Australia.

T F **6.** Australia produces more bauxite than uranium.

T F **7.** Cobalt is Australia's chief export.

T F **8.** Australia's coal mines are located in the country's eastern border.

T F **9.** Most of Australia's forests are located in the country's interior.

T F **10.** Australia produces more gold than silver.

T F **11.** Australia imports a large amount of manganese.

T F **12.** Australia has more natural resources than most other countries.

Answers are on page 318.

Writing Activity 2

Think about a time when you referred to a map to find a place you had never visited before. Write two paragraphs describing your experiences reading a map and the route you took.

Answers will vary.

Applying Ideas in Bar Graphs

Bar graphs make it easy to compare quantities. The longer the bar, the greater the quantity being measured. Bar graphs have two axes: the horizontal axis across the bottom and the vertical axis along the side. Generally, each axis is labeled and has a certain value.

To read a bar graph, you have to be able to tell the value at the top of the vertical bar. Read across from the top of the bar to the axis at its side. Sometimes the line across from the top of a vertical bar does not meet an exact value. You must then estimate your answer.

Use the graph below to practice reading bar graphs. Put a check in front of the correct answer to the questions that follow.

DOLLAR VALUE OF ORE FROM FRIGATE MINE

1. In which year was the dollar value of ore taken from the mine at the lowest point?

_____ (1) 1865

_____ (2) 1875

_____ (3) 1885

_____ (4) 1895

2. What was the approximate dollar value of ore taken from the mine in 1865?

_____ (1) $80 thousand

_____ (2) $70 thousand

_____ (3) $78 million

_____ (4) $80 million

3. Between which years was the greatest decline in the value of ore taken from the mine?

_____ (1) 1855 and 1865

_____ (2) 1865 and 1875

_____ (3) 1875 and 1885

_____ (4) 1885 and 1895

4. In which year was the dollar value of ore taken from the mine about $67 million?

_____ (1) 1855

_____ (2) 1865

_____ (3) 1875

_____ (4) 1885

To answer the first question, notice that the shortest bar is above the year 1895, choice (4), indicating the smallest dollar value for that year.

To answer the second question, find the bar labeled "1865" across the horizontal axis. Then read across from the top of the bar at 1865 to the points on the vertical axis. The top of the bar falls between "70" and "80," more than halfway up. Choice (3), *$78 million*, is correct.

The third question asks you to compare the dollar value of ore in two different years. The greatest decline occurs between *1885* and *1895*, choice (4).

For the fourth question, the bar for *1885*, choice (4), reached to about the $67 million mark.

EXERCISE 3

Directions: Study the bar graph shown below. Then fill in the blanks with the correct answers.

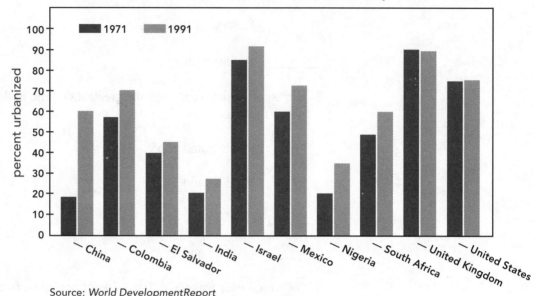

URBANIZATION IN SELECTED COUNTRIES, 1971–1991

Source: *World DevelopmentReport*

1. China and India are the countries with the greatest number of people. Which of the two had the greatest increase in urbanization from 1971 to 1991?

   _____

2. Which two countries experienced the least change in urbanization during this period?

   _____

3. Which country had the highest level of urbanization in 1991?

   _____

4. Which two countries were slightly less than 20 percent urbanized in 1971?

   _____

5. Which two countries had about the same percent of urbanization as the United States in 1991?

   _____

6. About how much did South Africa's urbanization rate increase from 1971 to 1991?

   _____

7. Which country had a higher percentage of urbanization in 1991—the United Kingdom or the United States?

   _____

8. Which country was more urbanized in 1971—Nigeria or El Salvador?

   _____

9. In which year was Colombia's urbanization rate at about 70 percent?

   _____

10. What can you infer from the figures for all countries during the years from 1971 to 1991?

    _____

Answers are on page 318.

EXERCISE 4

Questions 1–7 are based on the graphs below and the information given about them.

Notice that the graph on the left is labeled "millions" on the vertical axis. The graph on the right is labeled "thousands." In order to find the number of casualties, you need to multiply each number by 1,000. For example, in World War I there were some 320,000 casualties.

CASUALTIES IN PRINCIPAL U.S. WARS

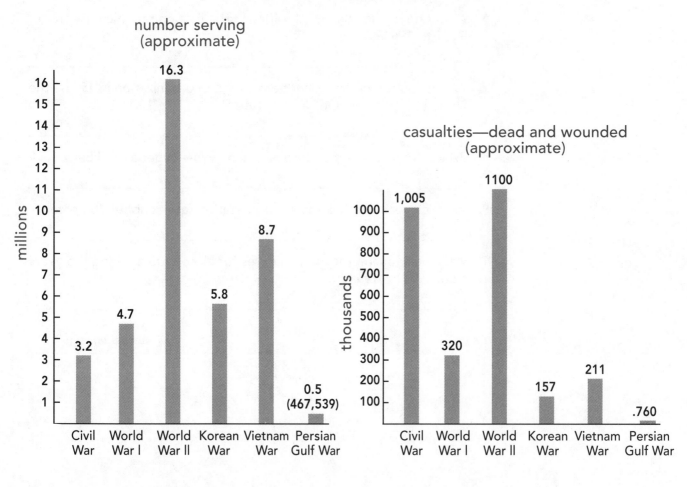

1. The fewest number of casualties occurred in which two wars?

   (1) Korean War and Vietnam War
   (2) Korean War and Persian Gulf War
   (3) World War I and World War II
   (4) World War I and Persian Gulf War
   (5) World War II and Korean War

2. Which war had the greatest number of casualties compared with the number of soldiers serving?

   (1) Civil War
   (2) World War I
   (3) World War II
   (4) Korean War
   (5) Persian Gulf War

3. In which war did the fewest number of soldiers serve?

   (1) Civil War
   (2) World War I
   (3) Korean War
   (4) Vietnam War
   (5) Persian Gulf War

4. In which two wars did the greatest number of casualties occur?

   (1) World War I and Persian Gulf War
   (2) World War II and Korean War
   (3) Civil War and World War II
   (4) World War I and Vietnam War
   (5) World War II and Persian Gulf War

5. About how many persons served in the Vietnam War?

   (1) 468 thousand
   (2) 3 million
   (3) 4.5 million
   (4) 6 million
   (5) 8.7 million

6. About how many casualties occurred during World War I?

   (1) 157 thousand
   (2) 211 thousand
   (3) 320 thousand
   (4) 1 million, 5 thousand
   (5) 1 million, 100 thousand

7. The data on the graphs support which of the following conclusions?

   (1) Modern weapon systems have accounted for a great increase in casualties.
   (2) The greatest number of American casualties took place during the Civil War and World War II.
   (3) Modern medical techniques have failed to save lives on the battlefield.
   (4) American war casualties have increased steadily during the twentieth century.
   (5) Modern military technology has resulted in a decline in casualties.

Questions 8–11 are based on the following map.

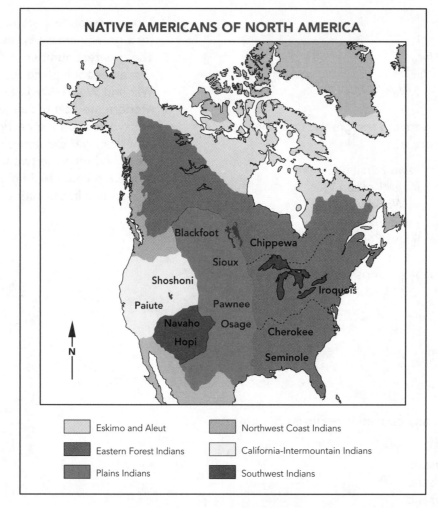

NATIVE AMERICANS OF NORTH AMERICA

Legend:
- Eskimo and Aleut
- Eastern Forest Indians
- Plains Indians
- Northwest Coast Indians
- California-Intermountain Indians
- Southwest Indians

8. The Pawnee were part of which group?

   (1) Eskimo and Aleut
   (2) Eastern Forest Indians
   (3) Plains Indians
   (4) Northwest Coast Indians
   (5) Southwest Indians

9. The far north of the continent was inhabited by which group or groups?

   (1) Eskimo and Aleut
   (2) Eastern Forest Indians
   (3) Plains Indians
   (4) Northwest Coast Indians
   (5) Southwest Indians

10. Which of the following tribes was Southwest Indians?

    (1) Cree
    (2) Paiute
    (3) Cherokee
    (4) Sioux
    (5) Hopi

11. The Cherokee were part of which group?

    (1) Eastern Forest Indians
    (2) Plains Indians
    (3) Northwest Coast Indians
    (4) California–Intermountain Indians
    (5) Southwest Indians

Questions 12 and 13 are based on the following graph.

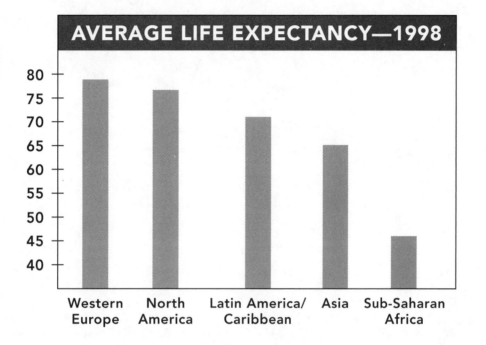

AVERAGE LIFE EXPECTANCY—1998

12. Which statement is best supported by the graph?

   (1) All the people in the regions shown have a shorter life expectancy than people in the United States.
   (2) The average person in Asia lives about ten years longer than the average person in Sub-Saharan Africa.
   (3) People in the Western Hemisphere live longer than people in the Eastern Hemisphere.
   (4) The region with a life expectancy most similar to North America is Western Europe.
   (5) People lived longer in 1998 than in 1900.

13. Which geographical areas have the longest life expectancy?

   (1) Asia, North America, Latin America and the Caribbean
   (2) Western Europe, Latin America and the Caribbean, and North America
   (3) Sub-Saharan Africa, Asia, and Latin America and the Caribbean
   (4) Western Europe, Sub-Saharan Africa, and North America
   (5) North America, Western Europe, and Asia

Answers are on pages 318–319.

Chapter 3

Analyzing Social Studies Materials

When you *analyze* something, you break it down into its basic parts. In social studies, you look at how material is organized in order to better understand the meaning of the whole passage or graphic. In this chapter, you will learn how to analyze social studies materials in these ways:

- comparing and contrasting ideas
- identifying cause-and-effect relationships
- finding out the sequence of events
- making inferences
- drawing conclusions

Fact and Opinion

A *fact* is a statement that can be proved. An *opinion* is a personal belief or feeling, like, or dislike that cannot be proved. While you are examining social studies material, you will come across statements that are facts and others that are opinions. Your own perspective may be based on whether you are able to recognize something as a fact or an opinion. If you read a statement and are unsure if it is a fact or an opinion, ask yourself if the statement can be proved, or if it is something the author believes or feels but cannot be proved.

One of the following two statements is a fact; the other is an opinion. Write *F* before the statement that is a fact and *O* before the statement that is an opinion.

_____ **1.** The U.S. Constitution is the greatest political document ever written.

_____ **2.** Twenty-six amendments have been added to the U.S. Constitution.

You were right if you thought the first statement was an opinion. The word *greatest* shows that the writer is expressing an opinion. The second statement is a fact that can be checked by looking at a copy of the Constitution.

EXERCISE 1

Directions: Read the statements below. Write *F* if the sentence is a fact, or *O* if the statement is an opinion.

_____ 1. The United States is a democracy in which people elect their government officials.

_____ 2. Democracy is the best form of government.

_____ 3. Local governments mismanage their responsibilities of police and fire protection.

_____ 4. Local governments have responsibility for public schools.

_____ 5. All citizens aged eighteen and over have the right to register and vote.

_____ 6. The vice president has the least important job in the entire federal government.

_____ 7. If the president dies in office, the vice president becomes the new president.

Answers are on page 319.

Comparison and Contrast

Writers use *comparison* when they want to examine similarities, or how things are alike, and *contrast* to look at differences between people, things, or ideas. For example, a social studies passage might compare and contrast various countries.

To show how countries are alike or different, such things as land use, number of cities, rivers and lakes, natural resources, climate and vegetation, languages, peoples, cultural customs, art, music, architecture, economic systems, types of industry, population patterns, religions, places of interest, educational systems, imports and exports, and types of government might be compared and contrasted.

EXERCISE 2

Directions: Use the information in the passage below to fill in the chart that follows.

Rich and Poor in the Cities

American cities are returning to a pattern similar to that of European cities during the Middle Ages. At that time, the rich and their servants lived in the inner city. The working classes and the poor lived on the city's outer edge.

In the United States for much of the twentieth century, wealthy people have lived in the suburbs and the poor have lived in the inner cities. However, in recent years, wealthy people have begun to move back to the central part of cities like New York and Chicago. Run-down living units are gradually being rehabbed for people with higher income levels. This move is called gentrification. The process of gentrification has restored parts of the downtown areas and the inner cities. At the same time, it has pushed the poor to live in the outer edges of the city or in the older suburbs.

CHANGES IN LIVING PATTERNS OVER TIME

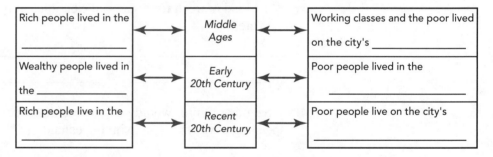

Answers are on page 319.

Information in Tables

A *table* is a list of numbers placed in columns and rows to make it easier to make comparisons. A table has a title at the top. The separate columns and rows within the table are also labeled. This way you will know what information they contain.

Look at the table on the next page. What does the table title tell you? The title tells you that the table has information on the amount of money the winners in Senate elections spent on their election campaigns.

The column headings at the top tell you that these figures cover the elections of 1976, 1984, and 1990. The row headings on the left tell you how much money was raised and how much money was spent.

FINANCIAL ACTIVITY OF WINNING SENATE CANDIDATES

(in millions of dollars)

	1976	*1984*	*1990*
raised	$21.0	$100.9	$121.5
spent	$20.0	$97.5	$115.4

See how well you do in reading this table by answering the questions below.

1. How much more money was raised in 1990 than in 1976?

   _____

2. Did the winning candidates in the years shown spend more money or less money than they raised?

   _____

3. What kind of trend for senatorial election campaigns do the figures indicate?

   _____

   _____

4. What other figures would you need to determine whether this increased spending pays off for the winning candidates?

   _____

   _____

The answer to the first question is *$100.5 million.* Look at the columns with the headings "1976" and "1990." Then read across the left-hand row labeled "raised" to the two columns. The difference between the $121.5 million raised in 1990 and $21.0 million raised in 1976 is $100.5 million.

The answer to question 2 is *less money than they raised.* If you compare the "raised" and "spent" columns for all three election years, you will see that the winning candidates raised more money than they spent. The year 1976 was close, however, with a $900,000 difference.

The answer to the third question is that *candidates have been raising greater sums of money to win the election from 1976 to 1990.* To answer question 4, you would need to know *how much the losing candidates spent.*

EXERCISE 3

Directions: Study the table below and then put a check in front of the correct answer to the questions that follow.

CONSUMPTION OF MAJOR FOOD COMMODITIES IN THE UNITED STATES PER PERSON PER YEAR

(in pounds)

	1970	1980	1990
red meat	132.0	126.4	112.4
fish	11.7	12.4	15.0
poultry products	33.8	40.6	55.9
eggs (number per year)	309.0	271.0	233.0
fats and oils	52.6	57.2	62.7
fresh fruit	79.4	87.0	92.6
selected fresh vegetables	88.8	92.7	110.9

1. Between 1970 to 1990, in which food category did consumption rise more than 50 percent?

_____ (1) red meat

_____ (2) fish

_____ (3) poultry products

_____ (4) fresh fruit

2. The information in the table supports which of the following conclusions?

_____ (1) Most Americans are becoming vegetarians.

_____ (2) Americans are consuming less red meat and more fruits and vegetables.

_____ (3) Americans consume too much sugar and salt.

_____ (4) The price of fresh vegetables has risen by 50 percent.

3. From 1980 to 1990, which of the following did Americans eat?

    _____ (1) fewer eggs and less chicken

    _____ (2) fewer eggs and more red meat

    _____ (3) more eggs and less chicken

    _____ (4) more fresh fruit and more fish

4. Americans decreased the consumption of which of the following foods between 1970 and 1990?

    _____ (1) poultry products

    _____ (2) fresh fruit

    _____ (3) red meat

    _____ (4) selected fresh vegetables

Answers are on page 319.

Cause and Effect

Writers frequently use a ***cause-and-effect*** pattern to organize social studies passages. They show how one event causes another event to happen. For example, the introduction of new technology has led to greater productivity for some companies. So a positive outcome has resulted. On the other hand, because the new technology allows machines to do much of the work that people had done in the past, workers in many industries are now out of work (a negative effect).

CAUSES	EFFECTS
development of new technology ⟶	more productivity
machines replace people ⟶	increased unemployment

How do you identify a cause-and-effect relationship? A good way to do so is to look for key words and phrases such as *because, since, therefore, as a result, consequently, if . . . then, the reason was, led to, the outcome was, the result was, brought about, was responsible for,* and *accordingly.*

EXERCISE 4

Questions 1 and 2 are based on the passage below.

Population Growth in the Third World

The term *Third World* refers to the developing nations. These are the poorest countries in the world. Unlike the United States, they do not have large industries. These countries remain largely agricultural, depending on farmland for survival.

In recent years, public health measures have greatly influenced the rapid growth of Third World populations. United Nations health efforts have had a big impact on controlling malaria, yellow fever, and other diseases. One result has been a great drop in infant mortality (the death rate of babies in the first year of life). In some countries, the infant mortality rate has dropped from 200 to 50 deaths per 1,000 births. This rapid decline in infant mortality is the main reason for increased population growth. Even further growth is expected because more young women will reach child-bearing age.

1. What has been a major cause of the reduction in infant mortality?

   (1) more young women at child-bearing age
   (2) public health measures that help control diseases
   (3) increased population growth
   (4) better food and housing conditions
   (5) malaria, yellow fever, and other diseases

2. What effect will increased survival of infants have on future population growth?

   (1) reduce it by increasing the demand for effective family planning
   (2) increase it because more young women will reach child-bearing age
   (3) decrease the number of child-bearing women
   (4) reduce population growth because of food shortages
   (5) reduce the need for public health measures

   Answers are on page 319.

Sequence of Events

Many social studies writers use a ***sequence-of-events*** approach to organizing information. Presenting events in the order in which they happened is especially common in history passages or time lines. As you read these materials, you need to keep in mind the series of events that the writer describes. Writers often use key words such as *first, second, third, before, after, next, then,* and *finally.*

EXERCISE 5

Questions 1 and 2 are based on the passage below.

The Cuban Missile Crisis

In October 1962, an American spy plane—the U-2—found signs of Soviet nuclear missile bases in Cuba. President Kennedy began a U.S. naval blockade of Cuba. He also threatened to invade Cuba and strike back at the Soviet Union, as Russia was known then, if the Soviets began an attack on the United States from the Cuban bases.

When the Soviets were shown photographs of the bases, they agreed to negotiate with the United States. First, the Soviets offered to remove their bases from Cuba if the United States removed its missiles from Turkey. But the United States refused to do so. Then, the Soviet Union agreed to withdraw the missiles and tear down its bases in Cuba. In turn, the United States ended its blockade and agreed not to invade Cuba.

1. When did the United States blockade Cuba?

   (1) when the Soviets asked the United States to remove its missiles from Turkey
   (2) when the Soviet Union first set up missile bases
   (3) when U.S.-Soviet negotiations broke down
   (4) when the United States discovered signs of Soviet nuclear missile bases in Cuba
   (5) when Cuba launched an attack from its bases

2. When did the United States end the blockade?

   (1) after the missile bases were dismantled
   (2) when the Soviet Union agreed to negotiate
   (3) before the Soviet Union agreed to dismantle its bases
   (4) when the Soviet Union removed the missiles from the bases
   (5) when the Soviet Union threatened to attack the United States

Answers are on page 319.

Writing Activity 3

Think about two countries that are currently at war or have fought with each other in the past. Write one paragraph explaining the causes of the war. Write a second paragraph describing the effects of the war on the countries' people, lands, and culture.

Answers will vary.

Ideas in Line Graphs

Line graphs show how one or more items of information have changed over time. A line graph has a series of connected points. Each point represents a value at a particular point in time. The points are then connected by a line. The line's movement up or down on the graph shows a trend. Like a bar graph, a line graph is plotted on a pair of axes. You can read down to find a value on the bottom (horizontal) axis. You can read across to find a value on the side (vertical) axis.

The following line graph shows the growth of world trade and world output, or production. Based on the graph, circle *T* for each true statement, or *F* for each false statement.

GROWTH OF WORLD TRADE AND OUTPUT

T F   **1.** World trade fell below world output in 1982.

T F   **2.** The lowest percentage of growth in world output took place in 1992.

T F   **3.** The percentage of growth in world trade and world output was about the same in 1984.

T F   **4.** The growth in world output reached its highest points in 1984 and 1988.

T F   **5.** The percentage of growth in world trade has been above world output ever since 1984.

T F   **6.** The percentage of growth in world trade fell below 0 percent in 1982.

T F   **7.** The percentage of growth in world output remained at about the same level between 1988 and 1992.

T F   **8.** The percentage of growth in world trade reached its highest point at more than 8 percent in 1984.

Statement 1 is *true*. The line showing world trade dropped to -2 percent. World output fell only slightly in 1982 to about 1 percent.

Statement 2 is *false*. The lowest percentage of growth took place in 1991, not 1992. World output was moving up in 1992.

Statement 3 is also *false*. In 1984, world trade reached its highest point in the years covered—more than 8 percent. World output grew only 4 percent.

Statement 4 is *true*. The line showing world output is clearly at its two highest points in 1984 and 1988.

Statement 5 is also *true*. Follow the line for world trade. You will see that it is above the line showing world output from 1984 to 1992.

Statement 6 is also *true*. The line for world trade fell to about -2 percent in 1982.

Statement 7 is *false*. The line showing world output consistently fell between 1988 and 1991 and rose slightly in 1992.

Statement 8 is *true*. The line for world trade rose slightly above the 8 percent level in 1984.

EXERCISE 6

Directions: Study the table to see which of the following four graphs matches it. Then put a check in front of the correct answer to the questions that follow.

PER CAPITA INCOME
in constant (1991) dollars

1982	$ 12,794
1983	13,057
1984	13,539
1985	13,940
1986	14,502
1987	14,856
1988	15,109
1989	15,439
1990	14,992
1991	14,617

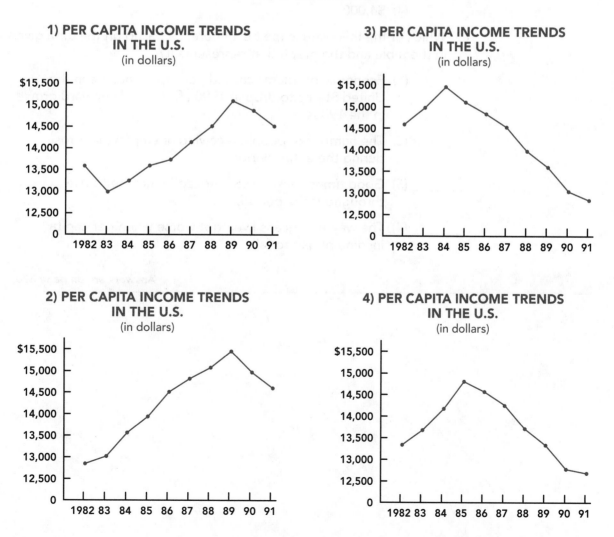

1. In which year was U.S. per capita income at its highest?

_____ (1) 1983

_____ (2) 1984

_____ (3) 1988

_____ (4) 1989

2. Which line graph sums up the table data most accurately?

_____ (1) graph I

_____ (2) graph 2

_____ (3) graph 3

_____ (4) graph 4

3. About how much did per capita income increase between 1982 and 1991?

_____ (1) $1,000

_____ (2) $2,000

_____ (3) $3,000

_____ (4) $4,000

4. Which of the following is the best inference based on the data given in the table and the graph that represents it?

_____ (1) Economic problems caused per capita income in the United States to drop in 1990 after steady upward growth in the 1980s.

_____ (2) The number of people receiving unemployment rose during the entire period.

_____ (3) Good times caused U.S. per capita income to rise throughout the period.

_____ (4) The way Americans lived got worse when per capita income began to fall.

Answers are on page 320.

EXERCISE 7

Directions: Study the two graphs below. Then answer the questions in the space provided.

POLITICAL DIVISION IN THE U.S. CONGRESS
1981–1995

Senate
(total: 100 members)

House of Representatives
(total: 435 members)

1. During which two-year period did the Democrats first control the Senate?

   _____

2. In which years was the number of Republicans in the House of Representatives the greatest?

   _____

3. Did the Republicans gain control of the House of Representatives at any time from 1981 to 1995?

   _____

4. During which years was Democratic membership in the Senate the lowest?

   _____

5. Did Republican membership in the Senate decline or increase from 1991 to 1995?

   _____

Answers are on page 320.

Inferences

In a previous chapter, you learned how to identify the main idea and locate supporting details. This type of reading skill is called **_literal understanding_**. It simply requires that you go back to the passage and understand information that is stated directly. Making **_inferences_** requires a reader to go beyond the directly stated information and find a meaning that is implied or suggested. An inference is a form of "educated guess" based on facts. Before you make an inference, you must be very sure of what the passage is stating directly.

Below is a short paragraph. The question that follows asks for an inference.

There is some evidence that people who take sleeping pills over long periods of time become irritable or depressed. One possible explanation is that sleeping pills inhibit normal dreaming. Thus, many doctors do not recommend the consistent use of sleeping pills.

Based on the passage, what inference can you make about dreaming?

_____ 1. Dreaming makes people depressed and irritable.

_____ 2. Too much dreaming is abnormal.

_____ 3. Not everyone needs to dream.

_____ 4. Sleeping pills do not affect dreaming.

_____ 5. Dreaming may be necessary for good mental health.

_____ 6. The sale of sleeping pills should be banned.

_____ 7. Most people have normal dreams.

_____ 8. Some sleeping pills are more harmful than others.

_____ 9. People often dream in color after taking sleeping pills.

_____ 10. Anyone who takes a sleeping pill gets depressed.

The answer is **5**. The paragraph shows a connection between the restraint of normal dreaming and irritability or depression. From this connection, you can infer that normal dreaming promotes mental well-being.

EXERCISE 8

Questions 1 and 2 are based on the paragraph below.

Until recently, the Catholic Church was tied very closely to the Spanish government. This meant that divorce and abortion were illegal. The Catholic religion was taught in schools. After the death of General Franco in 1975, the ties between church and state came apart. In 1978, a new constitution did away with the church's official position. While the Catholic Church was still an important institution, religion seemed to have become less important in people's daily lives.

1. What can you infer about religion in Spain?

    (1) Catholicism is the religion of a small majority of people in Spain.
    (2) Catholicism is the traditional religion of Spain.
    (3) Only the rich and powerful are Catholic.
    (4) People in Spain have no special religious affiliation.
    (5) Catholicism continues to guide the government of Spain.

2. What can you infer about Franco's government?

    (1) The government supported legal divorce and abortion.
    (2) The government gave the Catholic Church a special place under its constitution.
    (3) The government gave no special place to the Catholic Church under its constitution.
    (4) The government supported legal abortion, but not divorce.
    (5) The government supported legal divorce, but not abortion.

Questions 3 and 4 are based on the paragraph below.

Because of more than 400 miles of coastline in Rhode Island, water is its most abundant natural resource. Narragansett Bay forms an open door for trade in the Atlantic Ocean. It is also a popular recreation area that attracts many tourists. Several valuable fisheries are located in this area. Rhode Island is the world's leading costume-jewelry center and the home of the leading silversmiths in the United States. This state is also known for its manufacturing of fabricated metals, machinery, electrical and electronic equipment, and ships and boats.

3. Which of the following is probably NOT a popular sport in Rhode Island?

    (1) water skiing
    (2) swimming
    (3) boating
    (4) fishing
    (5) downhill skiing

4. Rhode Island is known for all of the following EXCEPT which industries?

    (1) silversmithing
    (2) metal fabricating
    (3) machine technology
    (4) foresting timber
    (5) making costume jewelry

Answers are on page 320.

Drawing Conclusions

The ability to draw conclusions is an important inference skill. You **_draw a conclusion_** when you predict the outcome of events or determine the relationship of facts in a passage.

What conclusion can be drawn from the following passage?

The federal government borrows large amounts of money for its spending. This causes the supply of available money for loans to become tightened. Interest rates for borrowing tend to rise. Thus, when companies borrow money, they pay more in interest. Companies usually pass this extra cost along to consumers.

If the government borrows a lot of money to finance a big increase in spending, what might happen to consumer prices?

_____ (1) Prices would fall.

_____ (2) Prices would rise.

_____ (3) Prices would fall and then rise.

_____ (4) Prices would rise and then fall.

_____ (5) Prices would stay about the same.

The correct conclusion is (2), prices would rise. The facts show that large-scale government borrowing leads to higher interest rates. Companies must spend more money when they borrow, so they usually raise their prices to make up the difference.

EXERCISE 9

Questions 1 and 2 are based on the passage below.

Credit Cards

There are advantages and disadvantages to having and using a credit card. On the positive side, a credit card, if used wisely, can be a wonderful convenience. You never have to worry about having ready cash when you want to buy something. You also don't have to pay the full price for an item right away. Instead, you can pay in monthly installments. You always have to pay either the full cost or a part of it when you get your credit card bill each month.

On the negative side, if you pay only part of your credit card bill, you'll be charged interest on the remaining amount. You will continue to pay interest until you pay the total amount you owe. You can end up spending much more for your purchase than if you had paid cash. So think twice before you charge big-ticket items with your credit card.

1. Which piece of advice is based on this passage?

   (1) Use credit cards because they are cheaper.
   (2) Never use a credit card, because you pay more.
   (3) Make sure that you can afford to pay monthly installments.
   (4) Always use cash because it is easier.
   (5) Use credit cards as a way to establish good credit.

2. Which is a disadvantage to buying with credit cards?

   (1) You will never have to have cash on hand.
   (2) You may forget to carry the cards with you.
   (3) You may underestimate how much you will pay for an item in the long run.
   (4) Interest rates are rising.
   (5) It is difficult to establish credit.

Question 3 is based on the paragraph below.

In the 1920s, psychologists Hugh Hartshorne and Mark May studied the development of honesty by testing 11,000 children. Hartshorne and May saw the children imitating adult and peer models a great deal. In other words, they found that the children did what they saw others do, not what they were told to do. If the children were surrounded by lying, cheating, and stealing, they tended to lie, cheat, and steal. If the people they imitated were honest, they tended to be honest.

3. According to Hartshorne and May, when are children likely to be honest?

   (1) when they are often in social situations
   (2) when the people around them are honest
   (3) when they are told they should be honest
   (4) when their families have plenty of money
   (5) when they are punished for dishonesty

Questions 4 and 5 are based on the graph below.

AMERICA MOVES TO THE CITIES
(percent of U.S. population living in urban areas)

Source: *Statistical Abstract of the United States*

4. Which statement about the graph is NOT true?

   (1) More people lived in urban areas in 1990 than in 1890.
   (2) Fewer people lived in urban areas in 1900 than in 1910.
   (3) The percent of people living in urban areas increased by about 4 percent from 1960 to 1970.
   (4) The decades with the lowest percent of increase in people living in urban areas were 1970 and 1980.
   (5) The percent of people living in urban areas almost doubled between 1900 and 1950.

5. Which of the following conclusions is best shown by this graph?

   (1) The percentage of people living in urban areas of the United States has steadily fallen.
   (2) The percentage of people living in rural areas of the United States has steadily risen.
   (3) The percentage of people living in a few major cities in the United States has risen greatly.
   (4) The percentage of people living in urban areas of the United States has risen greatly.
   (5) More people lived in the northeastern part of the United States in 1990 than in 1900.

Answers are on page 320.

Chapter 4

Evaluating Social Studies Materials

When you read, you *evaluate,* or judge the value or logic of an idea. You often ask yourself if you have enough information to answer a question or solve a problem. You also ask if the information you have is what you need.

For example, when you are thinking about buying a new car, you evaluate your financial situation and your transportation needs before you go out and look for the best deal. You judge to see if various cars are well made, how much they cost, and what features are offered with the car and which ones you will have to pay extra for. You ask which repairs are covered under warranty and what the loan rates are.

You also evaluate information when you read social studies passages, charts, maps, graphs, and political cartoons. You decide if the information is accurate or if it is based on sound logic.

In this section, you will learn how to evaluate social studies materials by:

- judging the value of information
- evaluating logic
- recognizing tone
- interpreting editorial cartoons

Judging Information

In order to judge the value of something, you must have standards to refer to. Standards allow you to judge, or evaluate, the value of something. The standard for a teacher is how well his or her students learn. The set of standards, or the criteria may be the students' standardized test scores. The value of a movie can be measured by its ability to entertain as well as its ability to make money. A newspaper article is judged on whether or not the facts are true and whether it is written clearly.

If you know and understand the criteria by which something is judged, you can evaluate it. For example, if you want to buy a house and you know the legal requirements for a good contract, then you can enter into one with confidence. Some of the criteria for a good legal contract are:

1. a clear written offer by the buyer or the person representing the buyer

2. a clear written acceptance of the offer by the seller or the seller's representative

3. once the buyer and the seller agree, then a settlement of the deal that is clear to both the buyer and the seller

4. a clear exchange of money between the buyer and the seller

In order to be legally binding, a contract must have the four criteria listed above. A legally binding contract is one in which both parties are obligated to keep up their end of the deal. Look at the situation below. If the situation represents a legally binding contract, write *yes* in the space next to it. If it does not, write *no* in the space next to it and write the number or numbers of the criterion that the situation does not represent.

_____ A husband and wife both shake hands with a neighbor in an agreement to purchase a used car for $5,000 from him. The neighbor in turn agrees to hand over the title of the automobile upon receipt of the money.

You should have written *No, 1 and 2*. Though an offer to purchase the car is made, and the seller accepts the offer, neither the offer nor the acceptance is in writing. Therefore, it is not a legally binding contract. By evaluating the standards for a legally binding contract and comparing them to the situation presented, you can make an accurate judgment about the situation.

EXERCISE 1

Directions: In the following cases, judge whether the situation described represents a legally binding contract. If it does, write *yes* on the line. If it does not, write *no* on the line.

_____ **1.** A buyer tells a woman that he will pay what she wants for her house.

_____ **2.** A farmer signs a note and promises to feed and house a worker who is willing to work in exchange for room and board. The worker signs the note, too.

_____ **3.** At a flea market, a buyer and seller go back and forth on the price for a chest of drawers. The buyer says he will only pay $300 less than the seller's final offer.

Answers are on page 320.

EXERCISE 2

Directions: Read the passage below. Be prepared to make judgments based on the theory described in the passage.

Erik Erikson was a psychoanalyst who studied social psychology. By 1950 he had written extensively about his theory of the social development of the individual. Erikson believed that although institutions vary greatly from one society to another, all societies develop institutions that help the individual develop. One such institution in our society is the elementary school. Elementary school is supposed to help each child not only learn, but also develop into an individual who can exist outside of his or her family unit. Erikson also believed that at each developmental stage of an individual there is a crisis the individual must face and successfully overcome. The purpose of the elementary school is supposed to help a child through the crisis of growing up and away from their family. For example, a child must learn how to leave home every day and go to school.

For each of the scenarios below, write (1) in the blank if the scenario would help support Erikson's theory, (2) if the scenario would dispute Erikson's theory, and (3) if the scenario would have no bearing on Erikson's theory.

_____ 1. A child writes a book report and does not receive a good grade because he has copied from the book.

_____ 2. A child is continually absent from school. When she does get to school she is upset that she is not at home.

_____ 3. Upon graduating from high school with a good grade point average, a teenager joins the army and quickly becomes a lieutenant.

Answers are on page 320.

Evaluation of Logic

After reading a passage ask yourself, "Does the writer make sense? Are the ideas logical?" To answer these questions, you must use *evaluation of logic*. This is another inferential reading skill, in which you make a judgment of the way writers present and use their ideas. When evaluating logic, you may have to draw on any or all of the reading skills you have already learned.

Probably the most important part of evaluating logic is judging the writer's logical consistency. *Logical consistency* means the writer's use of sound reasoning in developing an idea. You should especially be aware of the following two points.

- A writer's facts should support his or her conclusions.

- A writer should correctly apply his or her own ideas.

Read the passage below and put a check in front of the statement that is supported by the passage.

Critics of government assistance programs for the poor often claim that such aid does not work. However, nationwide studies show that students who participated in preschool Head Start programs showed improvement in their school performance in later grades.

_____ (1) Increased spending on education does not improve performance.

_____ (2) Early help in education has no relation to later performance.

_____ (3) Preschool children do well in later grades without these programs.

_____ (4) Early help in education can affect later academic performance.

The details in the passage support statement (4). The passage states that children who participated in preschool Head Start programs showed improved school performance in later grades. The details in the passage do not support any of the other statements.

EXERCISE 3

Directions: Read the passage below and put a check in front of the correct answer to the questions that follow.

The Rising Crime Rate

The soaring crime rate affects everyone in the United States. One explanation for the rise in crime is that society offers too many rewards for the criminal and too few reasons for people to do honest work. Many people turn to crime because they think of it as a quick way to get what they want. Crime must be made less desirable and work more attractive.

Another explanation is that most crime results from economic and social conditions. These conditions affect men and women who are unable to better their lives. They feel hopeless in a society that promises an equal chance for everyone.

1. Which conclusion is supported by the details in the passage?

    _____ (1) Crime does not pay.

    _____ (2) The rise in the crime rate has more than one cause.

    _____ (3) Getting rid of poverty would mean an end to crime.

    _____ (4) The crime rate is rising because society is too easy on lawbreakers.

2. According to the passage, different views of the causes of crime reflect different ideas about what?

    _____ (1) work

    _____ (2) the influences of society

    _____ (3) law enforcement

    _____ (4) the criminal justice system

Answers are on pages 320–321.

Recognizing Tone

A writer uses tone to influence the reader's reaction to a situation. *Tone* refers to a writer's own bias or opinion about a subject. Feelings such as delight or anger sometimes can be detected in a piece of writing. However, not all writing gives away the author's feelings. Many writers are straightforward and objective.

To recognize tone in writing, you must analyze the way a selection is written and the feeling that underlies it. Pay careful attention to the writer's choice of words. Look at the two paragraphs below.

Paragraph 1

Starvation is rampant, and hunger haunts the humble hovels of the needy. Will nothing be done about this? How can people continue to support a government that ignores the needs of the poor?

Paragraph 2

Not long ago, concern about hunger focused on the world's poorer nations. Lately, hunger has become an issue in the United States. Many people accuse the government of making the problem worse by cutting back on programs that help the poor. The government denies these charges, saying that it has always provided assistance to the needy.

In paragraph 1, the writer's tone is angry. Notice the writer's words. *Starvation is rampant*; *hunger haunts the humble hovels* (not homes) *of the poor*; the government *ignores the needs of the poor*. The goal of the first writer is to make the reader angry and upset about the hungry poor.

Paragraph 2 has an objective tone. The writer's own feelings are not clear. The words *hunger*, *the issue*, and *the needy* are not charged with emotion. The writer simply reports the opinions of two different sides on the subject of government responsibility for hunger.

EXERCISE 4

Directions: Read the following passage and put a check in front of the correct answer to the questions that follow.

We could see the two principal characters approaching the Senate chamber from opposite directions. The senator from North Carolina strode briskly and with confidence toward the Senate floor. He chatted amiably with reporters about strategy for the debate. Meanwhile, the senator from New York darted into sight and scurried down the hallway. He paused briefly to huddle nervously with his assistants about maneuvers in the debate.

1. Based on the passage, what does the writer feel?

_____ (1) He or she does not admire either senator.

_____ (2) He or she likes the North Carolina senator but dislikes the New York senator.

_____ (3) He or she has no feeling about either senator.

_____ (4) He or she dislikes the North Carolina senator but likes the New York senator.

2. Which word has a positive feel to it?

_____ (1) darted

_____ (2) scurried

_____ (3) amiably

_____ (4) nervously

Answers are on page 321.

Interpreting Editorial Cartoons

Cartoonists make fun of individuals, governments, and businesses by drawing them in a humorous or ridiculous way. *Editorial* or *political cartoons* express an opinion and bring attention to a social or political problem. Cartoonists make great use of irony—showing things in a way that is the opposite from the way they really are. Editorial or political cartoons have a main idea. They express the opinion of the artist. On the GED Social Studies Test, you will have to answer questions that are based on political cartoons.

When looking at an editorial or political cartoon, pay attention to the following features:

• the title or caption

• the characters (may be real people or symbols such as Uncle Sam for the United States)

• any labels or conversation (shown in balloons with the words printed inside)

Study the editorial cartoon shown below and put a check in front of the correct answer to the questions that follow.

1. What does the large bulldozer represent?

_____ (1) big business

_____ (2) a construction company

_____ (3) the federal government

_____ (4) city hall

2. What can you infer about the cartoonist's beliefs?

_____ (1) Small businesses will stay open no matter what the tax is.

_____ (2) Unfair taxation will hurt small businesses.

_____ (3) High taxes are fair for small businesses.

_____ (4) Small businesses will sweep away taxes.

For question 1, the bulldozer represents choice (3), *the federal government*. The bulldozer is labeled "taxes." The size of the bulldozer is much larger than needed to tear down the small business. The federal government determines the largest share of the taxes that people and small businesses pay. So the bulldozer represents the federal government.

For question 2, statement (2) is the best choice. The cartoonist believes that *unfair taxation will hurt small businesses*. The label "Fairness Construction Co." represents the government that levies the tax. The cartoonist uses the name "Fairness" to mean just the opposite, *unfairness*.

EXERCISE 5

Questions 1–3 are based on the following passage.

(1) The best political system ever developed is the two-party system of the United States. (2) Since the Civil War, no third party has been able to threaten the political power of either the Democratic Party or the Republican Party. (3) Every president of the last one hundred years has been a member of one of these two parties. (4) No third party has been able to gain control of either house of Congress. (5) The country has been spared the chaos that results when there are more than two parties. (6) And the people have not had to endure the tyranny of one-party rule.

1. Which of the following sentences from the passage are opinions?

   (1) sentences (1), (2), and (3)
   (2) sentences (2), (3), and (4)
   (3) sentences (3), (4), and (5)
   (4) sentences (4), (5), and (6)
   (5) sentences (1), (5), and (6)

2. Which of the following statements is supported by the passage?

   (1) A third-party candidate could win a national election if he or she had enough money to run a campaign.
   (2) The two-party system is outdated and is in urgent need of change.
   (3) The Republican and the Democratic parties are the only political parties that could be successful in the United States.
   (4) The United States is slowly turning toward a one-party political system.
   (5) Both the Democratic and the Republican parties have considerable strength and support in the United States.

3. Which statement best describes the tone of the passage?

   (1) The passage is completely straightforward and objective.
   (2) The passage reflects the author's bias for the two-party system of the United States.
   (3) The passage starts out being objective, then changes to an emotional tone.
   (4) The tone of the passage is angry and hostile.
   (5) The passage is bias-free.

Question 4 is based on the cartoon below.

4. What is the main idea of this cartoon?

   (1) Smoking is bad for your health.
   (2) Only people who live far away from other people should be allowed to smoke.
   (3) There are getting to be far fewer areas where people are allowed to smoke.
   (4) Automobile exhaust and cigarette smoke pollute the air.
   (5) Smokers won't bother anyone in the desert.

Questions 5 and 6 are based on the cartoon below.

5. What is the main idea of this cartoon?

   (1) People have a hard time cashing their Social Security checks.
   (2) The national debt is higher than ever.
   (3) Bankers have a hard time deciding on good credit risks.
   (4) People should stay away from banks.
   (5) People are worried about the Social Security system going broke.

6. What can you infer about the cartoonist?

   (1) He feels that the nation's economy is strong.
   (2) He has once worked as a banker.
   (3) He has little faith in the Social Security system.
   (4) He opposes loans to the federal government.
   (5) He feels that the Social Security system should be done away with.

Answers are on page 321.

Writing Activity 4

Find an editorial cartoon in a newspaper or magazine. What is the main idea of the cartoon? What symbols are used in the cartoon? Is the cartoon effective in getting its point across to you? Explain why or why not.

Answers will vary.

PART TWO

Understanding
Social Studies

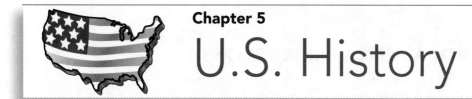

Chapter 5

U.S. History

In this chapter, you will study U.S. history. You study history to learn about important events that happened in the past. You often compare what happened in the past to what is happening now. As you read, try to keep in mind events today that are similar to those of the past. You may find that, indeed, history repeats itself.

Exploration of the New World: 1492–1783

> ### Key Word
>
> **indentured servant**—someone who worked for a specific period of time in the American colonies as payment of a debt

Many European powers explored and settled the Americas, North and South, to find new sources of wealth. Columbus represented Spain when he sailed across the Atlantic in 1492. He was trying to find a new route to India and the Far East. Instead, he found the Western Hemisphere, which Europeans called the New World. After that voyage, Spain took over many of the Caribbean islands, Mexico, and most of Central and South America. Spain took huge amounts of the silver and gold it found in its new colonies back to Europe.

England and France led the settlement of North America. England established colonies along the Atlantic coast in the 1600s in Jamestown, Plymouth, and Massachusetts Bay. France established settlements in what is now Canada, along the Ohio and Mississippi River valleys, and south to New Orleans near the Gulf of Mexico.

Many of the English colonies were started by Englishmen in search of fortunes. But the colonies were populated by people trying to escape prison or poverty in Europe. Between 50 and 75 percent of the colonists became indentured servants, bound to spend a certain number of years serving a master. This service was usually in payment for their passage to the New World. After this period of service, the indentured servants were free colonists. Slaves, on the other hand, were forcibly imported from Africa for cheap labor, often for a lifetime. They also became a large part of the colonial population. Other colonists, such as the Puritans, came to establish religious communities.

NORTH AMERICA PRIOR TO 1763

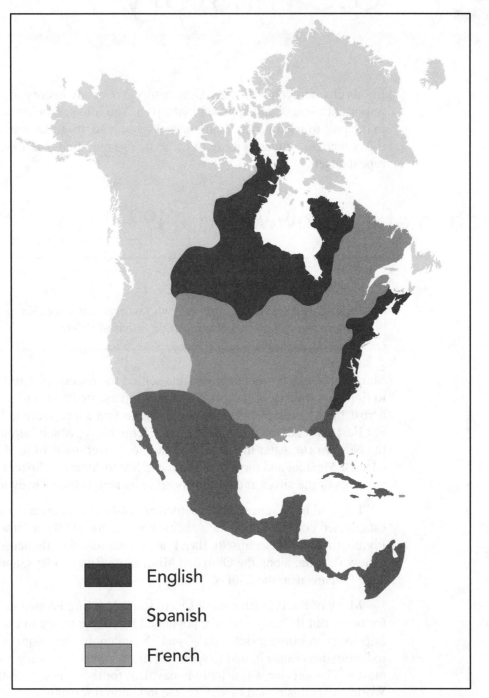

EXERCISE 1

Directions: Based on the passage and the map, answer the questions in the space provided.

1. Which person's explorations influenced other countries to explore America?

   _____

2. What did Spain find in the New World that was of great value?

   _____

3. Why did some people become indentured servants?

   _____

4. What is the difference between an indentured servant and a slave?

   _____

   _____

   _____

5. Which country settled in the central part of North America?

   _____

6. Which country claimed land in the northern part of North America?

   _____

7. Why did the Puritans come to North America?

   _____

8. About what percent of the colonists became indentured servants?

   _____

9. Which country did Columbus represent when he sailed across the Atlantic?

   _____

Answers are on page 321.

The Development of the American Colonies

Key Words

mercantilism—a seventeenth century practice in which the colonies supplied the mother country with raw materials and became a market for manufactured goods

representative—one who stands or acts for another through delegated authority

---

The English colonies developed an expanding trade in lumber, tobacco, and other agricultural products. Slave traders also made huge profits from the growing slave trade. The colonists began industries in shipbuilding, textiles, shoes, and iron making. Large and busy towns grew up around the seaports. England controlled trade with the colonies through a policy of mercantilism. England passed laws to slow the growth of colonial industries and to force the colonies to be dependent on England for their manufactured goods.

Each American colony had a governor and an elected representative body to pass laws on taxes and other matters. These representative bodies became the centers of opposition to English colonial policies. As the colonies grew, they tried to expand west. Their expansion was blocked by the French and the Indians. The long-standing competition between England and France came to a head during the French and Indian War (1756–1763). France lost the war and almost all of its North American territories to England. France could no longer block westward expansion.

EXERCISE 2

Directions: Put a check in front of the correct answer to the questions that follow.

1. Why did England try to stop the growth of industry in its colonies?

    _____ (1) to make the colonists dependent upon English manufactured goods

    _____ (2) to avoid a war with France

    _____ (3) to make colonists buy English agricultural products

2. Which of the following is true of government in the colonies?

    _____ (1) Governors ran each colony's affairs with an iron hand.

    _____ (2) Representative bodies had no power at all.

    _____ (3) Representative bodies became centers of opposition to English policies.

3. What happened as a result of the French and Indian War?

    _____ (1) The colonists no longer had to pay taxes.

    _____ (2) The policy of mercantilism ended.

    _____ (3) France lost most of its North American territories to England.

4. In the seventeenth century, colonies supplied the mother country with raw materials and also did which of the following?

    _____ (1) expanded westward

    _____ (2) bought manufactured goods

    _____ (3) took over Native American territories

Answers are on page 321.

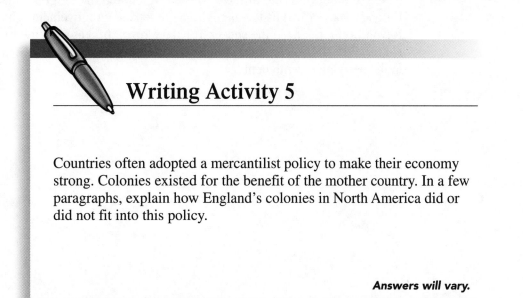

Writing Activity 5

Countries often adopted a mercantilist policy to make their economy strong. Colonies existed for the benefit of the mother country. In a few paragraphs, explain how England's colonies in North America did or did not fit into this policy.

Answers will vary.

The Road to Revolution and Independence

Key Word

tyranny—a government in which all power is in the hands of a single ruler

In 1763, England passed laws to tax the American colonists to help pay for the French and Indian War. The English also believed that the colonists should help pay the costs of government. Among the laws were the Sugar Act, the Stamp Act, and the Tea Act. The English also tightened political control over the colonial government and courts. The colonists protested these laws by dumping tea into Boston Harbor (called the Boston Tea Party). Colonial protesters cried out that English rule had become a tyranny. The colonists had no political representation in England, where the tax laws were passed.

The English responded to the Boston Tea Party with the Intolerable Acts. Boston Harbor was closed until the colonists paid for the destroyed tea. Colonists were forced to pay to house English soldiers. The powers of the colonial courts were also cut back. The governor had to approve any town meeting.

In response, the colonists called the First Continental Congress in 1774 to resist English control and to increase their rights. In April 1775, British troops and American colonists fought at Lexington and Concord, Massachusetts. The battles marked the beginning of the American Revolution. The Second Continental Congress met later in 1775. It voted for an army and named George Washington as commander-in-chief. In July 1776, the Congress adopted the Declaration of Independence. The colonists waged a five-year war with England. It ended in 1781 with the surrender of the British at Yorktown, Virginia. Independence was won.

The American Revolution established the principle that government must be based on the consent of the governed. It marked the first time that a European power had lost a colony to an independent movement. The American Revolution influenced the successful slave revolution against the French in Haiti (1795–1803) and later struggles in Latin America against Spanish rule in the early nineteenth century.

EXERCISE 3

Directions: Match the date on the left with the important event that happened in that year on the right. Write the correct letter on the line.

_____ **1.** 1774   (a)   The British surrendered in Yorktown, Virginia.

_____ **2.** 1775   (b)   The First Continental Congress was called to resist British control over the American colonies.

_____ **3.** 1776   (c)   Slaves began to revolt against the French in Haiti.

_____ **4.** 1781   (d)   The Second Continental Congress voted for an army and appointed George Washington as its commander-in-chief.

_____ **5.** 1795   (e)   The Declaration of Independence was adopted.

Directions: Put a check in front of the correct answer to the questions that follow.

6. What was the purpose of the Boston Tea Party?

_____ (1) to entertain English soldiers

_____ (2) to celebrate the Tea Act

_____ (3) to protest unfair British laws in the colonies

7. What effect did the American Revolution have on other colonies and countries?

_____ (1) Most other countries took on democratic forms of government.

_____ (2) Latin America rebelled against Spain's dominance.

_____ (3) The English made several new settlements in colonial America.

Answers are on pages 321–322.

EXERCISE 4

Directions: Read the passage below from the Declaration of Independence and answer the following questions.

We hold these truths to be self-evident, that all men are created equal, that they are endowed by their Creator with certain unalienable Rights, that among these are Life, Liberty, and the pursuit of Happiness. That to secure these rights, Governments are instituted among Men, deriving their just powers from the consent of the governed, That whenever any Form of Government becomes destructive of these ends, it is the Right of the People to alter or abolish it, and to institute a new government, laying its foundation on such principles and organizing its powers in such form, as to them shall seem most likely to effect their Safety and Happiness.

Put a check in front of the correct answer or answers.

1. What are "unalienable rights"?

    _____ (1) rights that came into being when the colonies were established

    _____ (2) rights given by a monarch

    _____ (3) rights that cannot be taken away

    _____ (4) rights that exist with the president's consent

    _____ (5) rights that exists only when they are written down

2. According to the passage, if a government becomes destructive of peoples' rights, which of the following can people do?

    _____ (1) change the government

    _____ (2) appoint a new monarch

    _____ (3) begin a new government

    _____ (4) stage a military coup

    _____ (5) assassinate the leader

Answers are on page 322.

The Triangular Trade Route

Fifteen million Africans were violently torn away from their homes and forced into slavery in the New World. Many American slave traders followed a triangular trade route. They took rum to Africa to trade for slaves and then sailed across the Atlantic to the West Indies. This second leg of the voyage was the awful "Middle Passage" in which the slaves were carried by ship in very close quarters, and many slaves died. In the West Indies, the slaves were sold for money or traded for molasses. The molasses was taken back to New England and distilled into rum for another trip to Africa.

Slavery proved to be very profitable. Each voyage produced between 100 and 1,000 percent profit. The slave trade provided cheap labor to run plantations in Brazil, the West Indies, and North America. More than 700 American ships were involved, and more than 100 New England distilleries supplied rum for trading. By the eighteenth century, the English controlled the slave trade. Profits were used to finance economic and industrial growth in England during the nineteenth century.

After 1808, it was illegal to bring slaves into the United States. But slavery itself did not end in the United States until after the Civil War.

TRIANGULAR TRADE ROUTE

EXERCISE 5

Directions: Based on the passage and the map, answer the questions that follow in the space provided.

1. Which three areas formed the basis of the Triangular Trade Route?

   _____

2. Why was molasses important in slave trade business?

   _____

   _____

3. Why were slaves important to the plantation system in colonial America?

   _____

   _____

4. How were American ship owners affected by slavery?

   _____

   _____

5. How did slavery benefit England in the nineteenth century?

   _____

   _____

6. When did slavery end in the United States?

   _____

Answers are on page 322.

Writing Activity 6

Write a few paragraphs describing what the Middle Passage might have been like. What hardships did slaves endure? Why would many slaves have died during this leg of the journey?

Answers will vary.

A New Nation Establishes Itself

After winning independence from England, great political disagreements took place over how much power should go to the federal government and how much to the states. When a strong Constitution was adopted in 1787, the federal government was able to slowly gain power over the states. The first president, George Washington, organized the various government departments. He also established taxes to pay for running these departments, and set up the federal courts.

The new nation had gained from England most of the land east of the Mississippi River. But disputes continued over forts on the Great Lakes. In 1800, France was back in North America. France got most of the Louisiana Territory from Spain and controlled the Mississippi River. In 1803, President Thomas Jefferson bought the huge territory from the French for $15 million. The area doubled the size of the country. It also put the Mississippi River firmly under American control.

The War of 1812 was fought over the issue of English interference with American merchant ships. The war ended with no clear winner. U.S. boundaries were unchanged. However, the War of 1812 was important for the United States for two reasons. First, it helped unite Americans by temporarily making national interests more important than sectional, or regional, interests. Second, the war proved that the United States was strong enough militarily to keep its independence. With new land available in the West and the removal of the English threat, the road to westward expansion was finally open.

EXERCISE 6

Directions: Put a check in front of the correct answer to the questions that follow.

1. When did the new United States face its most serious problems?

   _____ (1) when the British had control of forts along the Mississippi and the French had control of the Great Lakes

   _____ (2) when the British had control of forts on the Great Lakes and the Spanish had control of the Mississippi

   _____ (3) when the British had control of forts on the Great Lakes and the French had control of the Mississippi

   _____ (4) when the French captured U.S. merchant ships and the British controlled the Mississippi

2. As a result of the War of 1812, which of the following did the United States not gain?

   _____ (1) temporary unity around national interests

   _____ (2) stronger sectional, or regional, interests

   _____ (3) greater military strength

   _____ (4) an ability to stay independent

3. Based on the U.S. experience in the War of 1812, what can you conclude about governments facing a divided nation?

   _____ (1) A war can be used to temporarily unite the country.

   _____ (2) A war can be used to cause more divisions.

   _____ (3) A war can be used to prevent the growth of nationalism.

   _____ (4) A war can be used to strengthen the government.

Answers are on page 322.

Westward Expansion

> ### Key Words
>
> **Manifest Destiny**—the American belief that it was the country's destiny to take over the entire North American continent
>
> **annexation**—taking over of lands not originally part of one's country

From 1800 to 1850, Americans believed that it was their destiny to occupy the land from the Atlantic to the Pacific Ocean. This belief, and the policies that developed from it, came to be called Manifest Destiny. The country soon obtained Florida from Spain and Texas from Mexico.

The Mexican government gave grants of land to American settlers in its province of Texas during the 1820s. Later, these settlers rebelled against Mexico. They declared Texas an independent republic in 1836. The brief but fierce war was famous for the battle of the Alamo in San Antonio.

THE UNITED STATES EXPANDS, 1783–1853

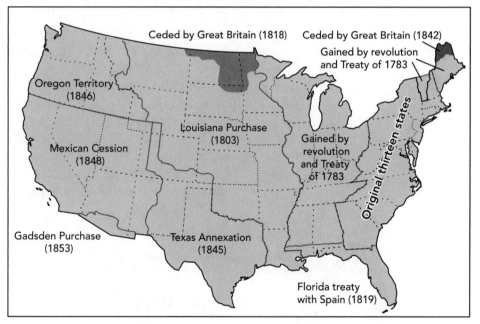

In 1845, the United States annexed Texas as a state. The annexation angered many Mexicans. When U.S. troops occupied a border region claimed by Mexico, the Mexican War began. The United States won the war and took control of even more land. This area now holds California, New Mexico, Arizona, Nevada, Utah, Texas, and parts of Colorado. The United States also reached agreement with England and acquired the Oregon Territory.

The new lands contained rich farmlands and vast pastures for cattle and sheep. There were boundless forests and rich stores of gold, silver, and other ores. All of these resources contributed greatly to the economic growth of the United States.

Economic Development and Sectionalism

Key Word

sectionalism—the economic, political, and social differences among the regions of the United States

---

Economic development was rapid during this period. Canal building and the development of the steamboat gave a big boost to trade and transportation by water. After the 1820s, railroad building became a major economic activity. By 1860, the United States was crisscrossed with about 30,000 miles of track.

The growth of the cotton industry brought in more money than all other exports combined. This boom began with Eli Whitney's invention of the cotton gin in the 1790s. The cotton gin cleaned large amounts of cotton so it could be used in manufacturing. The Industrial Revolution had led to the establishment of large, mechanized mills in England and New England to process this cotton. The demand for Southern cotton grew. Cotton was well suited for growing on large plantations. In this way, cotton helped firmly establish slave labor as the basis for the South's economy.

Territorial expansion and the development of different regional economies created political problems. The Southern economy was based on slavery and the export of cotton. The Western economy was based on several crops grown on small farms. The North, especially the Northeast, became the region of shipping, finance, and industry. These differences led to the growth of sectional feelings. For example, people were proud to be Southerners or Westerners. Under sectionalism, politicians in each region defended that region's economic interests. The Southern states argued strongly for the rights of states to do as they pleased without federal government interference. The growth of sectionalism was an important cause of the Civil War.

Writing Activity 7

Sectionalism has a long history in the United States. In a few paragraphs, write how sectionalism makes itself known in your region. Explain if sectionalism is more against other regions or more against the federal government.

Answers will vary.

EXERCISE 7

Directions: Study the map below. Then put a check in front of the correct answer to the questions that follow.

SECTIONALISM AND THE VOTE IN CONGRESS ON TEXAS ANNEXATION, 1845

(vote on passage of joint resolution)

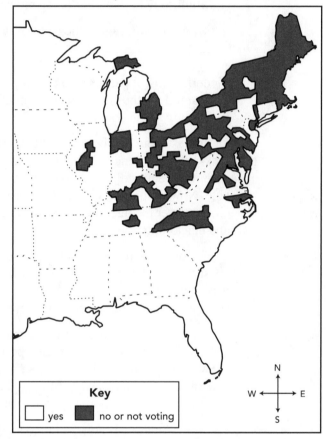

Key

☐ yes   ■ no or not voting

1. In which region did most states vote *no* on the question of the annexation of Texas?

   _____ (1) South

   _____ (2) West

   _____ (3) North

2. Which of the following can you infer from the voting pattern?

   _____ (1) The Northern states were opposed to another slave-owning Southern state in the Union.

   _____ (2) The Northern states supported Mexico's right to Texas.

   _____ (3) The Southern states preferred that Texas stay independent.

   _____ (4) The Northern states feared Texas's industrial competition.

Answers are on page 322.

Politics and Movements

Key Words

Jacksonian Democracy—an age of reform that roughly paralleled President Andrew Jackson's term in office

abolitionist—member of an antislavery movement before the Civil War

women's suffrage—the right of women to vote

Modern political parties also developed in the period from 1783 to 1850. They stood for the very real economic and political differences that were developing in the country.

Issues about democratic rights became important during Andrew Jackson's presidency (1829–1837). Before Jacksonian Democracy, most states had required people to own a certain amount of property in order to vote. Now property qualifications for voting were dropped. All white male citizens over the age of twenty-one could vote. However, Indians, women, and blacks still could not vote.

Reforms of this period also included the popular vote to confirm state constitutions. The filling of public office by elections rather than appointment was another reform. Horace Mann led a movement to establish free public schools. This is a basic right in a democracy.

An unhappy result of national growth was increasing conflict with the Indians. The federal government's policy was to move the Indians west of the Mississippi River. The Indians tried and failed to keep their homelands. Cherokees and Creeks were forcibly moved from the Carolinas, Georgia, and Alabama to the Oklahoma Territory in the late 1830s.

More Americans attacked the system of slavery. These people were called abolitionists. They wanted to abolish, or do away with, slavery altogether. The secret Underground Railroad helped slaves escape to freedom. The abolitionists helped create an antislavery feeling in the North and West. This feeling paved the way for popular support for the Union position in the Civil War.

Women continued to have few rights. But women were active in the early antislavery societies. This experience helped them in the fight for the vote, or women's suffrage. Elizabeth Cady Stanton and Lucretia Mott founded the first national women's organization at Seneca Falls, New York, in 1848. Its goal was women's rights.

EXERCISE 8

Questions 1 and 2 are based on the passage on the previous page.

1. Which of the following describes the extension of voting rights during Andrew Jackson's presidency?

   (1) All white males were allowed to vote.
   (2) All Americans were given the right to vote.
   (3) It included women with property.
   (4) It ended the three-fifths rule for counting slaves.
   (5) It has not changed since then.

2. The emergence of protest movements for social change as early as the 1820s shows what about these movements?

   (1) They were a very important part of U.S. history.
   (2) They were inspired by a handful of radicals.
   (3) They were shortsighted and achieved only limited goals.
   (4) They were not very important to the two-party system.
   (5) They were a threat to the democratic way of life.

Answers are on page 322.

EXERCISE 9

Directions: Match the person or term on the left with the description on the right. Put the correct letter on the line.

_____ **1.** Jacksonian Democracy

_____ **2.** Horace Mann

_____ **3.** Oklahoma Territory

_____ **4.** Underground Railroad

_____ **5.** Elizabeth Cady Stanton

(a) secret network that helped slaves escape

(b) leader of movement for free public schools

(c) nationwide movement concerned with the spread of democratic rights

(d) leader of the women's suffrage movement

(e) location that Creeks and Cherokees were forced to move to

Answers are on page 322.

EXERCISE 10

Directions: Read the letter below from a settler ready to head West and then put a check in front of the correct answer to the questions that follow.

Dear Sir:

We arrived here (St. Jo) on the 14th. All in good order or as good as could be expected. Some of our animals were stiffened by standing on the boat. The weather was very disagreeable and cold until yesterday. We put up in town one week to recruit our animals. . . . We bought two mules at St. Jo for $120.00. They are as good or better than an average of our other ones. After our arrival here, we concluded to sell one of our wagons and only take three. We sold it to some advantage. We are going to put four mules to two wagons and two mules to one.

Mules, oxen, corn, and oats can be had to some better advantage than in St. Louis but nothing else. They put the screws very tight to emigrants for all small jobs and articles the emigrants are obliged to get, and upon the whole, I think outfits can be had as cheap in St. Louis excepting livestock. . . .

There have been teams starting for several days past, heavy loaded with feed. The grass is very backward, and . . . for some distance on the prairies, little or no old grass to be had as it has been eaten and burned off. My intention is to haul feed to do us about 12 or 14 days. Consequently I want to see whether it is warm enough for grass to grow while we have feed, so that when our feed is out we can have some grass. There has not been any here yet but it begins to start or make appearance this morning since the rain. . . . My health is good at this time and has been since I left. . . . I have concluded not to go to Council Bluff as the season is late and that point so much north of this. There is at least 10 days difference in vegetation between this place and St. Louis. . . . There is large quantity of cattle starting and emigrants fitted out in every way, but their wagons are generally heavier than ours. We have as light wagons as any that I have seen and our teams look as well as any. There is some better and many not half as good.

From yours respectfully,
A. H. Wilson, 1852

1. What can you infer about the route these settlers planned to take?

_____ (1) It was well-known.

_____ (2) It was unexplored.

_____ (3) It was lightly traveled.

_____ (4) It was very rough terrain.

2. Why did the group have to bring animal feed?

_____ (1) The animals got sick from eating prairie grass.

_____ (2) The old grass had been eaten and burned off.

_____ (3) They planned to sell it to other settlers.

_____ (4) They planned to use some of it for seed.

3. What can you infer about merchants in St. Joseph?

_____ (1) They often charged more than merchants in St. Louis.

_____ (2) They earned more money from local townspeople.

_____ (3) They charged much less than merchants in St. Louis.

_____ (4) Their businesses could not handle the settlers.

4. Which things could the group buy more easily in St. Joseph than in St. Louis?

_____ (1) wagons

_____ (2) feed for the animals

_____ (3) heavy clothes

_____ (4) mules, oxen, corn, and oats

Answers are on pages 322–323.

The Problem of Slavery

Key Word

Dred Scott case—the controversial 1857 Supreme Court decision ruling that slaves were not citizens and that slaves were the property of their masters

---

Sectionalism continued to deepen in the country until 1860. Northern manufacturers wanted to build an industrial country based on manufacturing, free labor, and many kinds of farming. Southern plantation owners preferred a single-crop plantation economy based on slave labor.

The argument over slavery was at the heart of sectionalism. It grew sharper as the sections competed for control over the new western territories. Control of most of the western territories could tip the political balance in the U.S. Congress. The whole future development of the United States was at stake. Peace was kept only through a series of compromises.

The purchase of the huge Louisiana Territory raised the issue of "free soil versus slave soil." Antislavery forces wanted slavery banned. Proslavery forces wanted the future states to decide for themselves whether to be free or slave states. The Missouri Compromise of 1820 admitted Missouri as a slave state and Maine as a free state. Slavery was limited to the land stretching west from the southern border of Missouri. Still, large new areas were opened to the expansion of slavery.

In the *Dred Scott* case of 1857, the Supreme Court ruled that slaves were not citizens. They were the property of their masters. Slave owners' property rights were protected by the U.S. Constitution. So Congress could make no law prohibiting slavery. The *Dred Scott* decision created great anger against the South. People feared the further expansion of slavery.

Antislavery feelings grew with the publication in 1853 of Harriet Beecher Stowe's best-selling novel, *Uncle Tom's Cabin*. In 1859, John Brown, a militant abolitionist, attacked the federal arsenal at Harpers Ferry (now part of West Virginia). He tried to get weapons to arm slaves for rebellion. Brown failed and was hanged. Frederick Douglass, an exslave and eloquent spokesman against slavery, toured the North, raising support for abolitionism.

The newly formed Republican Party was opposed to the spread of slavery and in favor of economic growth. This position helped the Republican Party to grow rapidly. In 1860, its presidential candidate, Abraham Lincoln, won the election.

EXERCISE 11

Directions: Circle *T* for each true statement, or *F* for each false statement.

T F **1.** Slavery became the leading problem in sectionalism.

T F **2.** Control over new states created in the western territories threatened to tip the balance of power in the U.S. Congress.

T F **3.** The Missouri Compromise settled the issue of slavery in the territories once and for all.

T F **4.** The *Dred Scott* case protected the rights of property owners.

T F **5.** Harriet Beecher Stowe's novel, *Uncle Tom's Cabin*, helped build strong feelings against slavery.

T F **6.** The election of a Republican president in 1860 was not likely to please the South.

T F **7.** John Brown was hanged because he gave weapons to slaves so they could lead a rebellion.

T F **8.** Frederick Douglass attacked the federal arsenal at Harpers Ferry.

Answers are on page 323.

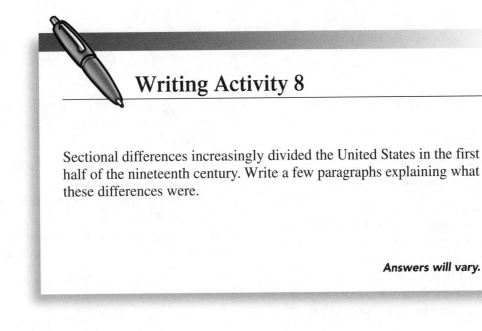

Writing Activity 8

Sectional differences increasingly divided the United States in the first half of the nineteenth century. Write a few paragraphs explaining what these differences were.

Answers will vary.

The Civil War

> ### Key Word
>
> **secession**—the act of a state seceding, or leaving, a country to which it belongs

---

The South believed that the balance of power had been permanently tipped against it by the 1850s. Northern political and economic strength grew with the admission of California, Oregon, and Minnesota into the Union. It was only a matter of time before a majority of free states would vote for a constitutional amendment abolishing slavery. The Southern leaders feared Lincoln and quickly moved for secession from the Union. They formed the Confederate States of America.

Lincoln was unwilling to allow the breakup of the Union, and war began in 1861 between the North and the South. The industrial North had more people and more resources to fight a war. The South had excellent military leaders and fought on their own land. However, Lincoln's Emancipation Proclamation in 1863 freed the slaves who lived in rebel territory. In addition, the recruitment of ex-slaves into the Union army helped to undermine the South. The war to save the Union turned into a crusade against slavery.

After four long years, the North's superior ability to maintain a modern army ground down the Confederate states. General Robert E. Lee's army surrendered in the spring of 1865.

PRE-GED PRACTICE

EXERCISE 12

Questions 1 and 2 are based on the passage above.

1. Southern leaders chiefly seceded from the Union for which of the following reasons?

   (1) They underestimated Lincoln.
   (2) They believed they could win the conflict.
   (3) They feared a majority of free states would vote to abolish slavery.
   (4) They wanted to stop abolitionists from provoking slave rebellions.
   (5) They wanted to extend slavery to the North.

2. According to this summary, what was the effect of President Lincoln's Emancipation Proclamation?

   (1) It turned the war to save the Union into a crusade against slavery.
   (2) It had no effect on the North's war effort.
   (3) It had little effect on the Confederacy.
   (4) It freed all slaves in the North and South.
   (5) It was welcomed by the Confederacy.

   Answers are on page 323.

Reconstruction

> ### Key Word
>
> **impeachment**—the process of charging a public officeholder with a crime or misconduct in office so that the person can be removed from office

The time of rebuilding following the Civil War is known as the Reconstruction era. President Lincoln and Andrew Johnson, his successor, tried to reunite the torn nation quickly. They were willing to let Southerners decide most questions of race relations in the defeated states. Both Lincoln and Johnson were willing to pardon Confederate officers and politicians. Many Confederate officials then returned to Southern legislatures in 1865. These legislatures passed so-called Black Codes. These laws severely restricted the rights of former slaves.

Radical Republicans in Congress were enraged by the actions of Southern state legislatures. They wanted far-reaching social changes in the South. They also wanted protection for the rights of freed slaves. The Radicals were in favor of a tough policy toward the South and former Confederate officials. Their plan was adopted.

The Radicals' conflicts with President Johnson became so heated that impeachment proceedings were brought against him. However, Johnson was not convicted by the Senate.

The Radicals sponsored many important reforms and constitutional amendments. The Thirteenth Amendment (1865) abolished slavery. The Fourteenth Amendment (1868) made blacks citizens who had equal rights under the law. The Fifteenth Amendment (1870) granted black men the right to vote.

The Radicals' Reconstruction plan temporarily forced many former Confederate officials out of office. For the first time, blacks were elected to statewide offices and to the U.S. Senate. In the South, the Freedmen's Bureau set up the first schools for blacks. Reconstruction ended in 1877. It was part of a compromise between conservative Republicans and Southern Democrats in the disputed presidential election of 1876. The compromise agreement gave Rutherford B. Hayes the crucial Southern Democratic support he needed for election. In return, Hayes pulled the remaining U.S. troops out of the South.

Reconstruction made few economic and social changes in the South. Ex-slaves did not receive the "40 acres and a mule" that they had been promised. Large plantations still remained. The freedmen had little land and no economic base from which to defend their newly won freedom. Many issues of justice and equality would not be settled for another hundred years.

EXERCISE 13

Directions: Match the term on the left with its description on the right. Write the correct letter on the line.

_____ 1. impeachment

_____ 2. Black Codes

_____ 3. Thirteenth Amendment

_____ 4. Fourteenth Amendment

_____ 5. Fifteenth Amendment

(a) made blacks citizens who had equal rights under the law

(b) abolished slavery

(c) gave black men the right to vote

(d) passed by Southern state legislatures to restrict the rights of former slaves

(e) charging a public official with a crime or with misconduct

Answers are on page 323.

PRE-GED PRACTICE

EXERCISE 14

Questions 1 and 2 are based on the table below.

COMPARISON OF RESOURCES BETWEEN NORTH AND SOUTH IN 1860

	North	South
population	71%	29%
railroad mileage	72%	28%
iron and steel	93%	7%
farm output	65%	35%

1. In which resource does the North have the greatest advantage compared with the South?

   (1) population
   (2) railroad mileage
   (3) iron and steel
   (4) farm output
   (5) production of cotton

2. Which of the following does this table illustrate?

   (1) that the South had a superior railroad system
   (2) equal regional economic development before the Civil War
   (3) the great agricultural wealth of the South
   (4) the economic advantages of the North
   (5) the agricultural weakness of the South

Answers are on page 323.

EXERCISE 15

Directions: Read the letter below sent by an ex-slave to his former master. Then answer the questions that follow.

To My Old Master

Sir:

I got your letter, and was glad to find that you had not forgotten Jourdon, and that you wanted me to come back and live with you again, promising to do better for me than anybody else can. I have often felt uneasy about you. I thought the Yankees would have hung you long before this, for harboring Rebs they found at your house. I suppose they never heard about your going to Colonel Martin's to kill the Union soldier that was left by his company in their stable. Although you shot at me twice before I left you, I did not want to hear of your being hurt, and am glad that you are still living. It would do me good to go back to the dear old home again. . . . I want to know particularly what the good chance is you propose to give me. I am doing tolerably well here, I get 25 dollars a month, with victuals [food] and clothing; have a comfortable home for Mandy, the folks call her Mrs. Anderson, and the children go to school and are learning well. . . . We are kindly treated. . . .

As to my freedom, which you say I can have, there is nothing to be gained on that score, as I got my free papers in 1864 from the Provost-Marshal-General of the Department of Nashville. Mandy says she would be afraid to go back without some proof that you were disposed to treat us justly and kindly; and we have concluded to test your sincerity by asking you to send us our wages for the time we served you. This will make us forget and forgive old scores, and rely on your justice and friendship in the future. I served you faithfully for thirty-two years, and Mandy for twenty years. At twenty-five dollars a month for me, and two dollars a week for Mandy, our earnings would amount to eleven thousand six hundred and eighty dollars. Add to this the interest for the time our wages have been kept back, and deduct what you paid for our clothing, and three doctor's visits for me, and pulling a tooth for Mandy, and the balance will show what we are in justice entitled to.

Please send the money by Adam's Express, in care of V. Winters, Esq., Dayton, Ohio. If you fail to pay us for faithful labors in the past, we can have little faith in your promises in the future. We trust the good Maker has opened your eyes to the wrongs which you and your fathers have done to me and my fathers, in making us toil for you for generations without recompense. Here I draw my wages every Saturday night; but in Tennessee there was never any pay-day for the Negroes anymore than for horses or cows. Surely there will be a day of reckoning for those who defraud the laborer of his hire.

From your old servant,
Jourdon Anderson

Directions: Put a check in front of the correct answer to the questions that follow.

1. What does the letter demonstrate about some ex-slaves?

_____ (1) They were miserable as freemen and wanted to return to their former homes.

_____ (2) They were easily attracted by the appeals of their old masters.

_____ (3) They had just as hard a time in the North as in the South.

_____ (4) They clearly understood how slavery had exploited them.

2. The letter expresses which view about slavery?

_____ (1) It had been beneficial to blacks.

_____ (2) It had reduced human beings to the level of animals.

_____ (3) It was preferable to the life Anderson has found in the North.

_____ (4) It had provided a good education for Anderson's children.

Answers are on page 323.

Changes in Society: 1865–1900

> ## Key Word
>
> **industrialization**—the development of large-scale industries and mass-production techniques

During the period from the end of the Civil War to 1900, some great changes occurred across the country. The foundations of modern America were laid in the factories, mills, mines, and cities of the Midwest and the East. The widespread settlement of the West meant the end of the frontier.

Western migration greatly increased after the Civil War. Indians who were pushed off their lands fought the U.S. cavalry from 1865 to 1890. The Indian wars finally came to an end in 1890 following the massacre by federal troops of more than 200 Sioux men, women, and children at Wounded Knee, South Dakota. At about the same time, the last of the western lands were settled and the land rush slowed down.

The eastern United States was rapidly becoming an industrial urban society. Northern businessmen had gained wealth and experience from the Civil War. After the war, they moved quickly to change civilian production. In doing so, they put America on the road to industrialization. Large-scale production began to dominate American economic growth.

EXERCISE 16

Directions: Circle *T* for each true statement, or *F* for each false statement.

T F **1.** From the Civil War to 1900, the foundations of modern America were laid in the Midwest and East.

T F **2.** The close of the western frontier and the end of the Indian wars took place at about the same time.

T F **3.** The massacre at Wounded Knee, South Dakota, brought an end to the Indian Wars.

Answers are on page 323.

Technology, Industrialization, and Urbanization

Key Word

urbanization—the growth of large cities, with a population shift away from rural areas

---

Inventions revolutionized all areas of life. The national railroad system greatly expanded. The telegraph established nationwide communication. The invention of the Bessemer and open-hearth smelt processes led to the creation of a giant steel industry. Tremendous growth in energy resources took place. New coal fields opened, the electric dynamo was invented, and oil well drilling developed.

Technical advances also revolutionized agriculture by mechanizing the farm. The McCormick Reaper drastically reduced the time and people needed to cut grain. The mechanization of agriculture freed more farm laborers to work in the new factories in the cities.

Industrialization caused a gigantic growth in the population of cities and towns. Americans moved to where the jobs were. The population shift from rural areas to the cities is known as urbanization. Industry centered around sources of raw materials, energy sources, and good transportation. Large cities like Pittsburgh and Chicago took shape around steel mills and factories. Even more new industry was needed to build housing and transportation for the new urban areas.

Immigration from Europe also played an important role in the growth of American cities. About 25 million Europeans were recruited to work in U.S. mines, mills, and forges. Agents were sent to Europe to encourage people to come to the United States. Millions of Europeans faced economic hardship and political repression in their homelands. They were eager to come to the United States to find a better life. Large numbers of Asians came to build the railroads in the West. Most of the new immigrants settled in the big cities. These people often faced poverty and discrimination.

A powerful new group of financiers and industrialists sparked America's industrialization. Andrew Carnegie, John D. Rockefeller, J. P. Morgan, Cornelius Vanderbilt, and others put together the giant companies that ruled American economic life. They created monopolies that centralized control of business in a few hands. This power was often misused to keep prices high and wages low. These company owners used their great economic power to dominate politics. They also got laws passed that were favorable to their businesses.

EXERCISE 17

Questions 1–6 are based on the passage on the previous page.

1. Which person was most directly responsible for technological advances in agriculture?

   (1) Andrew Carnegie
   (2) Cornelius Vanderbilt
   (3) Cyrus McCormick
   (4) John D. Rockefeller
   (5) J. P. Morgan

2. Europeans and Asians who came to America expected to find all EXCEPT which of the following?

   (1) freedom from economic problems
   (2) a better life in this country
   (3) freedom from political repression
   (4) a chance to work in U.S. factories or on the railroads
   (5) poverty and discrimination in housing and in the workplace

3. Financiers and industrialists did NOT create monopolies to do which of the following?

   (1) keep the control of business in the hands of a few
   (2) lower prices and keep wages high
   (3) dominate the political arena
   (4) have favorable laws passed
   (5) gain economic power

4. What was the impact of industrialization in America?

   (1) It affected only industrial technology.
   (2) It influenced only where people lived.
   (3) It had little effect on the number of immigrants.
   (4) It revolutionized the entire country
   (5) It affected only agriculture.

5. Which of the following is true about urbanization in the United States?

   (1) It caused industrialization.
   (2) It was caused by the growth and centralization of industry.
   (3) It took place faster in the South than elsewhere.
   (4) It took place by simply moving farmers into the cities.
   (5) It met all the hopes of European immigrants for a better life.

6. Which of the following can you infer from this section?

   (1) Large-scale social change is usually very smooth and free of conflict.
   (2) Changes in one part of society, such as the economy, lead to changes in all other areas.
   (3) Change can take place in one part of society and have little effect on any other part.
   (4) The settling of the West was the most important event of this period.
   (5) Immigration caused America to industrialize.

Answers are on page 323.

The Impact on the South

Key Words

sharecropper—a tenant farmer who pays a portion of the crop as rent for the land

Jim Crow laws—racial segregation laws passed in the South during the late nineteenth and early twentieth centuries

---

In contrast to the North and West, the urban and industrial growth in the South was slow. Large areas of the South were still characterized by a backward agricultural system of sharecropping. The situation was much like the old plantation because tenant farmer sharecroppers, both black and white, did not own the land. They also had to pay part of their crop as rent. The sharecroppers were in constant debt to the large landowners.

After the end of Reconstruction, a new system of segregation based on Jim Crow laws destroyed any remaining hopes for racial equality. Poll taxes and literacy tests kept both blacks and poor whites from their right to vote. These abuses continued until the civil rights protests of the 1960s led to federal laws outlawing such practices.

EXERCISE 18

Directions: Based on the passage above, fill in the correct answers in the spaces provided.

1. Sharecroppers paid rent by giving the landowners _____.

2. Racial equality in the South made no progress under the _____.

3. Two things which kept blacks and poor whites from voting

   were _____ and _____.

4. Urban and industrial growth were slowest in the _____.

Answers are on page 324.

The Workers and Farmers Respond

Workers and farmers saw very little of the new riches from rapid industrialization. Factory, rail, and mine workers often worked more than twelve hours each day for extremely low pay. In reaction to these conditions, workers began to organize. The Knights of Labor was the first truly national federation of trade unions. Local labor disputes were widespread. The first nationwide strikes took place on the railroads. A railroad strike in 1877 affected much of the eastern United States. Street battles took place between troops and labor union supporters in Pittsburgh and Chicago.

Union organizers were only mildly successful. A few skilled craft unions survived to form the American Federation of Labor (AFL). But organizing drives for most unskilled and semiskilled laborers failed. Violence was frequent. In the 1894 Pullman strike in Chicago, unions were defeated by a combination of private police, state militia, and federal troops. Thirty strikers died and labor leaders were put in jail. Meanwhile, rural areas were swept by waves of protests over high credit costs and steep railroad freight rates. Mechanization had increased farm production. Bankers and the monopolies, however, harvested the wealth. Farmers were urged by their leaders to "raise less corn and more hell." They did. Across the country, they organized the Farmers' Alliances to fight for their interests.

Protests against monopoly power led to the passage of the Interstate Commerce Act (1887) and the Sherman Anti-Trust Act (1890). Nevertheless, the influence of the monopolies was great. The antitrust law was eventually enforced more against unions and farmers than against the monopolies. The failure of reform laws such as the Sherman Act led to strong public support for the Populists (People's Party) in the 1890s. This third-party movement aimed to control the monopolies. The Populists won over a million votes in 1892. In 1896, its demands were incorporated into the Democratic Party platform. Republican candidate William McKinley was supported by big business. He defeated Democrat William Jennings Bryan. Later, many Populist ideas were adopted by both parties.

In the last thirty years of the nineteenth century, industrialization and urbanization changed America. The social and political problems created by these changes were not solved. They would come up again in conflicts during the twentieth century.

EXERCISE 19

Put a check in front of the correct answer to the questions that follow.

1. What was the Populists' goal?

 _____ (1) to help establish more monopolies

 _____ (2) to protect the rights of Indians

 _____ (3) to control the power of unions

 _____ (4) to help unions in their struggle with big business

2. Drawing on the experience of America, what should today's developing countries that try to industrialize expect?

 _____ (1) a smooth transition to a new society

 _____ (2) little political turmoil

 _____ (3) widespread changes combined with political and social turmoil

 _____ (4) unions, farmers, and business working in harmony

3. What effect did workers' efforts to organize unions in this period have?

 _____ (1) Their efforts got unlimited support from owners.

 _____ (2) Their efforts were limited to local areas.

 _____ (3) Their efforts were often met with violent resistance.

 _____ (4) Their efforts succeeded in establishing large, lasting unions of unskilled workers.

4. Which of the following is NOT a reason why workers tried to become unionized?

 _____ (1) twelve-hour workdays

 _____ (2) extremely low pay

 _____ (3) rapid industrialization

 _____ (4) low credit costs

Answers are on page 324.

EXERCISE 20

Study the graph below and then answer each question in the space provided.

UNITED STATES IMMIGRATION, 1821–1990

Sources: *Immigration and Naturalization Service, U.S. Justice Department*

1. During which ten-year period did immigration reach its peak?

   _____

2. Which ten-year period had the lowest number of people

   immigrating to the United States?_____

3. Put a check in front of the generalization that can be drawn from the passage and the graph.

   _____ (1) Immigration was not important to urbanization.

   _____ (2) Immigration reached its peak during the period of rapid urban and industrial growth.

   _____ (3) Most immigrants did not settle in the city.

   _____ (4) Although immigration reached its peak during the late 1800s and early 1900s, it was not related to industrialization.

Answers are on page 324.

EXERCISE 21

Read the passage below and answer the questions that follow.

Farmers' Protests

The mechanization of agriculture increased farm productivity, but it left the farmers poor because of increased debt, high transportation costs, and low prices. Farmers were desperate, and several farm organizations formed to fight for a better economic deal.

The most important of these was the National Farmers' Alliance. It began in Texas in 1877 as a buying and selling cooperative. However, cooperatives did not solve the farmers' problems, and the alliance turned to politics. It won some local elections, but these did not give the farmers enough political power to control the banks and railroads.

In 1892, the alliance moved into national politics through the People's Party of Populists. The new party favored such things as a progressive income tax, government control of the railroads and utilities, and inflated currency so the farmers could pay off their debts at a cheaper rate.

The Populist candidate, General James Weaver, polled more than one million votes in the presidential election of 1892, which was won by Grover Cleveland. In 1896, the Populists joined with the Democrats in order to run William Jennings Bryan for the presidency. Following his loss, the Populists rapidly faded away as an organized force.

Directions: Match the item on the left with its description on the right. Write the correct letter on the line.

_____ 1. People's Party

_____ 2. William Jennings Bryan

_____ 3. James Weaver

_____ 4. National Farmers' Alliance

_____ 5. inflated currency

(a) candidate of the Populist party in 1892

(b) organization that began as a buying and selling cooperative

(c) believed in political reform

(d) candidate who lost the presidential election of 1896

(e) part of Populist program to help farmers pay off their debts

Answers are on page 324.

The Progressive Era: 1900–1917

> ## Key Words
>
> **Progressive Era**—a period of many social and political reforms largely backed by presidents Theodore Roosevelt, William Howard Taft, and Woodrow Wilson
>
> **social class**—a group of people who share a common economic position in society
>
> **muckrakers**—writers who exposed corruption in business and politics during the early twentieth century

In the last quarter of the nineteenth century, the United States was transformed from a rural, farming society into an urban industrial society. By 1900, the United States had replaced Great Britain as the leading industrial producer in the world. The country was poised for even greater growth when Henry Ford developed the first modern factory production line. However, many Americans were concerned by worsening social conditions brought about by industrialization and urbanization. Labor strife continued. Abuses of child labor were widespread, and living and working conditions deteriorated in the cities.

At the same time, the economy became more concentrated in the hands of a small number of families. This concentration of economic power helped to cause a serious depression in 1907. Political institutions that had been suitable for a nation of farmers and small-business people could no longer deal with the problems of a large-scale industrial society. The developing economic, social, and political crises gave birth to a time known as the Age of Reform, or the Progressive Era. This period lasted roughly from 1900 to America's entry into World War I in 1917.

Industrialization had created a large new class of industrial workers and a very small class of wealthy industrialists and financiers. It also had created a large urban middle class. These people were professionals such as lawyers, doctors, engineers, and teachers. A rapidly expanding group of white-collar workers and small-business people was also created. Each of these social classes had its own ideas about how the country should make reforms. Many middle-class people feared that the large corporations were destroying America's free-enterprise system.

Radical journalists, called muckrakers, influenced many people. Lincoln Steffens exposed in his books and articles the corruption, poverty, and boss-run political systems in the large cities. Upton Sinclair's novel, *The Jungle* (1906), exposed the awful conditions in Chicago's meatpacking industry. This eventually led to the Meat Inspection Amendment and the Pure Food and Drug Act.

EXERCISE 22

Directions: The questions below are based on the passage on the previous page. Circle *T* for each true statement, or *F* for each false statement.

T F 1. Industrialization and urbanization brought about many improved social conditions.

T F 2. Industrialization was responsible for creating a large new class of industrial workers and a small class of wealthy industrialists and financiers.

T F 3. During the Progressive Era, the wealth of the nation was almost evenly spread among all the social classes.

T F 4. Living and working conditions deteriorated in the cities during this era.

T F 5. Muckrakers, such as Lincoln Steffens and Upton Sinclair, wrote about the terrible conditions of workers in large cities.

T F 6. In 1900, Great Britain replaced the United States as the world's leader in industrial production.

T F 7. Lincoln Steffens developed the first modern factory production line.

T F 8. America experienced a serious depression in 1907 as a result of having the country's economic power in the hands of the rich.

T F 9. Upton Sinclair's novel was partly responsible for the creation of the Pure Food and Drug Act.

T F 10. Political institutions were well-equipped to handle the problems of a large-scale industrial society.

Answers are on page 324.

Progressive Reforms

> ## Key Word
>
> **Social Darwinism**—the theory that the development of society is based on the survival of the fittest

The growing strength of radicals and the influence of the middle class forced the Democratic and Republican parties to take reform seriously. At first, reforms were carried out at state and local levels. Local reforms included sanitation laws, building codes, and child welfare laws.

Many private settlement houses, like Jane Addams's Hull House in Chicago, were built in poor neighborhoods. These houses provided some social and educational facilities for the poor. However, local reforms and their financial resources were limited. Reformers wanted the federal government to help solve the most serious problems.

Society was deeply divided over what to do. Some people supported Social Darwinism. Its main belief was that society is based on the survival of the fittest. Wealth was a symbol of survival. Nature intended for some people to succeed and for others to fail. Social Darwinists did not want government to take part in social reforms.

Others believed that reforms were necessary to keep the system from failing into economic disorder. Their spokesperson was the Republican President Theodore Roosevelt. He pushed for reforms to control the worst abuses of big business. By 1912, Roosevelt felt that the Republican Party had turned its back on reform. He split from the Republicans and formed the Progressive (Bull Moose) Party. The Republican vote was split. Woodrow Wilson, the Democratic candidate, was able to win.

The Progressive Era produced a long list of legislative reforms. Some of these included the regulation of railroads, the establishment of the Federal Trade Commission, and child labor protection laws. The basic questions of the Progressive Era centered on what role government should play in regulating economic and social conditions. What Progressive reform led to was the rule of the economy by private business. Limited government regulation would protect the general welfare. This solution has governed American society since. The Progressive Era ended with World War I, when the country turned its attention to international concerns.

EXERCISE 23

Questions 1–4 are based on the passage on the previous page.

1. Why did Theodore Roosevelt run for president in 1912 as a Progressive Party candidate?

    (1) The Progressive Era was over.
    (2) Social Darwinists had taken over the government.
    (3) The unprogressive Woodrow Wilson was the Democratic Party's candidate.
    (4) He believed the Republican Party had turned its back on reform.
    (5) The Socialists had become a major worry.

2. If the ideas of the Progressive Era reform were applied to environmental protection, what would the result be?

    (1) Companies could make all decisions about environmental protection.
    (2) Polluting companies would be run by their workers.
    (3) Polluting companies would be taken over by the federal government.
    (4) Polluting companies would be run by their local communities.
    (5) The government would regulate the worst abuses of polluting companies, but the owners would still control those companies.

3. Why did Progressive Era social reformers turn to the federal government for help in solving problems?

    (1) Reformers always believe in big government.
    (2) They did not want to resolve the problems themselves.
    (3) Private and local resources were limited.
    (4) The government demanded a voice in the situation.
    (5) They thought the federal government would be more sympathetic.

4. Social Darwinism was based on belief in which of the following?

    (1) social reforms
    (2) survival of the fittest
    (3) big business
    (4) international concerns
    (5) child labor protection laws

    Answers are on pages 324–325.

Writing Activity 9

Social workers and muckrakers faced social problems of the Progressive Era head-on. Both achieved considerable success in changing society. What problems would a muckraker write about in today's society? Select a problem and discuss what should be done about it.

Answers will vary.

EXERCISE 24

Directions: Read the speech below and then put a check in front of the correct answer to the questions that follow.

Women's Suffrage Movement

"Women even more than men need the ballot to protect their special interests and their right to earn a living. . . . We want a law that will prohibit home-work. . . . We hear about the sacredness of the home. What sacredness is there about a home when it is turned into a factory, where we find a mother, very often with a child at her breast, running a sewing machine? Running up thirty-seven seams for a cent. Ironing and pressing shirts seventy cents a dozen, and children making artificial flowers for one cent. . . . These women have had no chance to make laws that would protect themselves or their children.

[Men] discriminate against the class that has no voice. Some of the men say, 'You women do not need a ballot; we will take care of you.' We have no faith in man's protection. . . . Give us the ballot, and we will protect ourselves."

—Inez Haynes Irwin, *Uphill With Banners Flying*

1. What is the writer's position in this passage?

_____ (1) The ballot will not help the working woman.

_____ (2) Men cannot be depended on to protect women and children.

_____ (3) Men should protect the well-being of women and children.

_____ (4) Giving women the right to vote will destroy the sanctity of the home.

2. The law "that will prohibit home-work" specifically refers to putting an end to what?

_____ (1) work on one's home

_____ (2) schoolwork

_____ (3) factory-like production at home

_____ (4) sewing

Answers are on page 325.

Foreign and Domestic Policy: 1890–1945

Key Words

imperialism—a policy by which a nation extends its control over other lands

gunboat diplomacy—U.S. practice of sending troops into countries of the Western Hemisphere to protect U.S. interests

---

The Monroe Doctrine of 1823 proclaimed that the United States would not tolerate any new European colonization or interference in the Western Hemisphere. After this doctrine was announced, the United States did little to enforce it. The country was not much interested in world affairs until the 1890s.

By 1890, however, the West was largely settled and the frontier was closed. Then Americans became serious about taking over lands outside the United States. It began the policy called imperialism. European countries were building up large colonial empires in Africa and Asia. The United States did not want to be left out in the race to gain colonies.

The Cuban struggle for independence from Spain gave U.S. imperialists the opportunity they needed. To help Cubans win their struggle, the United States fought a three-month war with Spain in 1898. Cuba became independent but with strong U.S. controls for a number of years. The United States took outright control of the Spanish colonies of Puerto Rico, the Philippines, and Guam.

In 1898, the United States also took over the Hawaiian Islands. After 1900, the United States helped Panama become independent in exchange for a canal through Panama built and controlled by the United States. During the next few years, the United States sent troops to Mexico, Nicaragua, Haiti, and the Dominican Republic. It believed these actions were necessary to protect U.S. interests. But the people in these countries resented this gunboat diplomacy.

Some Americans were against imperialism. They wanted more foreign trade, but they did not want the United States to have a colonial empire. So they founded the Anti-Imperialist League. The writer Mark Twain was one of its most outspoken members.

EXERCISE 25

Directions: Answer the questions below in the space provided.

1. American imperialism became most prominent when the United States fought a war with _____ .

2. In 1898, the United States annexed a group of islands that today is the state of _____ .

3. U.S. military intervention, called _____ , caused a great deal of resentment in the countries of Latin America and the Caribbean.

4. Taking over lands beyond a country's borders is called

    _____ .

5. Anti-imperialists wanted _____ but not a _____ .

6. Part of the Monroe Doctrine of 1823 declared that the United States would not allow _____ or _____ in the Western Hemisphere.

7. European countries built up large colonial empires in

    _____ and _____ .

8. The United States fought with _____ to help Cuba win its independence.

9. One of the most outspoken members of the Anti-Imperialist League was _____ .

Answers are on page 325.

EXERCISE 26

Directions: Study the map below and then answer the questions in the space provided.

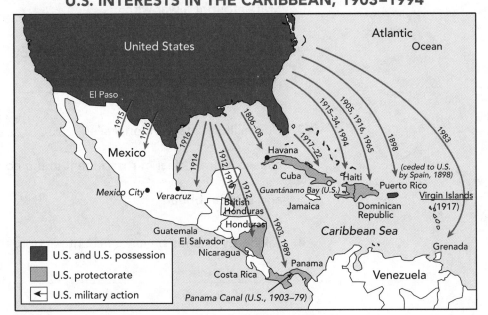

U.S. INTERESTS IN THE CARIBBEAN, 1903–1994

1. How is U.S. military action in the region shown?

   _____

2. In what year did the United States invade Grenada?

   _____

3. Name the present U.S. possessions in the region.

   _____

4. From the number of U.S. military actions in the Caribbean region, which of the following conclusions can be drawn about the United States?

   _____ (1) It had no interest in the region.

   _____ (2) It was enforcing the Monroe Doctrine.

   _____ (3) It was interested in Cuba but not Haiti or the Dominican Republic.

   _____ (4) It was interested only in Mexico.

Answers are on page 325.

World War I and After

> ### Key Words
>
> **isolationism**—national policy or attitude that a nation will do better if it pays more attention to domestic matters than to international affairs
>
> **armistice**—a stopping of fighting between countries

In 1914, Archduke Francis Ferdinand, the heir to the Austro-Hungarian throne, was assassinated. This sparked a war between rival groups of European nations—the Allies and the Central Powers. The United States stayed out of this war until 1917. Then Germany stepped up its submarine attacks on U.S. passenger ships and unarmed merchant ships. These attacks led to the loss of many American lives. The United States was forced into the war on the side of the Allies.

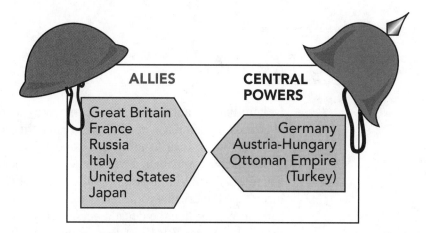

ALLIES

Great Britain
France
Russia
Italy
United States
Japan

CENTRAL POWERS

Germany
Austria-Hungary
Ottoman Empire
(Turkey)

By that time, the warring countries were tired of fighting and neither side seemed able to win. U.S. soldiers helped break this stalemate. On November 11, 1918, the Germans signed an armistice. Today we celebrate that date as Veterans Day.

The war made the United States a major world power. President Woodrow Wilson proposed Fourteen Points to make a lasting peace. However, the other Allied leaders decided that the enemy, especially the Germans, needed to be taught a lesson. The peace treaties were harsh. Republican leaders in the U.S. Senate opposed to Wilson kept the United States from signing the peace treaties and joining the League of Nations. This international body, similar to today's United Nations, was set up to ensure peace and world security. The United States wanted to keep its freedom of action. The country retreated into isolationism, where it stayed until forced into war again in 1941.

EXERCISE 27

Questions 1 and 2 are based on the passage on the previous page.

1. Which of the following describes the United States' actions from 1890 to 1941?

   (1) It alternated between active involvement in foreign affairs and periods of isolation.
   (2) It did not let trade influence its foreign policy.
   (3) It followed only a policy of isolation.
   (4) It always followed George Washington's advice of avoiding entangling alliances.
   (5) It did not use the military in expanding its influence.

2. Why did the United States enter World War I?

   (1) Great Britain forced it to do so.
   (2) German submarine attacks led to the loss of American lives.
   (3) It had made too many loans to the Allies and feared it wouldn't get its money back.
   (4) Public opinion favored joining the fight.
   (5) It was reacting to the assassination of Archduke Francis Ferdinand.

   Answers are on page 325.

The Roaring Twenties

Isolationism meant that world affairs were quiet for the United States in the 1920s. At home, however, a lot was happening. President Calvin Coolidge said that "the business of America is business." That certainly seemed true in the 1920s. Giant companies developed and expanded modern forms of production and marketing. With mass production assembly lines, more goods could be made, and Americans were ready to buy. They bought telephones, radios, and automobiles. When the decade began, only 9 million cars were registered in the United States. By 1930, there were more than 26.5 million cars.

The consumer age was born. Chain stores and department stores replaced many of the small shops. Industrial production rose 64 percent between 1919 and 1923. Many workers' real wages (wages adjusted for inflation) rose 24 percent. Stockholders' dividends often increased by 100 percent. Expanding industry caused changes in the work force. Women took jobs as secretaries and clerical workers. The Nineteenth Amendment (1920) gave women the right to vote.

Black workers continued to migrate from the South to work in factories in the North. There they could earn higher wages. Blacks brought with them a kind of African American music called jazz, which became popular with whites. They danced to a form of jazz, called swing, played by the big bands in the 1930s. Blacks also had their own cultural life in the Harlem Renaissance of New York City. Discrimination, particularly from a revived Ku Klux Klan, and race riots were common. The black nationalist leader Marcus Garvey founded the Universal Negro Improvement Association to combat discrimination and end imperialism in Africa.

Americans distrusted foreigners during this period. Congress followed the public mood by establishing strict quotas and lowering the number of immigrants allowed into the country.

The best-selling nonfiction book in 1926 was Bruce Barton's *The Man Nobody Knows,* a businessman's version of the life of Christ. Many writers during the 1920s were turned off by the emphasis on material things. Some of them, such as Ernest Hemingway and F. Scott Fitzgerald, moved to Europe.

EXERCISE 28

Directions: Circle *T* for each true statement, or *F* for each false statement.

T F **1.** Mass production made more goods available to consumers during the 1920s.

T F **2.** The main business of America during the 1920s was business.

T F **3.** When war production ended, women no longer remained in the work force.

T F **4.** African-American culture remained strictly in the South and had no influence on the rest of the nation.

T F **5.** Immigration was cut back by Congress during the 1920s.

T F **6.** Some American writers disliked the emphasis on material goods and went to Europe.

T F **7.** Swing music has its roots in African American jazz.

Answers are on page 325.

The Great Depression and the New Deal

> ### Key Words
>
> **collective bargaining**—meeting between labor representatives and employers to settle disputes about hours, wages, and working conditions
>
> **industrial unionism**—organizing of unskilled and semiskilled factory workers chiefly by the Congress of Industrial Organizations (CIO)

The era of economic prosperity ended suddenly with the stock market crash of 1929. Manufacturers could not sell their goods. Workers lost their jobs. Farmers lost their farms. Unemployment in some cities rose to 60 percent. People without jobs faced being put out of their homes because they could not pay the rent. When the Depression began, the United States had no unemployment insurance. It had very little public welfare and no Social Security. Private relief agencies had difficulty caring for so many people. Millions of people had no money, no work, and no hope. Farmers killed their livestock and destroyed crops rather than lose even more money by selling at very low prices.

World War I veterans marched on Washington, D.C., to collect their army bonus, which the government had promised them. They were driven out by the army. Councils for the unemployed were formed to keep people from being evicted from their homes.

President Hoover's actions did little to restore confidence or the economy. With the country on the verge of economic collapse, Franklin D. Roosevelt was overwhelmingly elected president in 1932. Roosevelt's New Deal programs, including Social Security and Federal Unemployment Insurance, were designed to prevent the worst features of the Great Depression from taking place again. The Works Progress Administration (WPA) gave public works jobs to thousands of unemployed people.

The New Deal did not get the United States out of the Depression. But it did establish the idea that government is responsible for seeing that people are free from economic anxiety through income support programs and the creation of jobs. At the same time, the New Deal greatly increased the government's role in regulating the economy.

Labor unions made great gains during the Depression. New Deal legislation guaranteed workers the right of collective bargaining. The Congress of Industrial Organizations (CIO) was formed in 1935 to promote industrial unionism. The older American Federation of Labor (AFL) was craft-oriented and had paid little attention to unskilled industrial workers. Between 1935 and 1937, the CIO organized four million workers.

EXERCISE 29

Directions: Study the graphs below and put a check in front of the correct answers to the questions that follow.

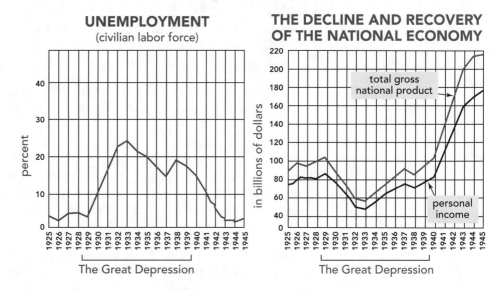

UNEMPLOYMENT
(civilian labor force)

THE DECLINE AND RECOVERY OF THE NATIONAL ECONOMY

1. Which of the following groups were most hurt at the beginning of the Great Depression?

_____ (1) People who received government assistance.

_____ (2) People who organized protest movements.

_____ (3) People who depended largely on private charities.

_____ (4) People who were recent immigrants.

2. What do the two graphs show about unemployment?

_____ (1) It increased from 1929 to 1933, and the gross national product declined.

_____ (2) It decreased from 1929 to 1933, and the gross national product decreased in the same period.

_____ (3) It declined continuously since 1933.

_____ (4) Unemployment and the gross national product both increased in 1938.

3. What was the most lasting effect of the New Deal?

_____ (1) It brought the country out of the Depression.

_____ (2) It set a policy that government would not interfere in labor disputes.

_____ (3) It established the idea that government was responsible for people's basic economic needs.

_____ (4) It established the policy of creating economic growth by making payments to business and cutting welfare.

The Road to World War II

> ### Key Words
>
> **communism**—a system of government in which private ownership of property was not permissible and a single, authoritarian party controlled state-owned means of production
>
> **fascism**—a political system that puts the state above the individual, and which usually has a dictator to carry out its social and economic policies

The entire world was gripped by the Great Depression of the 1930s. The dictator Joseph Stalin tried to make the Soviet Union into an industrial power based on communism. The Russian people suffered greatly in the process; the brutal Stalin allowed no opposition.

In Germany and Italy, fascist dictators rose to power on the misery of the people. The dictators believed that fascism, expansion, and conquest could solve their countries' economic problems.

The Japanese military began the road to war by conquering Manchuria in 1931 and invading China in 1937. Italy's Benito Mussolini conquered Ethiopia in Africa in 1935. Japan, Italy, and Germany formed an alliance that became known as the Axis Powers.

In 1936, Germany's Adolf Hitler started his march to world conquest. He took over the Rhineland, Austria, and Czechoslovakia without a fight. In Germany, Hitler murdered or jailed his opponents and began a systematic extermination of the Jews.

When Germany attacked Poland in 1939, Great Britain and France declared war. Germany quickly conquered most of Europe with its blitzkrieg (lightning war). Hitler next turned on the Soviet Union. The Japanese sneak air attack on the U.S. fleet at Pearl Harbor, Hawaii, brought the United States into the war in December 1941. Japan's Axis allies in Europe then declared war on the United States.

World War II was truly a "world" war. Fighting raged in Europe, Asia, Africa, and in the Pacific islands until 1945. President Roosevelt met with Premier Stalin and British Prime Minister Winston Churchill at several Big Three conferences. They agreed that the Allies would fight until their enemies surrendered unconditionally. The Germans were finally defeated in May of 1945. The Japanese surrendered only after atomic bombs were dropped on the cities of Hiroshima and Nagasaki in August 1945.

EXERCISE 30

Directions: Match the item on the left with its description on the right. Write the correct letter on the line.

_____ 1. Ethiopia

_____ 2. Poland

_____ 3. Big Three

_____ 4. Axis Powers

_____ 5. Hiroshima

_____ 6. Japan

_____ 7. Manchuria

_____ 8. Great Depression

_____ 9. 1937

_____ 10. Stalin

_____ 11. Hitler

_____ 12. 1945

(a) invasion of this country caused England and France to declare war on Germany

(b) alliance of Germany, Italy, and Japan

(c) sneak attack by this country at Pearl Harbor brought United States into World War II

(d) African nation conquered by Italy in 1935

(e) Asian area first conquered by Japan

(f) agreed that Germany and Japan must surrender unconditionally

(g) Japanese city on which an atomic bomb was dropped

(h) when the Japanese military invaded China

(i) introduced a communist system into the Soviet Union

(j) when World War II ended

(k) began when the stock market crashed in the 1930s

(l) responsible for systematic extermination of the Jews

Answers are on page 326.

EXERCISE 31

Directions: Read the passage below and then put a check in front of the correct answer to the questions that follow.

The Flint Sit-Down Strike of 1936

The Flint sit-down happened Christmas Eve, 1936 . . . The second shift had pulled the plant. It took about five minutes to shut the line down. The foreman was pretty well astonished.

We had guys patrol the plant, see that nobody got involved in anything they shouldn't. If anybody got careless with company property . . . he was talked to. You couldn't paint a sign on the wall or anything like that. . . . They'd assign roles to you. When some of the guys at headquarters wanted to tell some of the guys in the plant what was cookin', I carried the message. . . .

We have a ladies auxiliary. They'd visit the homes of the guys that was in the plant. They would find out if there was any shortage of coal or food. Then they'd maneuver [scheme] amongst themselves until they found some place to get a ton of coal. Some of them even put the arm on Consumer Power if there was a possibility of having her power shut off.

Finally we got the word: THE THING IS SETTLED. My God, you had to send about three people, one right after the other, down to some of those plants because the guys didn't believe it. Finally, when they did get it, they marched out of the plants with the flag flyin' and all that stuff.

When Mr. Knudsen put his name to a piece of paper and says that General Motors recognizes the UAW-CIO—until that moment we didn't even exist. That was the big one.

—Excerpted from *Hard Times: An Oral History of the Great Depression* by Studs Terkel

1. What did the Flint sit-down strike show?

_____ (1) the helplessness of business resistance to unionism

_____ (2) manipulation by a handful of outside troublemakers

_____ (3) how to organize a complicated strike

_____ (4) the inability of union workers to influence business

2. Which of the following most likely explains why the company did not remove the strikers?

_____ (1) There was public support for the strike.

_____ (2) The workers would destroy the plant equipment.

_____ (3) The company thought the strikers could be starved out.

_____ (4) The company thought the strike would be over quickly.

Answers are on page 326.

U.S. Foreign Policy: 1945–2000

> ## Key Words
>
> **Cold War**—the period of conflict between the United States and the former Soviet Union and their allies after World War II
>
> **containment**—U.S. foreign policy to block further expansion of communism after World War II
>
> **arms race**—a continuous buildup of large amounts of weapons and of a huge military force by one country in order to gain an advantage over another country

The United States became the strongest world power after World War II. Much of Western Europe and Japan were in ruins. The other major world power was the Soviet Union. The two superpowers had joined together during the war to defeat Hitler. When the war ended, they became hostile. This was a struggle between two different social and economic systems. It was also a struggle between two giants competing for spheres of influence. This period of struggle was called the Cold War. It lasted from the late 1940s until the late 1980s.

The Soviet Union set up communist governments in several Eastern European countries. These countries were called satellites because they depended upon Soviet occupation forces and economic ties. Communists also came to power in China by 1949.

The Marshall Plan helped Western European countries rebuild their war-torn economies. Americans feared that the communists might take over the world. Therefore, it drew up a containment policy to limit communism to areas where it was already established. To support containment, the United States, Canada, and the Western European countries formed a military alliance called the North Atlantic Treaty Organization (NATO). The Soviet Union and its satellites formed the Warsaw Pact military alliance.

A long period of open hostility and an arms race began between the two superpowers. The Cold War turned "hot" during the Korean and Vietnam wars, but the United States and the Soviet Union avoided direct military conflict during this time.

EXERCISE 32

Directions: Circle *T* for each true statement, or *F* for each false statement.

T F **1.** The United States and the Soviet Union kept up their wartime cooperation for many years after defeating the Axis powers.

T F **2.** The countries that the Soviet Union controlled in Eastern Europe were called colonies.

T F **3.** The containment policy was supposed to keep Soviet communism from expanding into more countries.

T F **4.** The United States and its allies formed a military alliance called the Marshall Plan.

T F **5.** The Korean War was fought to prevent communist expansion in Asia.

Answers are on page 326.

The Third World

> ## Key Word
>
> **Third World**—developing nations of Asia, Africa, and Latin America, many of which gained their independence after World War II and were not allied with either superpower

Outside of the conflict between the United States and the Soviet Union, political struggles also took place in Africa, Asia, and Latin America. Nationalist movements in European colonies fought for independence. There were also movements against wealthy local elites who upheld unjust social and economic conditions. The Europeans had been weakened by World War II, so they had difficulty trying to hold on to their colonies. The Soviet Union supported local opposition forces in order to gain influence in Third World countries. By the 1960s and 1970s, most Third World countries had become independent.

The Cold War dominated U.S. policy toward the Third World. Once a British colony itself, the United States sometimes found it awkward to support colonial rule rather than a nationalist movement. But when the nationalism movement was supported by the Soviet Union, the United States seemed to have little choice. Most Third World nations tried to steer an independent course between the two superpowers.

The worst fears of the United States were realized in 1959 in Cuba. Fidel Castro overthrew a military dictatorship and set up a revolutionary communist government.

EXERCISE 33

Directions: Put a check in front of the correct answer to the questions that follow.

1. Which choice describes U.S. foreign policy toward the Third World?

_____ (1) The United States stressed foreign aid to Cuba.

_____ (2) The United States linked nationalist movements to communist expansion.

_____ (3) The United States was opposed to all independence movements.

_____ (4) The United States was concerned only with protecting U.S. business interests.

2. Which action describes Third World nations?

_____ (1) Third World nations sided with the United States against the Soviet Union.

_____ (2) Third World nations sided with the Soviet Union against the United States.

_____ (3) Third World nations had complicated social and economic movements that had no relation to international politics.

_____ (4) Third World nations were kept in line by whichever superpower gave them the most money.

3. Where did U.S. fears of communism in the Third World come true?

_____ (1) Mexico

_____ (2) South Africa

_____ (3) India

_____ (4) Cuba

Answers are on page 326.

The United States and Vietnam

Key Words

guerrilla—a person who fights behind the lines and carries out acts of sabotage, strike-and-run military action, or terror against the enemy

domino theory—the argument that if one nation faces great danger, so will its neighbor and then the next country until a whole region falls

The containment policy applied to Vietnam as well. When the French left in 1954, Vietnam was divided in two. North Vietnam was a communist country led by Ho Chi Minh. It sponsored guerrilla activity in South Vietnam, a weak country. To stop the domino theory from working, the United States sent aid to South Vietnam so that the communists would not take over the country. American military and economic aid climbed steadily under all presidents from Dwight D. Eisenhower to Richard M. Nixon.

U.S. troop strength in Vietnam reached 543,000 by 1969. More tons of bombs were dropped by air on North Vietnam than were dropped on Germany, Italy, and Japan in World War II. It did little good. Eventually, the United States signed the Paris Peace Agreement in 1973 and pulled out of Vietnam. Two years later, the communists united Vietnam under their leadership.

The Vietnam War created enormous difficulties at home. Antiwar activism was the greatest in U.S. history. The cost of the war weakened the economy. The war also forced U.S. foreign policy makers to take a new look at how the United States should deal with the Third World.

EXERCISE 34

Directions: Based on the information in the passage, underline the correct answer to the questions below.

1. North Vietnam supported guerrillas in (China, South Vietnam).

2. U.S. military aid to (North Vietnam, South Vietnam) increased steadily through the 1960s.

3. The (containment policy, domino theory) meant that if communism won in one country, the neighboring countries were also in danger.

4. You might infer from the passage that the war in Vietnam caused greater problems for the United States (at home, with its allies) than it did with the Soviet Union.

Answers are on page 326.

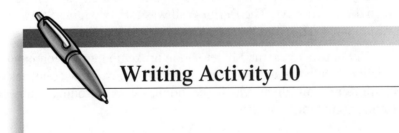

Writing Activity 10

President Richard M. Nixon had been a longtime enemy of communism. In 1973, however, he decided to renew U.S. relations with communist China. Write a few paragraphs explaining why Nixon might have done so at that time.

Answers will vary.

The End of the Cold War

> ### Key Words
>
> **détente**—a policy that called for more peaceful cooperation between the United States and the Soviet Union
>
> **market economy**—another name for free enterprise where buyers and sellers, not the government, determine prices and output

Both superpowers saw that the Vietnam War was dangerous because it could lead to a direct struggle between the United States and the Soviet Union. President Nixon worked out a policy of deténte with the Soviet Union and met with the leaders of China. By the late 1970s, however, deténte returned to Cold War when the Soviet Union invaded Afghanistan and the communist government in Poland took strong action against the Solidarity workers' movement.

In 1981, President Ronald Reagan decided to build up U.S. military forces to overtake the might of the Soviet Union. By the mid-1980s, a young leader, Mikhail Gorbachev, took charge of the Soviet Union. He realized that the Soviet economy could no longer keep up the arms race. The country withdrew from Afghanistan. By 1990 it allowed the East European satellites to go their own ways. The Berlin Wall was torn down in 1989 and Germany was reunited. The Cold War was over.

Within two years, the Soviet Union broke up into fifteen independent republics. Old-style communism survived in only a few countries such as North Korea and China. Market economies were introduced in nearly every former communist country.

While communism was breaking up, nationalism took its place. Ugly fighting broke out in Yugoslavia, which split into several independent countries. Many African countries faced economic decline, hunger, and heavy debt. The Middle East continued to be a battleground. Acts of terrorism occurred everywhere, even in the United States. All of these things created great problems for the United States because the country was now the only remaining superpower. The United States continues to serve as the world's peacekeeper because the world looks to it for leadership.

EXERCISE 35

Part A

Directions: Match the item on the left with its description on the right. Write the correct letter on the line.

_____ 1. Cold War

_____ 2. terrorism

_____ 3. nationalism

_____ 4. Berlin Wall

_____ 5. peacekeeping

_____ 6. détente

(a) relaxing of tensions and increased cooperation between the United States and the Soviet Union

(b) ended in 1989 with the Soviet satellites going their own ways

(c) its destruction led to the unification of Germany

(d) became a more important force in world affairs with the breakup of the Soviet Union

(e) a major problem that knows no borders and affects innocent people

(f) role the United States often assumes in the post-Cold War period

Part B

Directions: Based on the passage on the previous page, answer the questions below in the space provided.

1. President _____ established a policy of deténte with the former Soviet Union and met with Chinese leaders.

2. The communist government opposed the _____ movement among workers in Poland.

3. A market economy is a system in which buyers and sellers determine

_____ and _____.

4. The person responsible for easing up on the arms race in the former Soviet Union

was _____.

Answers are on page 327.

EXERCISE 36

Directions: Study the cartoon below and then put a check in front of the correct answer to the question that follows.

What do you think is the cartoonist's message?

_____ (1) Germany does not believe in wasting bricks.

_____ (2) Germans believed the Berlin Wall was a good idea and can be applied to unwanted immigrants.

_____ (3) Immigration is a major problem in Germany.

_____ (4) Germany has learned no lessons from the past in facing the current problem of immigration.

Answers are on page 327.

U.S. Domestic History: 1945–2000

Several important themes run through American domestic history since World War II. These themes include the impact of U.S. foreign policy on politics, the appearance of mass movements for social change, and the government's role in the economy and in meeting social needs.

A FAST-CHANGING WORLD

1989	Germany—Berlin Wall comes down Poland—Solidarity victory in free elections Afghanistan—Soviet Union withdraws last troops
1990	Nicaragua—Pro-Communist Sandinistas voted from office Iraq—invades Kuwait; defeated by U.S.-led coalition
1991	Soviet Union—breaks up into 15 independent republics Yugoslavia—Croatia and Slovenia declare independence
1992	El Salvador—end of 12-year civil war Bosnia and Herzegovina—declare independence; civil war Somalia—U.S. troops sent to guard food deliveries
1993	Israel—signs peace agreement with Palestinian Liberation Organization (PLO) in Washington Russia—Boris Yeltsin survives impeachment by former communists
1994	South Africa—black majority rule begins with election of Nelson Mandela as president Rwanda—civil war, mass flight and death of refugees Jordan—ends 46 years of war with Israel Haiti—military rulers defy world; refugee problem worsens

Source: World Almanac 1994

Key Word

McCarthyism—careless and groundless attacks on people suspected of being communists; associated with Senator McCarthy's anti-communist tactics

---

The fear of communism led to a "witch hunt" in the 1950s. Senator Joseph McCarthy of Wisconsin and his followers accused many Americans of being communists or communist sympathizers. In Congress, the House Un-American Activities Committee made its own investigations. Thousands of Americans lost their jobs as a result of McCarthyism. In 1954, Senator McCarthy's colleagues in the U.S. Senate condemned his actions.

As we have seen, the government's conduct in the Vietnam War had a widespread effect on the American people in the 1960s and early 1970s. The attempt to contain communism led instead to a large antiwar movement and a discrediting of the presidency and U.S. foreign policy. The cost of American involvement increased inflation and made it difficult to keep up with costly domestic social programs.

Americans seemed to have shaken the trauma of the Vietnam War by the 1980s. The end of the Cold War, however, meant that new thinking about the direction of U.S. foreign policy was needed. It was not clear what long-term direction it would take. Besides, Americans had become more concerned about the U.S. economy and making a living.

EXERCISE 37

Questions 1 and 2 are based on the passage on the previous page.

1. Why might the U.S. Senate have condemned McCarthy's actions?

   (1) He accused too many senators of being communists.
   (2) He was a discredit to the U.S. Congress.
   (3) The communist threat had ended.
   (4) His charges were proved correct, and the accused were put in jail.
   (5) The United States had become friendly with the communist countries.

2. Because by the late 1960s polls showed that the majority of Americans disapproved of U.S. involvement in Vietnam, what can you infer?

   (1) The cost in American lives and money was too high.
   (2) Americans increasingly sympathized with the North Vietnamese.
   (3) Americans feared that the Soviet Union would send in troops.
   (4) Americans favored isolationism and wanted to pull out.
   (5) Americans wanted the troops to be stationed in other countries.

Answers are on page 327.

Writing Activity 11

With the end of the Cold War, the United States had to refocus its attention from fighting communism to a great number of other problems and areas, such as terrorism, the international drug trade, renewed nationalism, the Middle East, and Central America. In a few paragraphs, describe what you believe U.S. foreign policy should be.

Answers will vary.

Movements for Social Change

In the period after World War II, several large protest movements that sought
basic changes in society grew up. In 1954, the Supreme Court banned racial
segregation in public schools in its *Brown v. Board of Education* decision. The
court did not consider segregated schools to be equal under the law. Protests
against all forms of racial segregation and discrimination developed.

A young and skillful speaker, Dr. Martin Luther King, Jr., became the
leader of this civil rights movement. He got black and white support for
nonviolent protest against discriminatory laws. Student sit-ins and local
boycotts were part of the nonviolent disobedience that produced the Civil
Rights Act (1964) and the Voting Rights Act (1965).

Although King was assassinated in 1968, the movement continued. The
Voting Rights Act allowed hundreds of African Americans and members of
other minorities to be elected to public office. In 1992, 38 African Americans,
17 Hispanics, and 47 women were elected to the House of Representatives.
In that same year, one African American woman (the first ever), five other
women, and one Native American were elected to the Senate. The civil rights
movement by African Americans led women, Hispanics, Native Americans,
gays and lesbians, and other groups to seek similar rights.

By the 1970s, many Americans became interested in protecting or cleaning
up the environment. This echoed the concern of the Progressives in the early
1900s and the conservationists of the New Deal of the 1930s. A number of
private groups such as the Sierra Club and the National Wildlife Federation
lobbied Congress and backed candidates in elections who supported their
views. A number of acts of Congress were aimed at curbing pollution,
cleaning up the land and water, and disposing properly of toxic and nuclear
wastes. The Environmental Protection Agency was set up. The continuing
goal is to improve the environment—and thus the quality of life—for all
Americans.

EXERCISE 38

Directions: Based on the previous passage, underline the correct answer that completes each statement below.

1. *Brown v. Board of Education* was a Supreme Court decision banning (segregation, integration) in (private, public) schools.

2. The civil rights movement led by Dr. King favored (violent, nonviolent) means to obtain racial justice.

3. Judging from the information on the 1992 election, you can infer that the Voting Rights Act was (successful, unsuccessful).

4. The number of private groups and public laws favoring environmental protection indicates that the movement had (little, widespread) support.

Answers are on page 327.

President Lyndon B. Johnson's Great Society Legislation

Economic Opportunity Act (War on Poverty)
- Head Start
- Job Corps
- Volunteers in Service for America (VISTA)
- Upward Bound

Civil Rights Act

Voting Rights Act

Equal Employment Opportunity Commission

Medical Care Act
- Medicaid (for welfare recipients)
- Medicare (for the elderly)

Immigration Act (ended quotas of 1924 act)

Public housing and rent supplements

Food stamps

By the 1980s, the government's role in maintaining social programs clashed with the need to cut government spending and reduce the national debt. Inflation made programs with built-in cost-of-living increases very costly, and many of them were cut.

By the 1990s, millions of Americans were without medical insurance because the country had no national health insurance program. In addition, people who needed public assistance but were not covered by a particular government program had to seek private help or depend on limited local or state funds. The AIDS epidemic and the revival of other diseases thought to be under control (such as tuberculosis) put further strains on the nation's health care system. The Clinton administration proposed universal coverage, but it ran into great opposition in Congress.

EXERCISE 39

Directions: Study the political cartoon below and then put a check in front of the correct answer to the questions that follow.

—By permission of Gary Varvel and Creators Syndicate, Inc.

1. What is the likely meaning of this cartoon?

_____ (1) President Bill Clinton is chiefly concerned that people know the health care plan is his.

_____ (2) Taxpayers have no idea how much Clinton's health care plan will cost them.

_____ (3) Clinton is not concerned about the cost of his plan.

_____ (4) Clinton has not worked out the details of his health care plan.

2. What does the cartoonist think of Clinton's health care plan?

_____ (1) He favors it somewhat.

_____ (2) He is 100 percent for it.

_____ (3) He is concerned about its cost.

_____ (4) He is worried about the details of insurance coverage.

Answers are on page 327.

The Government's Role in the Economy

> ## Key Words
>
> **national debt**—the total amount of money owed by the federal government of the United States to its creditors
>
> **trade deficit**—an excess of the value of imports over the value of exports; also called unfavorable balance of trade

The United States emerged from World War II with a strong economy that led the world in output. Pent-up demand for goods brought prosperity at home that continued through the 1950s and 1960s.

During the 1970s, however, the U.S. economy faced great inflation. This was caused in part by the Vietnam War spending and rising oil prices. The national debt increased enormously.

The American love for large, gas-guzzling automobiles forced the country to import much larger amounts of oil from overseas. This worked well until the Organization of Petroleum Exporting Countries (OPEC) decided to raise the price of oil and take a greater share of the profits for themselves. In addition, U.S. manufacturers faced powerful competition from Japanese and West German products. These countries had rebuilt their industries and used the most modern technology. The United States, on the other hand, continued to use old factories with outmoded equipment. The U.S. trade deficit, particularly with Japan, worsened.

U.S. businesses downsized, or cut back, in order to be more efficient. This worked well for the companies, who then became more competitive in the world market. But thousands of Americans lost their jobs. President George Bush's lack of attention to the economy probably cost him the election in 1992.

People continue to question government intervention in the economy. Despite wide differences, the consensus is that government must provide some degree of economic regulation and some form of economic security for its citizens.

EXERCISE 40

Directions: Study the graph below and then put a check in front of the correct answer to the questions that follow.

U.S. NATIONAL DEBT, 1940–1992

Source: *American Almanac 1994*

1. During which ten-year period did the national debt show the largest dollar increase?

_____ (1) 1940–1950

_____ (2) 1960–1970

_____ (3) 1970–1980

_____ (4) 1980–1990

2. Spending on which of the following accounted for the rapid growth of the national debt between 1940 and 1950?

_____ (1) New Deal

_____ (2) World War II

_____ (3) Social Security

_____ (4) Korean War

Answers are on page 327.

EXERCISE 41

Questions 1–3 are based on the passage below.

Cleaning Up America's Rivers

The Nashua's pollution grew up with America. For more than a century wood, wool, shoe, cotton, and paper mills had dumped waste into its quiet flow. By the mid-1960s, the river was classed as unfit even to receive sewage. Because of dumped dyes, people used to bet on whether it was going to be red, orange, blue, green, or white the next day. Then a woman named Marion Stoddart started a campaign to restore the Nashua and its tributaries. It's been called a one-woman crusade, but in many ways it worked because it wasn't. . . .

Stoddart built coalitions with businessmen, labor leadership, and paper companies—the worst polluters. She focused on economic as well as environmental issues. She gave bottles of dirty river water to key officials. At a hearing before the state water pollution-control board to reclassify the river's quality rating, which would force the cleanup, she demanded a goal many thought unthinkable: water safe for swimming. "Come on, be realistic," she was told. She didn't back down.

Within a few years people cleaned up their businesses, changed state law, and testified before Congress. And with federal help eight treatment plants have been built or upgraded, and a broad conservation buffer zone called a greenway has been created along about half of the Nashua and two major tributaries. Today most of the industry is still there—and many parts of the river are safe for swimming.

—Michael Parfit, *National Geographic*, November 1993

1. What was Marion Stoddart's goal?

   (1) to drive the paper companies out of business
   (2) to set up water treatment plants throughout New Hampshire
   (3) to make the Nashua River and its tributaries safe for swimming
   (4) to build dams on the Nashua River
   (5) to lobby in Washington for the Clean Water Act

2. How did Marion Stoddart go about achieving her goal?

   (1) making coalitions with business, labor, and the companies that caused the pollution
   (2) making coalitions with government and labor against the polluting companies
   (3) writing a series of articles in the newspaper on water pollution
   (4) making demands and, when those were met, making further demands
   (5) dumping varied colored dyes into the river to attract attention

3. Based on the passage, what could you infer?

   (1) One person can accomplish major changes in the environment.
   (2) Environmental changes can be made only by the federal government.
   (3) Companies that pollute the environment will not to change their ways.
   (4) People working together can bring about environmental change.
   (5) State and local government will do nothing about the environment unless private citizens take action.

Answers are on page 327.

READING EFFICIENCY A

Directions: This activity will help you to improve your reading efficiency. Before you start to read, write the present time at the top of the page. When you have completed the reading and all 5 questions, write your finishing time. Subtract to find how long you took. Score your answers. Then turn to page 340 to find your E-Factor and graph your progress.

Finishing Time	☐
Starting Time −	☐
Reading Time =	☐
Number of Answers Correct	☐

In the 1960s, the women's movement came alive in the United States. The movement was based on the idea of feminism. During the nineteenth and early twentieth centuries, American women worked hard to win the right to vote. The 19th Amendment was added to the Constitution in 1920. Many people thought women and men now had the same rights and were equal.

But women still had fewer chances to get an education. Men grew up knowing that they could almost anything they wanted to be. Women grew up believing that they only belonged in the home.

In 1963, Betty Friedan wrote a book called *The Feminine Mystique*. In her book, she wrote about the idea that many women were unhappy. Betty Friedan thought that women were unhappy because they were not able to develop their minds and use their talents to work outside their homes.

Feminists argued that even if women did work outside the home, they were treated unfairly. Women made less money than men did for the same job. Women had fewer chances to get better jobs.

More and more women joined the women's movement. Some women met in groups to talk about ways to become equal with men. A large, organized group called the National Organization for Women (NOW) began in 1966. NOW worked hard to pass equal rights laws.

1. Which of the following rights would be guaranteed under equal rights laws?

   (1) women get as many sick days as they need
   (2) female workers get free childcare
   (3) women doing the same job as men get the same pay
   (4) women do not have to go to jury duty
   (5) women pay lower interest rates on bank loans

2. Which of the following conclusions can you draw from reading this passage?

   (1) Women in America have been treated equally since 1920.
   (2) Women who have an education are more likely to get better jobs.
   (3) Women should have the right to work outside the home.
   (4) All women should join NOW.
   (5) Even though the Constitution says men and women are equal, they are not always treated the same.

3. The author of this passage

   (1) would most likely want equal rights for women
   (2) believes the women's movement is not needed
   (3) thinks that women should join NOW
   (4) thinks equal rights would hurt family life
   (5) believes that women have always been treated fairly

READING EFFICIENCY A

4. What does *feminism* mean?

   (1) the right of women to vote
   (2) the idea that women should have the same rights and chances as men
   (3) the belief that women are better at some jobs than men
   (4) the promise that women get a college education
   (5) the idea that women are an important part of the labor force

5. Which of the following contributed most heavily to the women's movement?

   (1) fewer men working
   (2) the change in what is taught in school
   (3) factories needing more workers and turning to women
   (4) a change in women's voting patterns
   (5) more women in politics

Answers are on page 328.

Directions: This activity will help you to improve your reading efficiency. Before you start to read, write the present time at the top of the page. When you have completed the reading and all 5 questions, write your finishing time. Subtract to find how long you took. Score your answers. Then turn to page 340 to find your E-Factor and graph your progress.

Finishing Time	
Starting Time −	
Reading Time =	
Number of Answers Correct	

The U.S. Civil War had a number of causes. Some people name slavery as the main cause. Others say sectional division was the root of the war.

In the early 1800s, the North and South were very different. They had different economies. They had different ways of life.

Farming was important in the North. But it was quickly becoming a business region. The cooler climate and rocky soil were not good for large plantations. The North's economy turned to trade. This economy favored the growth of cities. Immigrants came to the North. They lived and worked in the cities. Factories opened. They employed many northern workers. Workers received pay. They had the right to leave their employers. They could look for better jobs. This system of work was called *free labor*.

In the South, the economy was based on cotton and tobacco. The South had fertile soil and a warm climate. Early settlers grew many crops. They brought in black slaves from Africa. The slaves worked on plantations. A farm economy developed. This economy depended on slave labor. Owners fed and housed slaves. They did not pay them for work they did. Plantation owners made a lot of money. They did not want to change the system. Most white Southerners did not own slaves. But they believed in the need for slavery.

1. Which factor(s) favored an agricultural economy in the South?

   (1) skilled laborers
   (2) a cool climate
   (3) rich soil and a long growing season
   (4) limited available land
   (5) access to both railroads and water transportation

2. Which statement best describes the economy of the North?

   (1) The North had a strong economy because it had farms as well as industry.
   (2) The North's economy was weak because it did not use slave labor.
   (3) Northerners did not want factories built in their cities.
   (4) The North's economy boomed once slave labor was allowed in factories.
   (5) The climate of the North favored an agricultural economy.

3. All of the following would promote the growth of northern cities and the economy EXCEPT

   (1) more business and industry
   (2) better communication
   (3) improvements in transportation
   (4) increased demand for goods
   (5) fewer workers

4. The plantation system was profitable because

   (1) there was a greater supply of cotton than there was demand
   (2) there were no labor costs
   (3) most slaves were highly skilled workers
   (4) it costs less to run a plantation than a farm
   (5) slaves worked harder than free laborers

5. More than 70 percent of Southerners did not own slaves. Which of the following would NOT be a reason that nonslave owners supported slavery?

   (1) Slavery determined how most southerners made a living.
   (2) Slavery gave all whites status by limiting all blacks to menial jobs.
   (3) Southern nonslave owners believed that blacks were equal to whites.
   (4) Small farmers feared that freed slaves would become rivals for land.
   (5) Racial prejudices were deeply ingrained.

   Answers are on page 328.

Chapter 6

World History

The First Civilizations

> ### Key Words
>
> **Homo sapiens**—the term used to identify human beings, which means "thinking men"
>
> **civilization**—an advanced state of human living in which people have cities and an organized government

Human beings, called *Homo sapiens,* have been around for about 300,000 years. For most of that time, however, they had no written history. These early humans left nothing for us to read. During this time of prehistory, humans spent most of their waking hours moving from place to place, hunting for food, building crude shelters, and protecting themselves from wild animals.

About 7,000 years ago, things slowly began to change. For the first time, humans started to settle down in one place. They began growing their own food and building permanent homes. Cities were formed. People began using metals, such as copper and bronze, instead of stones to make tools. Then, about 5,000 years ago, they created a system of letters and began to write. This new form of living was called civilization.

People needed water for drinking and for their crops so they settled near rivers. One such place, called Mesopotamia, was established between the Tigris and Euphrates Rivers in what is now the nation of Iraq. The capital of this new civilization was the city of Babylon. To keep peace among people living so closely together, they needed rules. King Hammurabi, who lived nearly 4,000 years ago, drew up a set of laws. The Code of Hammurabi set down harsh penalties for those who broke the laws. The sentence fit the crime. We get the expression "an eye for an eye and a tooth for a tooth" from Hammurabi. These early laws provided everyone, regardless of their class or rank, at least some protection from their neighbors. Some of Hammurabi's laws sound quite modern. There were, for example, laws governing the fees medical doctors could charge. The poor were charged less than the rich.

EXERCISE 1

Directions: Put a check in front of the correct answer to the questions that follow.

1. Why do we know so little about *Homo sapiens* who lived a hundred thousand years ago?

_____ (1) their written laws are confusing

_____ (2) they left no written history

_____ (3) their books have all been lost

2. History began when people learned to do which of the following?

_____ (1) write

_____ (2) hunt

_____ (3) farm

3. Where were early civilizations started?

_____ (1) along the oceanfront

_____ (2) on mountaintops

_____ (3) near rivers

4. What was Babylon the name of?

_____ an early city

_____ a river valley

_____ a king

5. What was the Code of Hammurabi?

_____ a design for making new copper and bronze tools

_____ a new alphabet

_____ a set of laws

Answers are on page 328.

The Ancient Egyptians

> ## Key Words
>
> **pharaohs**—the rulers of ancient Egypt
>
> **pyramids**—giant stone tombs built for the pharaohs
>
> **hieroglyphics**—an ancient form of Egyptian writing that used pictures

Another early civilization was founded by the Egyptians in the valley of the Nile River. The waters of the Nile, the longest river in the world, were essential to the development of ancient Egypt. Every year the river gently flooded the valley, enriching the soil with silt and minerals. This fertile black soil made it possible for the Egyptians to grow a wide variety of foods. Without the Nile River, Egypt would have been nothing more than an empty desert. It was no wonder, then, that people often called Egyptian civilization "the gift of the Nile."

If the Nile River made it possible for Egyptians to live well, it also made it possible for the rulers of Egypt to live *really* well. These rulers built large palaces to show off their wealth. In time the rulers became known as pharaohs. The word *pharaoh* means "big house."

It wasn't enough for a pharaoh to live in a great house; he also had to be buried in one. The pharaohs used slaves to build massive tombs called pyramids. Each new pharaoh wanted a grander tomb than the last pharaoh's. The pyramids kept getting bigger and bigger. The largest tomb, called the Great Pyramid, was built in 2530 B.C., and its base covered 13 acres.

The Egyptians developed their own system of writing using pictures called hieroglyphics. The pictures showed common objects such as a human eye. Later, a group of people known as Phoenicians used pictures or symbols to represent sounds. This was an important first step toward the creation of a true alphabet.

EXERCISE 2

Directions: Study the map below. Then put a check in front of the correct answer to the questions that follow.

ANCIENT MIDDLE EAST

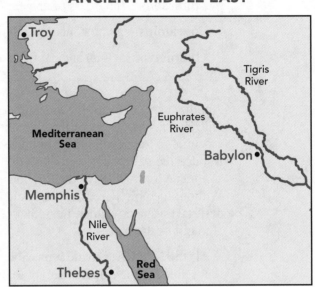

1. Where were the cities of Memphis and Thebes located?

_____ (1) on the Mediterranean Sea

_____ (2) on the Tigris River

_____ (3) on the Nile River

2. Into which of the following does the Nile River flow?

_____ (1) the Mediterranean Sea

_____ (2) the Red Sea

_____ (3) the Euphrates River

Answers are on page 328.

EXERCISE 3

Directions: Circle T for each true statement, or F for each false statement.

T F 1. The Egyptians benefited from the yearly Nile floods.

T F 2. The rulers of ancient Egypt were called pharaohs because they lived in big houses.

T F 3. Pharaohs had massive tombs, called pyramids, built for themselves.

T F 4. Hieroglyphics was a writing system that used ordinary letters.

Answers are on page 328.

The Ancient Greeks

> *Key Words*
>
> **democracy**—a form of government in which the people rule
>
> **city-states**—independent Greek cities with their own governments and laws

The pharaohs in ancient Egypt held absolute power. About 2,500 years ago, the Greeks set up a very different form of government that became known as *democracy*. In a democracy the people rule themselves. (Even so, not everyone in Greece was equal since only free men were allowed to vote.) Each Greek city, or *city-state*, was like an independent country because each one had its own government and its own laws.

The Greeks made many major contributions to the development of Western civilization. For example, their architecture is still copied today. Modern theater is based on the principles established by the Greeks. The Greeks also made key discoveries in mathematics, science, and medicine. Euclid discovered the basic rules of geometry. Archimedes found out how to measure the circumference of a circle as well as the law governing floating objects in water. Hippocrates attacked the use of magic in medicine and wrote a code of ethics for doctors.

But their greatest contribution of all came in the field of philosophy. The word *philosophy* means "love of wisdom." The ideas of Greek philosophers such as Socrates, Plato, and Aristotle, who lived in the city-state of Athens, have shaped and guided the way Westerners have thought through the ages. They asked hard questions about the meaning of life, the true nature of the world, and the proper role of citizens.

This "golden age" of Greece didn't last forever. One reason was that the Greeks constantly fought each other. Sparta and Athens, for instance, waged war against each other for many years. This Peloponnesian War weakened the city-states and made them vulnerable to invasion. In 338 B.C. Philip of Macedonia conquered Greece. His son Alexander the Great went on to conquer most of the lands between Greece in the west, Egypt in the south, and India in the east.

EXERCISE 4

Directions: Study the chart below and match the person on the left with the description on the right. Put the correct letter on the line.

Name	Field of Interest	Contribution
Plato	philosophy	described the ideal form of government in his book <u>The Republic</u>
Euclid	mathematics	discovered the principles of geometry
Hippocrates	medicine	wrote a code of ethics that doctors still follow
Aristophanes	theater	first playwright to write comedy and poke fun at politicians
Archimedes	science	while taking a bath, he discovered that different objects displace different amounts of water

_____ 1. Euclid (a) made discoveries about the displacement of water by different objects

_____ 2. Archimedes (b) wrote a book about the ideal form of government

_____ 3. Hippocrates (c) wrote a code of ethics for doctors

_____ 4. Aristophanes (d) established the principles of geometry

_____ 5. Plato (e) made people laugh with his plays

Answers are on page 328.

The Roman Empire

> ## Key Words
>
> **republic**—a form of government in which the people elect representatives
>
> **senate**—a body of elected officials
>
> **Pax Romana**—a long period of peace under Roman rule

The great Roman Empire had a humble beginning. The region around the present-day city of Rome was first settled by farmers in about 750 B.C. These settlers were soon overrun by a northern tribe, the Etruscans. The Etruscans improved the land by draining swamps. They also built excellent roads, established trade, and developed new architectural techniques including the arch.

In 509 B.C. the Romans drove the Etruscans and their king out of the city. The Romans did not like a monarchy so they established a new type of government called a republic. In the Roman republic, the voters elected representatives to run the government. These elected officials served in the senate. But Rome was not a true democracy. Only the most wealthy and powerful citizens were allowed to serve in the senate.

Soon Rome grew more powerful and began conquering its neighbors. The Greeks in southern Italy fell first, and then the Romans defeated Hannibal and the Carthaginians from northern Africa. The Roman empire added additional provinces in France (called Gaul), Britain, and the Middle East. The genius of the Romans was their ability to govern their far-flung empire well. They did this through a unified set of laws, a skilled civil service, and a well-disciplined army. The peace they established throughout their vast empire lasted many years and was called the Pax Romana, or Roman Peace.

All was not so peaceful back in Rome, however. Powerful army generals could control elections. One such leader was Julius Caesar, who defeated his rivals and made himself the sole ruler of Rome. On March 15 (the Ides of March) in 44 B.C. a group of rivals assassinated Caesar. This led to a long line of emperors. The old republic was dead.

EXERCISE 5

Directions: Based on the passage on page 157, underline the correct answer to the questions below.

EXAMPLE: The early settlers were conquered by the
(<u>Etruscans</u>   French   Greeks).

1. In 509 B.C. the Romans set up a new type of government called a (democracy   monarchy   republic).

2. The Roman senate was open to (only the rich and powerful   everyone   only winners in the Colosseum).

3. Hannibal and the Carthaginians came from (Britain   northern Africa   the Middle East).

4. The Romans are best remembered for their genius in (government   science   medicine).

5. Pax Romana refers to Roman (buildings   peace   roads).

6. Julius Caesar was a (Roman general   foreigner   senator).

7. Julius Caesar was assassinated on (his birthday   New Year's Day   the Ides of March).

Answers are on page 328.

Early Asian Civilizations

> ## *Key Words*
>
> **caste system**—India's system of dividing people into classes based on birth
>
> **dynasty**—a period of time during which one group ruled over China

Two of the world's great early civilizations arose in Asia. One developed in India more than 4,000 years ago in the valley of the Indus River. (The Indus River today flows through the nation of Pakistan.) Like the early settlers in Mesopotamia and Egypt, the people of the Indus River valley enjoyed an ever-improving standard of living. For example, they learned to use bronze and copper to make weapons as well as cooking utensils. The major city of Mohenjo-Daro had streets paved with bricks and lined with shops.

Little is known about what happened to these people. What we do know is that around 1500 B.C. another people called Aryans invaded the region from the north. The Aryans recorded their history and beliefs in four sacred books called the Vedas. These texts became the foundation for Hinduism, their religion. Over time, the Aryans divided all people into different classes based on birth. Under this caste system the priests, or Brahmans, ranked the highest and the "untouchables" ranked the lowest.

India was also the birthplace of Buddhism. In 563 B.C., a prince named Siddharta Gautama was born in northern India. As a young, man he wandered the streets of India trying to figure out why people suffered so much. He came to believe that human pain was based on too much human greed and selfishness. Siddharta's followers called him the Buddha or the Enlightened One.

The other great early Asian civilization developed in about 1500 B.C. along the banks of the Hwang Ho River in northern China. As in other early civilizations, power shifted from one group to another. Whichever Chinese group was in power at the time was said to be a dynasty. Each dynasty ruled until overthrown by another group which in turn would set up its own dynasty. China also developed its own religion based on the ethical teachings of Confucius, who was born about 551B.C.

The Chinese constantly worried about invasions by what they called "barbarians" from the interior of Asia. So in the third century B.C., they built the Great Wall of China to protect themselves. The Great Wall stretched some 1,500 miles across the north of China and remains the only human-made object on earth that can be seen from space.

EXERCISE 6

Directions: Study the time line below and answer the questions that follow.

1. What two events occurred in Asia around 1,500 B.C.?

_____

_____

2. Who was born first—Buddha or Confucius?

_____

3. The Great Wall of China was finished around what year?

_____

Answers are on page 328.

EXERCISE 7

Directions: Answer the question below in your own words.

1. What did the early civilizations mentioned in this passage have in common?

_____

_____

_____

_____

_____

_____

Answers are on page 328.

The Fall of Rome and the Byzantine Empire

Key Words

Christianity—the religion founded on the teachings of Jesus

mosaics—art works created by piecing together colorful bits of glass and stone or other material

icons—sacred paintings and statues used to decorate churches

The Roman Empire, which at one time included about 100 million people, lasted for 500 years. The emperors during this long period ranged from good and just, such as Augustus, to evil and corrupt, such as Nero. Despite the ups and downs of the leadership at the top, the Roman Empire remained remarkably stable. This was due in large part to competent government officials at all levels. A strong economy and robust trade also helped. But, over time, the immense cost of maintaining such a vast empire became too much even for Rome to handle. The economy was hit by inflation and high unemployment. Crime rose. Barbarians from Germany began mounting attacks against the weakened Roman Empire. Finally, in 476 A.D., after a long and steady decline, Rome fell.

Christianity developed during the time of the Roman Empire. Jesus, a Jew, lived about 2,000 years ago in the region called Palestine, which was then under Roman control. Jesus preached against violence and hatred and in favor of brotherhood and love. After his death in 33 A.D., his disciples, or followers, spread his message to all who would listen. At first the Romans tried to wipe out this new religion. They were unsuccessful, and more and more people became Christians. Then, in 395 A.D., Christianity became the official religion of the Roman Empire.

Earlier, in 330 A.D., the Emperor Constantine, sensing trouble ahead, moved his capital east to the city of Byzantine in what is now Turkey. The city was rebuilt and renamed Constantinople. While the western half of the Roman Empire collapsed, the eastern half did not. In fact, the Byzantine Empire thrived in many ways. Emperor Justinian codified the old Roman law into a clearer and more systematic form. The Byzantine Empire also excelled in architecture and art. The church of Hagia Sophia, built in the shape of a Greek cross, was a masterpiece of engineering and design. Byzantine artists made mosaics—the composition of colorful bits of glass and stone into lovely patterns. They also created icons, beautiful religious images used to decorate churches.

EXERCISE 8

Directions: Put a check in front of the correct answer to the questions that follow.

1. The strength of the Roman Empire rested primarily on which of the following?

   _____ (1) its constantly wise and just emperors

   _____ (2) the spread of Christianity

   _____ (3) its efficient and orderly government

   _____ (4) the fact that the empire never grew too large

2. Which of the following best describes the fall of Rome?

   _____ (1) sudden and unexpected

   _____ (2) caused by the teachings of Jesus

   _____ (3) the result of an invasion by the Byzantine Empire

   _____ (4) a long and gradual decline

3. What was the first reaction of the Romans to Christianity?

   _____ (1) to try to wipe it out

   _____ (2) to make it their official religion

   _____ (3) to build new churches in Constantinople

   _____ (4) to change their laws to reflect the teachings of Jesus

4. Which of the following statements about the Byzantine Empire is true?

   _____ (1) It outlived the western half of the Roman Empire.

   _____ (2) It excelled in art and architecture.

   _____ (3) It codified Roman law.

   _____ (4) all of the above

Answers are on page 328.

The Muslim World and the Mongols

> ### Key Words
>
> **Mohammad**—the founder of the religion of Islam
>
> **Koran**—the holy book of Islam based on Allah's messages to Mohammad
>
> **pilgrimage**—a religious journey to a holy place

The Middle East was the birthplace of two of the great world religions, Judaism and Christianity. It was also the birthplace of a third great world religion: Islam. The founder of Islam was Mohammad, who was born about 570 A.D. on the Arabian Peninsula in the city of Mecca. One day around 610 A.D., Mohammad was praying in a cave when he had a vision. An angel appeared and spoke to Mohammad. The angel told Mohammad that there was just one God and that his name was Allah. Subsequently, Mohammad received many more messages and recorded them in a book called the Koran.

Not everyone accepted Mohammad as Allah's prophet, and fighting broke out between his supporters and his opponents. In 622 A.D., Mohammad and a few followers fled Mecca for the city of Medina. Within 10 years, however, Mohammad's forces had captured just about all of the Arabian Peninsula. Mohammad established peace and outlined a set of duties for his followers. One duty was to pray five times a day while facing in the direction of the holy city of Mecca. Another duty was to make a pilgrimage to Mecca at least once during a person's life.

Islam soon spread far beyond the Arabian Peninsula. By around 750 A.D., Muslims, as the followers of Islam were called, had converted others throughout the Middle East, across northern Africa, as far east of the Indus River valley, and as far north as Spain and eastern Turkey.

Meanwhile, in Asia, the Mongols united under Genghis Khan. Khan and his successors spread Mongol rule over most of Asia. Not known for their cultural or scientific contributions, this nomadic people made a series of military conquests that were thorough and marked by brutality and destruction. Kublai Khan, Genghis Khan's grandson, established the Yuan dynasty in China in 1260. This dynasty lasted until 1368 when the Mongols were overthrown and a new dynasty—the Mings—was established.

EXERCISE 9

Directions: Study the map below and answer the questions that follow.

THE SPREAD OF ISLAM, 750 A.D.

1. Which cities shown on the map were *not* converted by Muslims by 634 A.D.?

   _____

2. When Mohammad fled Mecca for Medina, in which direction was he headed?

   _____

3. A Muslim living in Jerusalem would pray in what direction five times a day?

   _____

Answers are on page 329.

EXERCISE 10

Directions: Circle T for each true statement, or F for each false statement.

T F 1. From the beginning, people accepted Mohammad as God's prophet.

T F 2. All Muslims have a duty to visit Mecca at least once.

T F 3. The Mongols were famous for their cultural contributions.

T F 4. The Mongols established the Ming dynasty in China.

T F 5. The expansion of Mongol power ended with the death of Genghis Khan.

Answers are on page 329.

The Middle Ages

The thousand or so years following the collapse of the Roman Empire are called the Middle Ages (because they span the years between the ancient world and the modern world), or the medieval period. The first several centuries of this time are often referred to as the Dark Ages. They were "dark" because in Europe, at least, education declined, science stagnated, and trade slowed greatly. The most famous leader during this time was Charles the Great, or Charlemagne. He ruled over what is today France, Switzerland, Belgium, and the Netherlands as well as parts of Germany, Spain, and Italy. Pope Leo III crowned Charlemagne as the Holy Roman Emperor in 800 A.D. This kept alive the idea of the old Roman empire, but at that time it was an empire in name only.

After Charlemagne's death, his lands were divided among his sons. Now there was no central government to protect people from attacks by the Vikings, a group of sea raiders who came from the region now known as Scandinavia. People sought protection wherever they could find it. This led some weaker lords to pledge loyalty to a stronger lord. In exchange for protection, the weaker lord, or vassal, promised to fight as a knight for the stronger lord. This highly complex system of lords and vassals became known as feudalism. Peasants protected themselves by tilling the fields of a nearby lord.

In 1095, Pope Urban II called on the people of Europe to recapture the Holy Lands in the Middle East from the Muslim Turks who ruled the region at the time. Over the next 200 years, the Christians of Europe launched one crusade after another against the Muslims. At first they succeeded in taking Jerusalem and other places, but in the long run the Crusades failed. The Holy Lands returned to Muslim control. The crusades did, however, benefit the Europeans in one way. They opened European eyes to the superiority of Muslim culture, especially in fields such as science and medicine.

One great achievement of Europeans during the Middle Ages was building cathedrals to honor God. These massive stone churches towered over all the other buildings. Their most striking features were graceful flying buttresses and colorful stained-glass windows. Two prime examples of these churches are Notre Dame Cathedral in France and Salisbury Cathedral in England.

EXERCISE 11

Directions: Match the item on the left with its description on the right. Write the correct letter on the line.

_____ 1. medieval   (a) regained control of Holy Lands after the crusades

_____ 2. feudalism   (b) sea raiders from Scandinavia

_____ 3. Vikings   (c) another term for the Middle Ages

_____ 4. cathedrals   (d) a weaker lord in the feudal system

_____ 5. Charlemagne   (e) ordered the first crusade in 1095

_____ 6. vassal   (f) towering Christian churches made of stone

_____ 7. Pope Urban II   (g) a medieval system of mutual obligations

_____ 8. Pope Leo III   (h) crowned Charlemagne emperor

_____ 9. Christians   (i) his empire died with him

_____ 10. Muslims   (j) tried to conquer and keep the Holy Lands

Answers are on page 329.

Europe and the Renaissance

> ## Key Words
>
> **humanism**—a movement to focus interest on the real lives of humans
>
> **monarchy**—a form of government headed by a king or queen
>
> **exploration**—the search for new trade routes

The Middle Ages ended, and the modern world began, with the Renaissance. The Renaissance started in Italy in the mid-1300s and slowly moved north. It brought great changes in the way ordinary people looked at the world. Previously, the focus was on God, church, and life in the next world. During the Renaissance, however, people grew more concerned with the here and now, and with real human issues in this world. This new outlook became known as humanism. The Renaissance also sparked a revival of interest in the ancient Greeks and Romans. In fact, the word "Renaissance" means "rebirth"—a rebirth of interest in classic civilizations.

The Renaissance transformed the worlds of science, art, literature, and politics. The invention of the printing press by Johannes Gutenberg in 1452 turned the world upside down. Books, once copied by hand, could now be produced in large numbers and made available to many more people. The church's old monopoly over learning was broken. People could read and think for themselves. Scientists such as Copernicus and Galileo shattered the traditional belief that Earth was immovable and fixed at the center of the universe. Artists such as Michelangelo and Leonardo da Vinci painted the human form as it really was. Writers such as Desiderius Erasmus and Martin Luther attacked superstition and meaningless church ceremonies. The Renaissance also promoted unified political power under a monarchy. Spain, France, and England, in particular, were now ruled by powerful kings or queens.

The Renaissance awakened European interest in foreign trade and the rest of the world. This led to the "age of exploration." Sailors from Portugal and Spain began to explore for new water routes to Asia. Previously the only way to Asia was over land by caravan the way Marco Polo did it in the 13th century. Now explorers such as Bartholomeau Dias and Vasco Da Gama sailed south from Europe to find an all-water route to India around the tip of Africa. Then Christopher Columbus, seeking a shorter all-water route to Asia, sailed west across the Atlantic Ocean in 1492 and discovered America. Five years later, in 1497, John Cabot became the first European since the Vikings to set foot on the mainland of North America.

EXERCISE 12

Directions: Based on the passage on page 167, underline the correct answer to the questions below.

1. The Renaissance was the bridge to the modern world from the (ancient world   Middle Ages).

2. Humanism was focused on (this life   the next life).

3. Renaissance artists were inspired by (classic civilizations   medieval life).

4. Gutenberg's printing press meant that (kings   the Catholic Church) no longer had a monopoly on knowledge.

5. Before Copernicus and Galileo, most people believed that Earth (was fixed and immovable   rotated around the sun).

6. Marco Polo traveled to Asia by (sailing around Africa   going over land).

7. Columbus sailed west across the Atlantic Ocean looking for (Asia   America).

Answers are on page 329.

EXERCISE 13

Directions: Study the map and answer the questions below.

THE AGE OF EXPLORATION

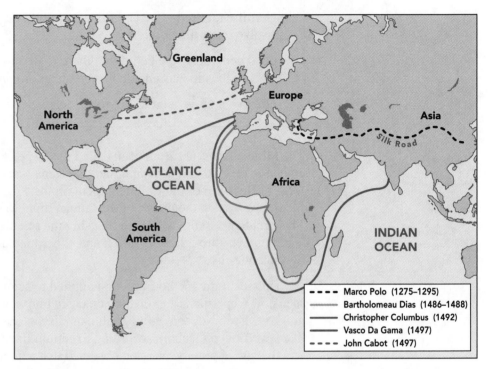

1. Whose voyage lasted the longest?

   _____

2. Who reached India in 1497?

   _____

3. Which explorer reached the mainland of North America?

   _____

4. After leaving Europe, in which direction did Dias and Da Gama sail?

   _____

Answers are on page 329.

The Age of Enlightenment

Key Words

scientific method—the careful use of observation and experimentation to solve scientific problems

social contract—the belief that there is an unwritten agreement between the citizens and their government to protect human rights

reform—a movement to improve society

The Middle Ages has often been called the "Age of Faith" because of the emphasis on God and heaven. Later, the Renaissance led the way for the "Age of Reason," or the Enlightenment, in the 17th and 18th centuries. The focus now was on the power of the human mind to solve human problems. This problem solving was done by using the scientific method. That means learning facts through observation and experimentation that can be repeated by someone else.

This scientific method was first applied to science problems. We have seen how Copernicus and Galileo changed our view of the earth's place in the universe. Issac Newton, an Englishman, discovered that the world operated like a well-oiled machine according to certain fixed laws. One of these laws was the law of gravity. Newton observed that apples always fall to the ground rather than flying off into space, and from this he concluded that they are pulled down by the gravity of the earth.

Europeans also applied reason to areas other than science. They figured that if the world was governed by natural law, then maybe human life was, as well. The philosopher John Locke argued that all people have "natural rights" given by God. These included the rights of life, liberty, and property. So any government that did not protect these rights was violating natural law. Locke said a "social contract" existed between the government and its citizens. If the government broke the contract by denying people's rights, the people could set up a new government. This is the argument Thomas Jefferson would later use in the Declaration of Independence.

In France, philosophers such as Voltaire, Rousseau, and Diderot tried to reform society. Voltaire fought against prejudice and in favor of tolerance. He said that while he might disagree with what a person said, he would fight for the person's right to say it. Rousseau advocated freedom, especially in education, and believed that all people were naturally pure and good. In his view, it was civilization that corrupted people. Diderot put all the learning of his age into a series of 35 books. His encyclopedia gave readers facts about all branches of learning.

EXERCISE 14

Directions: Study the chart below and answer the questions that follow.

GREAT IDEAS FROM THE AGE OF REASON			
Inventor	Country	Year	Invention
Galileo	Italy	1583	pendulum
Janssen	the Netherlands	1590	microscope
Galileo	Italy	1609	telescope
Kepler	Germany	1611	astronomical telescope
Harvey	England	1628	circulation of human blood
Pascal	France	1642	adding machine
Leeuwenhoek	the Netherlands	1676	bacteria
Fahrenheit	Germany	1714	mercury thermometer

1. Who invented the adding machine?

   _____

2. Who invented the pendulum and the telescope?

   _____

3. In what year was bacteria discovered?

   _____

4. What did Harvey discover?

   _____

5. What was invented in 1611?

   _____

6. Who invented the microscope?

   _____

7. In what country was the mercury thermometer developed?

   _____

Answers are on page 329.

The French Revolution

Key Words

estates—the three different classes in France before 1789

revolution—the overthrow of a ruler or government by the governed

reign of terror—a period of mass executions during the French Revolution

guillotine—a device used by the French to behead people

New ideas about natural rights led to revolutions first in America in 1776 and then in France in 1789. In both cases, the revolutionaries said that they were fighting to regain their natural rights. In France, the society was divided into three estates, or classes. The First Estate was the clergy, the Second Estate was the nobility, and the Third Estate was everyone else—merchants, lawyers, teachers, peasants, etc. The vast majority of people belonged to the Third Estate. Yet the First and Second Estates had almost all the political power and wealth, especially in terms of land.

On July 14, 1789, the French people stormed the Bastille, a prison in Paris, and launched the French Revolution. King Louis XVI asked a duke if it was a revolt. "No," answered the duke, "It's a revolution." A revolution is a total change in the way a country is governed. In the beginning, the French Revolution wasn't particularly violent. Then, in 1792, a group of radicals took over and began the bloody "reign of terror." The king, his queen, and thousands of others lost their heads to a new device called the guillotine. By mid-1794, the leaders of the terror lost popular support and they, too, went to the guillotine.

A new government was set up, but it was weak and corrupt. Then a strong new leader named Napoleon Bonaparte appeared. He took over the government in 1799 and five years later crowned himself emperor. Although Napoleon reformed many aspects of society—adopting a new uniform legal code, improving the school system, etc.—he did great harm, as well. His army invaded and conquered most of Europe. Many thousands of people died as a result. To rule these new conquests, Napoleon placed members of his own family on the various thrones. Later, there would be revolts against this foreign rule.

There were two nations, however, that Napoleon couldn't conquer—Russia and Great Britain. In 1812, Napoleon attacked Russia with an army of 500,000 soldiers. A brutal Russian winter and the stubborn determination of the Russians forced him to retreat with only a small fraction of his army intact. Napoleon's final defeat came at the hands of the British and their allies in 1815 at the Battle of Waterloo. Napoleon was then exiled to St. Helena, a small island in the South Atlantic where he died in 1821.

EXERCISE 15

Directions: Study the list of events below and rearrange them in the proper chronological order by writing them in the spaces on the right. The first event goes on the top line.

1. Reign of Terror began _____

2. Bastille stormed by citizens _____

3. Napoleon crowned emperor _____

4. Napoleon sent to St. Helena _____

5. The Battle of Waterloo _____

6. Louis XVI executed _____

Answers are on page 329.

EXERCISE 16

Directions: Study the map below and circle the correct answers to the True or False questions that follow.

NAPOLEON'S EMPIRE—1810

T F 1. Norway was allied to Napoleon.

T F 2. The Kingdom of Spain was part of the French Empire.

T F 3. The Russian Empire was not part of the French Empire but was under Napoleon's control anyway.

T F 4. The Grand Duchy of Warsaw was subject to Napoleon's rule.

T F 5. The Kingdom of Prussia and the Austrian Empire were not ruled by Napoleon but were allied with him.

T F 6. The Kingdom of Naples was part of the French Empire.

Answers are on page 329.

The Dynasties of Asia

Key Words

Taj Mahal—one of the great masterpieces of Islamic architecture

shogun—the supreme military ruler in Japan

samurai—Japanese warriors who lived up to a strict code of conduct

---

After 1707, the British gradually replaced the Moguls as the rulers of India. The Mogul Empire was undone by a series of civil wars and religious conflicts with the Hindus. Meanwhile, the British East India Company slowly gained power and even acted as a kind of government in parts of India. Some Indians resented this and rose up in rebellion but they were defeated. By the mid-1800s, all of India was under the control of the British. In 1877, Queen Victoria of the United Kingdom became the Empress of India. India was now the crown jewel in Britain's colonial empire.

The Moguls, however, left behind one of the most beautiful buildings in the world—the Taj Mahal. Shah Jahan had it built with white marble as a tomb for his wife in the city of Agra. Started in 1623, it took 20,000 workers and nearly 20 years to finish. The top of the dome is 243 feet high and can be seen from many miles away.

In Japan, a warrior society emerged in the 12th century. While Japan had an emperor, power rested in the hands of the shogun, or supreme military general. Like Europe, Japan developed a feudal society with its own forms of lords and vassals. The emperor and the shogun were at the top. Just below them came the loyal samurai, who adhered to a strict code of conduct that lasted into the 20th century. All other classes fell below them.

Beginning in the early 17th century, the Japanese deliberately cut themselves off from the rest of the world. No one was allowed to leave Japan and anyone who did was not allowed to return. That changed only when an American sailor named Matthew Perry sailed to Japan in 1853. He greatly impressed the Japanese with his guns and machines. The Japanese, unlike the Chinese, soon decided to adopt some Western ways.

Meanwhile, in China, the Manchu Dynasty replaced the Ming Dynasty in 1644. Before their fall, however, the Mings built the awesome Forbidden City in their new capital city of Beijing. Only members of the royal family and government officials were allowed inside its walls. When Europeans came to China, they won trade concessions from the Chinese and, in the 19th century, gained more and more control over the country. The Chinese, clinging to old traditions and beliefs, were almost powerless to stop this foreign domination.

EXERCISE 17

Directions: Put a check in front of the correct answer to the questions that follow.

1. Why was the Taj Mahal built?

_____ 1. as a government center

_____ 2. as a mosque

_____ 3. as a tomb

2. What was the role of the shogun in Japan?

_____ 1. He held the real power.

_____ 2. He obeyed the orders of the samurai.

_____ 3. He was outside the feudal system.

3. Which of the following best describes the samurai?

_____ 1. gardeners

_____ 2. warriors

_____ 3. government officials

4. Which of the following best describes Japan before the arrival of Matthew Perry?

_____ 1. a closed society

_____ 2. ruler of many smaller nations in Asia

_____ 3. a Western society

5. When Westerners came to China, the Chinese did which of the following?

_____ 1. quickly adopted the ways of the West

_____ 2. clung to their old ways

_____ 3. formed an alliance with the Japanese

Answers are on page 329.

The Rise of Nations and the Industrial Revolution

Key Words

nationalism—the desire of a certain group of people to have their own nation

technology—methods that make production cheaper and more efficient

factory system—the use of large buildings and machines for manufacturing

urbanization—the movement of people in large numbers from rural areas to cities

---

After the Wars of Napoleon, Europe had a few large kingdoms or empires, such as the Kingdom of France and the Austrian Empire, and many small states. Some of the countries that are prominent today didn't even exist in 1815. There was, for example, no Germany or Italy. As the 19th century moved along, a spirit of nationalism developed. People with the same language and culture wanted to have their own country. Germany, however, was just a scattering of many states. Italy was also divided into small states and, even worse, the Italians were ruled by a foreign power—the Austrian Empire.

Germany began to unify under its largest state—Prussia. More and more of the smaller northern German states joined Prussia. A successful war with France in 1870 encouraged the last southern German states to unite with Prussia. Finally, in 1871, the nation of Germany was born with William of Prussia as its emperor. In Italy, after several false starts, the Italians finally defeated Austria on the battlefield, and the modern state of Italy was born in 1870.

If the 19th century was the age of nationalism, it was also the age of industrialism. James Watt's invention of the steam engine in 1769 launched the Industrial Revolution. Previously, everything had been done by hand, usually at home. Now there was an explosion of technology that has continued to this day. During the 1800s, steam-driven machines increasingly did the work once done by human hands. This was especially true in the textile industry. Machines were, however, far too large and expensive to be used at home. So buildings called factories were built to house the machines. This system created a new and modern class of labor—the factory worker. In order to be close to their work, factory workers moved into new cities that sprang up around the factories.

This urbanization changed the face of Europe. In 1800, there were no cities with more than a million people. By 1900, however, there were several European cities with more than a million people. The population of London, for example, exceeded 6 million. This rapid urbanization caused many problems—diseases from poor garbage removal, bad housing, inadequate police.

Steam also changed how people traveled. Before the invention of the steam engine, the fastest a person could travel over land was on horseback. Someone such as Julius Caesar traveled as fast as, say, George Washington. Steam-powered boats and steam-powered railroads, however, reduced travel time dramatically in the 19th century.

EXERCISE 18

Directions: Underline the correct answer that completes each statement below.

1. The Age of (Industrialism   Nationalism) began when James Watt invented the (steam engine   railroad).

2. The first major industry to be industrialized was the (automotive   textile) industry.

3. During industrialization, workers moved (into cities   back to farms) so they would be closer to (stores   factories).

Answers are on page 330.

Colonialism

> ## Key Words
>
> **protectorate**—a weak country controlled by a stronger one
>
> **colonization**—the act of one country taking over direct control of another
>
> **imperialism**—the total domination of one country by another

The British once bragged that the sun never set on the British Empire. That was true in the 1800s and early 1900s. The British Empire spanned the globe. The British had colonies and protectorates in Asia, Africa, the Middle East, the Pacific region, and in the Americas. So at any given moment, the sun was already high in the sky shining on one or more of these possessions. The empire included India, "the crown jewel of the Empire," Australia, Hong Kong, Egypt, Nigeria, and South Africa, among others.

Other European nations tried to keep pace with Britain. These nations, too, thought that having colonies added to their national strength. So they developed colonization policies of their own. France, for example, established protectorates in Cambodia, Laos, and in northern and central Vietnam. It turned southern Vietnam into a colony. France also had colonies in Africa and South America. Portugal had colonies in Africa and China. Even the Netherlands had colonies in Africa and South America as well as the West and East Indies. New nations, such as Germany and Italy, joined the race by establishing colonies in Africa.

The imperialism of Europe was made possible by its industrial strength. Europeans could dominate native peoples because the European countries were economically and militarily so much stronger. The one great exception to this rule was Japan. Because the Japanese so quickly adopted certain Western ways, they became strong enough militarily to defeat Russia in a war in 1905. Japan even became an imperial power in its own right, taking over Taiwan and Korea.

Between 1870 and 1914, the European colonial race often led to conflict among the Europeans themselves. In South Africa, for example, the British fought Dutch settlers, called the Boers. The Boer War (1899–1902) ended in a British victory.

EXERCISE 19

Directions: Put a check in front of the correct answer to the questions that follow.

1. Which of the following was *not* once under British rule?

_____ (1) India

_____ (2) Australia

_____ (3) Egypt

_____ (4) Angola

2. The French established protectorates in which of the following?

_____ (1) Cambodia and Laos

_____ (2) southern Vietnam and Morocco

_____ (3) the East and West Indies

_____ (4) Japan and China

3. In South Africa, the Boers fought which of the following?

_____ (1) the French

_____ (2) the Portuguese

_____ (3) the British

_____ (4) the Russians

4. Which Asian nation had its own form of imperialism?

_____ (1) Vietnam

_____ (2) China

_____ (3) Japan

_____ (4) Cambodia

5. Which country did the Japanese defeat in 1905?

_____ (1) Britain

_____ (2) Russia

_____ (3) Portugal

_____ (4) the Netherlands

Answers are on page 330.

World War I

> ## Key Words
>
> **alliance**—an agreement between or among nations to come to the aid of an ally if that ally is attacked
>
> **stalemate**—a situation in conflict when neither side can gain a clear advantage
>
> **armistice**—a temporary halt to hostilities

The " 'isms" of the 1800s and early 1900s—nationalism, imperialism, and industrialism—helped to create conflict among Europeans. Nations tried to gain power and influence at their neighbor's expense. No single nation, however, felt powerful enough to stand alone. So most nations formed military alliances. If one member of an alliance was attacked, the other members would come to its aid. One such alliance was made up of Britain, France, and Russia. Another alliance was made up of Germany, Austria-Hungary, and the Ottoman Empire (Turkey).

Then, on June 28, 1914, a single act sparked a world war. A nationalist from Serbia shot and killed the Austrian archduke and his wife in Sarajevo, Bosnia, as the couple drove through the streets. Austria, backed by Germany, declared war on Serbia, which was supported by Russia. The alliances clicked into gear and World War I began. On one side were the Central Powers—Germany, Austria-Hungary, Turkey, and Bulgaria. On the other side were the Allies— Britain, France, Russia, Italy, and several other countries. The United States joined the Allies in 1917 after German submarines attacked American ships.

In the beginning, most people thought the war would be brief and glorious. How wrong they were! The war lasted four long bloody years. On the Western Front, both sides dug trenches and fought to a stalemate. Neither side could gain the upper hand—until the arrival of the Americans tipped the balance in favor of the Allies.

World War I ended in 1918 when a new German government asked for an armistice, or temporary peace agreement. The actual fighting ended at 11 A.M. on the 11th day of the 11th month of the year. By then more than 8 million soldiers on both sides had died.

World War I changed the map of Europe. The old monarchies in Russia, Germany, and Austria-Hungary disappeared. New nations such as Poland, Yugoslavia, Czechoslovakia, Finland, Estonia, Latvia, and Lithuania emerged. In addition, Germany was forced to sign the harsh Treaty of Versailles. To prevent a repetition of World War I, the Allies created the League of Nations. The hopes of this world peace-keeping body were crushed, however, when the United States refused to join.

EXERCISE 20

Directions: Study the chart below and answer the questions that follow.

THE TOLL OF WORLD WAR I			
Nation	Total # of soldiers	Percent killed	Percent casualties (killed and wounded)
France	8.4 million	16.0%	67.0%
British Empire	8.9 million	10.2%	33.6%
Russia	12.0 million	14.1%	55.4%
Germany	11.0 million	16.4%	55.0%
Austria-Hungary	7.8 million	11.8%	58.0%
United States	4.0 million	1.1%	5.8%

1. Which nation had the largest army?

   _____

2. Which nations had casualty rates over 50%?

   _____

3. Which nation had the highest percentage of its soldiers killed?

   _____

4. Which nation, in terms of the percentage soldiers killed and total casualties, suffered the least?

   _____

Answers are on page 330.

EXERCISE 21

Directions: Match the item on the left with its description on the right. Write the correct letter on the line.

_____ 1. alliance	(a) a temporary peace agreement
_____ 2. stalemate	(b) England, France, Russia, the United States, and others
_____ 3. armistice	(c) also called the Ottoman Empire
_____ 4. Central Powers	(d) a military agreement to support another
_____ 5. Allies	(e) Germany, Austria-Hungary, Turkey
_____ 6. Turkey	(f) when no one can gain a clear advantage

Answers are on page 330.

The Rise of Communism in Russia

Key Words

communism—the belief that all productive properties should be owned by the people as a whole

soviets—communist city councils made up of workers and soldiers during World War I

abdicate—to give up a throne

collectives—Russian farms run by large groups of peasants working together

---

Although Russia was allied with the winning side in World War I, it had a lot of problems during and after the war. The old Russian government under Czar (Tsar) Nicholas II was overthrown during the war. In 1917, Nicholas was forced to abdicate, or give up, his throne. (He and his family were arrested and later executed by the communists.) A new government, soon under Vladimir Lenin, took over. In March 1918, Lenin signed a treaty ending the war with Germany.

This Russian Revolution completely changed Russian society. The old nobility was crushed and a small group of dedicated communists took over the reins of government. Under communist philosophy, these rulers would stay in power until the people were ready to rule themselves.

Despite the peace with Germany, Lenin still had a war on his hands—a civil war. Many Russians did not want to be governed by the communists. Neither did many non-Russian nationals, such as the Finns, Poles, and Ukrainians. This civil war between the Reds (communists) and the Whites (their opponents) was a bloody affair. Millions of Russians were killed in the fighting or died as a result of famine or disease. In the end, the communists prevailed.

In 1922, Russia became the Union of Soviet Socialist Republics, or the U.S.S.R. The country, most often called simply the Soviet Union, had 15 republics, one for each major national group. The communists, now in total control, began to reorganize society. One step was to get rid of private farms. In their place, the communists organized "collectives," or farms, run by the peasants collectively. All the peasants farmed the land together and sold their crops to the government.

EXERCISE 22

Directions: Study the time line below and answer the questions that follow.

World War I begins		Communists take over Russia		Communists execute Nicholas II and family			U.S.S.R. created	
August 1914	March 1917	November 1917	March 1918	July 1918	November 1918	December 1922	January 1924
	Nicholas II abdicates his throne		Russia signs treaty with Germany		World War I ends		Lenin dies

1. Which happened first: the execution of Nicholas or the end of World War I?

   _____

2. Which happened later: the creation of the U.S.S.R. or the death of Lenin?

   _____

3. T   F   Germany defeated Russia in World War I.

4. T   F   The communists took control of the Russian government before the end of World War I.

Answers are on page 330.

Fascism and Democracy

> ## Key Words
>
> **dictatorship**—a government in which one person has absolute authority over a nation
>
> **Nazis**—the political party of Adolf Hitler
>
> **Fascism**—a government headed by an oppressive dictator and usually based on nationalism and racism

Many Europeans craved strong leadership in the uncertain world of the 1920s and 1930s. They wanted someone who could get results and who could restore national pride. In Russia, they got more than they bargained for in Joseph Stalin. He took over after the death of Lenin in 1924. Stalin ruled with an iron fist, never flinching to eliminate anyone who opposed him. He was, however, just one of the dictators who emerged out of the ashes of World War I.

The Weimar Republic ruled Germany immediately after World War I. It was a democratic form of government with constitutional guarantees for freedom of speech and religion. Its leaders, however, had great difficulties dealing with the economy and the war debts left over from World War I. A new party arose in the 1920s with different answers. It was called the Nazi party and its leader was Adolf Hitler. Hitler hated democracy and he hated the Jews. He tried unsuccessfully to seize power in 1923. Hitler was arrested and sent to prison. There he wrote *Mein Kampf* (My Struggle), which outlined his plans for Germany.

Once out of prison, Hitler resumed his political activity. Many Germans were drawn to his program. Then, in 1933, they voted him chancellor, or prime minister, of Germany. Before long, he gained total control over the country. He did revive the economy through large-scale building programs. But his followers also burned books. They attacked Jewish businesses and synagogues. And they began forcing Jews to wear a yellow star on their clothing. Despite such actions, Hitler enjoyed popularity with most Germans during the 1930s.

In Italy, another dictator came to power. He was Benito Mussolini, the head of the Fascist party. Mussolini shared many of Hitler's beliefs. He believed in dictatorship with a single party and a single leader. The Fascists wanted Italy to be a strong and powerful country again. Like Hitler in Germany, Mussolini turned his country into a totalitarian state.

The Nazis and the Fascists, however, wanted more. They soon built strong armies to threaten their neighbors. Hitler took over German-speaking territories on Germany's border. Italy invaded Ethiopia in Africa. Meanwhile, the democracies—principally Britain and France—did nothing to stop them. In 1938, the British and the French, wanting to avoid war at all costs, gave in to Hitler at a meeting in Munich, Germany. Hitler had demanded the right to take over the non-German nation of Czechoslovakia.

EXERCISE 23

Directions: Study the map below and answer the questions that follow.

HITLER'S TERRITORIAL GAINS, 1936–1939

■ Rhineland *(acquired March 1936)*	■ Sudetenland *(acquired Sept. 1938)*	■ Czech lands *(acquired March 1939)*	■ Austria *(acquired March 1938)*

1. List the territorial acquisitions of Hitler in chronological order starting with the first.

   _____

   _____

2. Reread the section on Hitler's acquisitions. Which was the only one that had a population that was not German-speaking?

   _____

3. What strip of land separated Prussia from Germany?

   _____

Answers are on page 330.

World War II

> ## Key Words
>
> **nonaggression pact**—an agreement between countries to not go to war against each other
>
> **Third Reich**—the name of Hitler's government
>
> **concentration camps**—places where the Nazis used forced labor and where they executed those unfit for work

At the Munich meeting, Hitler had promised he would make no more territorial demands after Czechoslovakia. He lied. Hitler had much greater ambitions for his government, which was known as the Third Reich. But first he had to deal with the Soviet Union. Although both countries were ruled by dictators, the communists hated the Nazis and vice versa. Yet they agreed on one thing. They did not want to fight each other—at least, not yet. So in 1939, the two enemies signed a nonaggression pact. Freed from his worry about a war with the Soviet Union, Hitler attacked Poland on September 1, 1939. Two days later, Britain and France finally declared war on Germany. The war that the democracies had tried so hard to avoid had now begun.

After crushing Poland, Hitler turned west and attacked France, which fell in June of 1940. There was now only one free nation left standing in the Western Europe—the United Kingdom. Hitler tried to bomb England into surrender with a Blitzkrieg, or lightning war. But somehow England held out. After ten months of an air war in the skies over England, Hitler quit. He had lost the Battle of Britain.

Then, in June 1941, Hitler broke his nonaggression pact with Stalin by attacking the Soviet Union. The move caught Stalin by surprise. The Germans pushed deep into Russian territory. But Russia wasn't a pushover like Belgium or France had been. It proved to be too vast, its winters too cold, and its people too stubborn. Eventually Hitler was forced to retreat, after suffering massive losses.

Meanwhile, on December 7, 1941, the Japanese bombed Pearl Harbor, and the United States declared war on Japan. Hitler, an ally of Japan, then declared war on the United States. The United States and Britain agreed it was more important to defeat Germany first. But the Allies were too weak and Germany was still too strong to attack Europe directly. So they attacked German forces in North Africa first and then defeated Germany's other ally, Italy. Finally, on June 6, 1944, a day known as D-Day, the Allies landed in France. Meanwhile, the Russians were pushing back the Germans in the East. Soon victory was in sight.

At last, in May, the Germans surrendered. Hitler committed suicide in his bunker in Berlin. It was only then that the Allies discovered the full extent of the horrors that had occurred during the war. The Germans had set up concentration camps, where they sent Jews and other groups of people they did not like. More than six million people died in these camps.

In the Pacific, American forces began to close in on Japan by moving from one island to another. Then, in August of 1945, the United States used a new and horrible weapon on Japan. Americans dropped atomic bombs on two Japanese cities, Hiroshima and Nagasaki, killing a couple of hundred thousand people. On August 14, 1945, Japan surrendered, and World War II was over.

EXERCISE 24

Directions: Study the bar graph below and answer the questions that follow.

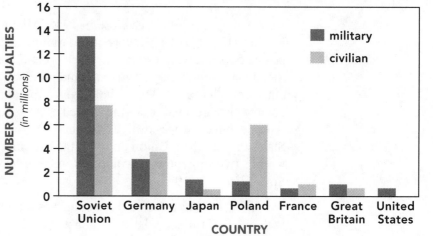

WORLD WAR II: CIVILIAN AND MILITARY CASUALTIES

1. Which nation suffered no civilian casualties?_____

   Why? _____

2. Which nations had fewer than one million total casualties?

   _____

3. In terms of total casualties, which nation suffered the most?

   _____

4. Which nations had higher civilian casualties than military casualties?

   _____

5. The Japanese home islands were never invaded. Why, then, were there 300,000 civilian casualties?

   _____

   _____

Answers are on page 330.

The Postwar World

> ### Key Words
>
> **United Nations**—an international organization created in 1945 to promote peace throughout the world
>
> **Cold War**—the state of hostilities, not involving actual fighting, that developed after World War II between the Soviet Union and the United States

As World War II drew to a close in 1945, Allied leaders created the United Nations (U.N.). The U.N. was meant to replace the League of Nations. Most people hoped it would promote peace around the world. That did not happen. Small wars kept breaking out here and there. Sometimes the U.N. helped, but other times it didn't. One of the biggest problems the U.N. faced was the fact that the strongest nations—the United States and the Soviet Union—were sworn enemies. It was difficult for the U.N. to do anything if either the United States or the Soviet Union opposed the action. This Cold War between the world's two superpowers would last more or less until the final breakup of the Soviet Union in 1991.

The Cold War affected three countries directly. They were divided in two with one half ruled by the communists and the other half by non-communists. Germany was divided into East Germany (run by communists) and West Germany (a democracy). The city of Berlin itself was divided in half. The communists built the Berlin Wall to seal off their half of the city. (Germany was finally reunited in 1990.)

Korea was also cut in half, with the communists controlling the north and the non-communists presiding over the south. In 1950, North Korea invaded South Korea. This time the U.N. took action and sent troops to stop the North Koreans. The Korean War (1950–1953) ended in a stalemate. As a result, there is still a communist North Korea and a non-communist South Korea.

Another country that was split in half was Vietnam. The split took place in 1954 and when elections to reunite the country were not held in 1956, the communists in the north felt cheated. So they began a campaign to topple the non-communist government in the south. The United States, trying to stop the spread of communism, fought on the side of the South Vietnamese. The North Vietnamese and their communist allies in South Vietnam, called Viet Cong, eventually won the war. In 1975, Vietnam was reunited under communist rule.

In the Middle East, a country was not divided in half, but a special region was. About 6 million Jews died in Nazi concentration camps. The Jewish people swore, "Never Again." One way to make sure such future tragedies were avoided was to give Jews their own country. Throughout most of their long history, the Jews had no home. They lived in the nations of other peoples. In 1948, the Jews declared the new nation of Israel in Palestine to be the home of the Biblical Jews. The region was already occupied by Palestinian Arabs, however, so since 1948 Israel and her Arab neighbors have fought four wars that have settled little. Tensions remain high today.

EXERCISE 25

Directions: Circle *T* for each true statement, or *F* for each false statement.

T F 1. After World War II, most people hoped that the League of Nations would protect world peace.

T F 2. The struggle between the United States and the Soviet Union was called a Cold War because there was no actual fighting.

T F 3. During the decades following World War II, the world's two superpowers were the United States and Nazi Germany.

T F 4. Berlin was once divided into a communist half and a non-communist half.

T F 5. In 1950, South Korea invaded North Korea.

T F 6. The Korean War is a good example of the U.N.'s inability to do anything in time of conflict.

T F 7. The Korean War ended in an overwhelming victory for the North Koreans.

T F 8. The canceled 1956 elections in Vietnam were meant to reunite the country.

T F 9. Palestine is the ancient home of both Jews and Arabs.

T F 10. The U.N. has been very effective in ending the conflict between the Jews and the Arabs.

Answers are on page 330.

The Modern World

Key Words

global culture—certain customs and desires shared by many of the world's people

Common Market—the name given to the first European effort to eliminate trade barriers between and among member nations

European Union—the current European organization that promotes economic growth and free trade

Euro—the new European currency meant to replace national currencies

ethnic cleansing—widespread murder meant to eliminate certain ethnic groups

---

In many ways the world has become a much, much smaller place since World War II. Thanks to high-speed trains, superhighways, and the jet plane, travel time has been cut drastically. Thanks to the fax machine, e-mail, and the computer, communication is virtually instant. Also, the world, which was once rich in clearly distinct cultures, is increasingly becoming one global culture. Travel almost anywhere in the world and you can easily find people wearing blue jeans, eating a Big Mac, or drinking a Coke.

The growing global culture is the flip side of the growing global market. Western Europeans saw what a vast free market did for the United States. A person in Oregon can sell any legal product thousands of miles away to a person in Florida without any trade barriers or special taxes. But someone in France could not do the same with someone just a few miles away in Belgium or Spain. So the idea of a large "free market" attracted Europeans. They wanted something similar to the United States for themselves. So in 1957, six nations formed the European Common Market. The goal of this Common Market was to reduce the barriers to trade and to boost economic growth. Later, other nations joined and the Common Market was replaced by the European Union (E.U.). The E.U. had the additional goal of pledging to aid its weaker members.

Europeans even adopted a single currency—the Euro—to replace old national currencies, since those separate currencies had to be exchanged for trade across national borders. In North America, the United States, Canada, and Mexico eliminated trade barriers when they signed a new trade agreement called NAFTA (North American Free Trade Agreement).

While in many ways the world is coming more and more together, in some ways it is falling apart. Ethnic and religious conflicts are the new plague. Today, nations don't fight each other so much as different groups within a country fight each other. During the 1990s, for example, Yugoslavia broke up. In the process, certain groups tried what has been called ethnic cleansing. That meant killing members of other ethnic groups. Similar things have happened in recent years in Rwanda, Somalia, Indonesia, and other places. Internal conflicts have also haunted many of the nations in Central and South America.

EXERCISE 26

Directions: Study the chart below and answer the questions that follow.

EUROPEAN UNION MEMBER NATIONS			
Nation	Population	Per capita income	Major ethnic groups
Austria	8,139,299	$21,400	German
Belgium	10,182,034	$23,200	Flemish, Walloon
Denmark	5,356,845	$23,200	Scandinavian
Finland	5,158,372	$20,000	Finn
France	58,978,172	$22,700	French
Germany	82,087,361	$20,800	German
Greece	10,707,135	$13,000	Greek
Ireland	3,632,944	$16,800	Celtic, Irish
Italy	56,735,130	$21,500	Italian
Luxembourg	429,080	$33,700	French, German
Netherlands	15,807,641	$22,000	Dutch
Portugal	9,918,040	$15,200	Portuguese
Spain	39,167,744	$16,400	Spanish, Basque
Sweden	8,911,296	$19,700	Swedish
United Kingdom	59,113,439	$21,200	English, Scottish, Irish

1. This list shows the full member nations in the E.U. as of 1999. How many were there? _____

2. Which nation has the largest population? _____ the smallest population? _____

3. Which nation has the highest per capita income? _____ the lowest per capita income? _____

4. Germans are a major ethnic groups in which nations?

_____

5. How many E.U. nations have per capita incomes of at least $20,000?

_____

The World in the 21st Century

> *Key Words*
>
> **fossil fuels**—sources of energy found in the earth such as oil, gas, and coal

The 20th century witnessed stunning technological change. In terms of motorized flight, for instance, humans were stuck on the ground until the Wright Brothers took a brief flight in 1903. Just 66 years later, humans stood on the moon. Similar advances took place in communication, biology, medicine, and dozens of other fields. There is little reason to think that the pace of scientific progress will slow down in the 21st century.

There are dark clouds on the horizon, however. One is the growth of population. At the beginning of the 20th century, the world's population stood at 1.6 billion. By the end of the century, it stood at more than 6 billion. Medical and technological advances made it possible for people to live longer than at any other time in history. However, that meant there were almost four times as many mouths to feed in 2000 than there had been in 1900. Technology has made it possible to feed most of these people. But how long can technology outrun population growth?

Another problem is the environment. Human activity has polluted much of the land, water, and air. In addition, scientists worry about the loss of the rain forests. These oxygen-producing forests are being cut down to make way for more farms to feed the growing population. Global warming and melting ice caps also trouble scientists. How will a warmer environment affect our ability to grow food? Then there is a question of fossil fuels, such as oil, coal, and natural gas. Our growing demand for them has forced us to invade ecologically fragile regions. How long can this last?

On the other hand, humans have faced tough problems before and have usually found a solution. There will be one difference in the 21st century, however. We will be less likely to look for solutions as citizens of a certain community or nation and more likely to look for solutions as citizens of the world.

EXERCISE 27

Directions: Study the table below and answer the questions that follow.

WORLD POPULATION: NOW AND IN THE FUTURE			
Continent	Population in 1999	Projected in 2025	Projected in 2050
Asia	3.6 billion	4.8 billion	5.4 billion
Africa	775 million	1.4 billion	2.0 billion
Europe	725 million	700 million	600 million
South America	345 million	451 million	520 million
North America	475 million	617 million	725 million

1. Which is the only continent with a projected loss of population?

   _____

2. North America's projected population in 2050 will equal what continent's actual population in 1999?_____

3. About how many more people will Asia gain during the first half of the 21st century?_____

4. In terms of percentage increase, which continent's population will grow the fastest over the next 50 years?_____

   _____

Answers are on page 331.

READING EFFICIENCY C

Directions: This activity will help you to improve your reading efficiency. Before you start to read, write the present time at the top of the page. When you have completed the reading and all 5 questions, write your finishing time. Subtract to find how long you took. Score your answers. Then turn to page 340 to find your E-Factor and graph your progress.

Finishing Time	
Starting Time	−
Reading Time	=
Number of Answers Correct	

One of the earliest cultures began in Mesopotamia. Mesopotamia was between the Tigris and Euphrates Rivers. The valley was called the Fertile Crescent. This area is now part of Syria, Turkey, and most of Iraq.

In the late spring the rivers overflowed their banks. The flooding left rich soil on the farmlands. However, the long, hot summers made farming difficult. Farmers developed a system for water control. Irrigation made it possible to grow good crops.

In about 3500 B.C., the Sumerians came to the region. These settlers started several city-states Their cities were built out of mud bricks. They built a temple for the chief god or goddess. It was the most important building in the city. The Sumerians worshiped about three thousand gods and goddesses.

Most of the people farmed for a living. They also wove cloth. They made pottery and metalwork.

The Sumerians invented the world's first writing system. It was a form of picture writing. This writing was called cuneiform.

The city-states grew. Wars were common. City-states fought each other. They wanted to control the land and water. Invaders threatened the city-states. In 1792 B.C., the Babylonians took over the region. Hammurabi was the king. He is best remembered for his laws. He treated the people in his lands justly.

1. Which word best describes the relationships between the city-states?

   (1) cooperative
   (2) respectful
   (3) peaceful
   (4) neutral
   (5) aggressive

2. What was notable about King Hamurabi?

   (1) He invented cuneiform writing.
   (2) He began a legal code based on strict justice.
   (3) He built an irrigation system.
   (4) He settled a Sumerian city-state in 3500 B.C.
   (5) He traded with other empires.

3. What is the author's purpose in this passage?

   (1) to explain the Code of Hamurabi to the reader
   (2) to compare Mesopotamia and Iraq
   (3) to persuade the reader to learn more about the Fertile Crescent
   (4) to inform the reader about an early culture
   (5) to make judgments about the Sumerians

READING EFFICIENCY C

4. What was a positive effect of the overflowing of the Tigris and Euphrates Rivers?

(1) an increased need for irrigation
(2) cooler summer weather
(3) the deposit of rich soil on farmlands
(4) more clay for pottery making
(5) better transportation between the city-states

5. Which of the following conclusions can you draw from this passage?

(1) The economy of the Sumerian city-states was based on trade.
(2) Religion was an important part of Mesopotamian life.
(3) Mesopotamians were well known for their educational system.
(4) Men and women had equal rights in Mesopotamian society.
(5) Life in Mesopotamia improved under foreign rule.

Answers are on page 331.

READING EFFICIENCY D

Directions: This activity will help you to improve your reading efficiency. Before you start to read, write the present time at the top of the page. When you have completed the reading and all 5 questions, write your finishing time. Subtract to find how long you took. Score your answers. Then turn to page 340 to find your E-Factor and graph your progress.

Finishing Time	
Starting Time −	
Reading Time =	
Number of Answers Correct	

On November 11, 1918, Germany surrendered to the Allies. World War I ended. In January, delegates from the Allied nations met in Paris. They wanted to make a final peace settlement. They did not want another world war.

President Woodrow Wilson had a plan for lasting peace. It was called the "Fourteen Points." Great Britain wanted to make the Germans pay for the war. France wanted national safety. Italy wanted to gain lands held by Germany. The defeated nations made separate treaties.

The Treaty of Versailles was the most important. The Germans thought it was a harsh peace. They were unhappy with the reparations section. Germany had damaged the Allied countries. The treaty ordered Germany to pay for the losses. The Allies threatened to invade if Germany did not pay.

There were many terms of the treaty. Germany gave up land in Europe. It lost overseas colonies. The treaty limited Germany's armed forces. Germany had to pay $33 billion dollars.

The peace settlement soon came under attack. Some countries thought it was too weak. Others felt it was too harsh. Within twenty years of signing the treaties, Europe was again at war.

1. Why was making the peace settlement a difficult job?

    (1) The countries had different plans for the peace agreements.
    (2) Germany would not accept the peace terms.

    (3) Another war had already begun.
    (4) The Senate did not approve the treaty.
    (5) The delegates could not find a place to meet.

2. Which of the following was not one of the Allied nations?

    (1) United States
    (2) Great Britain
    (3) France
    (4) Germany
    (5) Russia

3. Why did the Germans finally agree to the terms of the Treaty of Versailles?

    (1) They wanted to start another war.
    (2) They felt guilty about the damage that they had caused in Europe.
    (3) They felt they had no alternative.
    (4) They wanted to trade with the United States.
    (5) They thought that the terms of the treaty were fair.

4. Why were the European countries concerned with the reparations section?

    (1) They wanted to purchase more land.
    (2) They wanted to become richer than Germany.
    (3) They wanted to build bigger armies.
    (4) They wanted to pay the United States for helping win the war.
    (5) They suffered severe losses during the war.

READING EFFICIENCY D

5. Which of the following conclusions can you draw from reading this passage?

   (1) The peace treaties strengthened European governments.
   (2) The American people supported the Treaty of Versailles.
   (3) $33 billion was not enough money to rebuild Europe.
   (4) The peace treaties were not effective.
   (5) President Wilson's plan was the best.

   Answers are on page 331.

Chapter 7

Civics and Government

Political science is the study of the institutions of government and how they work. Political scientists study governmental structure and policy making, political parties, political behavior, interest groups, and international relations.

A *political system* is an institution that organizes power relationships in a society. People have created a wide variety of political systems from simple tribal organizations to very complex nation-states like the United States. The earliest political systems had no formal governmental structure. Important decisions were often made by one person or a council. As societies became more complex, people created more complicated governmental structures.

A *government* is the body or institution that makes and administers society's laws. The police and the courts are the part of government that maintains order in society. Armed forces provide security against attack by other countries. Most governments promote some form of general welfare in health, safety, education, and help to the needy.

Three necessary functions underlie all governments:

- executive (administers the operations of the government)

- legislative (makes the laws)

- judicial (interprets the laws)

All governments possess the power to make decisions and carry them out. Some rule by direct force or by the threat of force against its citizens. Others rule with the support of their citizens.

When the people believe that the government is not working in their interest, governmental authority can break down. If a government uses force against the people, the struggle can escalate. Some governments have been overthrown by revolution, such as the American colonists' fight against the English government.

Governments may also be overthrown by a small group rather than by a popular uprising. This kind of action is called a coup d'état, meaning a "blow against the state."

People try to influence the government in many ways. For example, political parties are a part of the American political system, but they are not a part of the government. Citizens also can become involved in the American political system by petitioning, demonstrating, and lobbying.

Types of Government

There are four main types of government. They are monarchy, democracy, oligarchy, and dictatorship.

Monarchy

Monarchies are one of the oldest forms of government in the world. A king or a queen is the head of the government. Queen Elizabeth II of Great Britain and Queen Beatrix of the Netherlands are monarchs. Countries that have constitutions, such as the United States, but also have monarchs, are called constitutional monarchies. Great Britain is a constitutional monarchy. The queen's tasks are chiefly ceremonial. She reigns but does not rule. Instead, the queen has a prime minister, a cabinet, and a permanent civil service who carry out the day-to-day job of governing according to the laws passed by Parliament, the legislative branch of government.

Countries where the monarch's word is the law are called absolute monarchies. King Fahd of Saudi Arabia is an absolute monarch. The country has no constitution, no parliament, and no political parties.

France and Russia used to be absolute monarchies, but the people overthrew King Louis XVI during the French Revolution in 1792 and Tsar Nicholas II in the Russian Revolution of 1917. Sometimes absolute monarchs claim to rule by divine right, which means that they believe their right to rule comes from God.

Democracy

A second type of government is a democracy. The power to rule in a democracy comes from the people. (In Greek, *demos* means people, and *cracy* means power or form of government.) The United States is a democracy in which the people take part in the government. Other countries, such as France and India, are also democracies.

Democracy has deep roots in Western political tradition. It can take different forms ranging from the direct democracy, or participatory democracy, of the Greek city-states or the representative democracy found in the United States.

The United States is too large for everyone to gather to discuss and vote on laws. The people elect representatives to carry out the wishes of the people according to the Constitution. In a representative democracy, all people over a certain age have the right to vote. This was not always so. In the United States, only white men could vote until after the Civil War. Then black men were given this right by the Fifteenth Amendment (1870). Women did not get the right to vote until 1920, when the Nineteenth Amendment was passed.

The largest democracy in the world is India, which has a population of 900 million. However, the country is divided by many ethnic groups, languages, and religions. The result is that India is difficult to govern.

Oligarchy

A third type of government is an oligarchy, which means government by a few. Before the Industrial Revolution, England was considered an oligarchy. Even though it had a monarch whose powers had by then become limited, the real power was in the hands of a few members of Parliament. Voting was limited to people with a certain income. So the aristocracy and rich merchants—the upper class—controlled the government.

Some of the ancient Greek city-states were oligarchies ruled by a few leading families. The seafaring Republic of Venice was ruled by a merchant elite. The rest of the people had no say in the government.

Some countries today might be considered oligarchies even though they would not call themselves that. Although conditions change rapidly, certain developing countries, particularly in Latin America, have long been ruled by the leading families who control the economies of these countries.

Dictatorship

A widespread form of government is the *dictatorship*. A dictator is a person who has complete control over a country. A dictator rules somewhat in the manner of an absolute monarch but does not use royal titles like *king* or *emperor*. In modern times, dictators have become totalitarian rulers. Under totalitarianism, the dictators have complete control over all political, economic, and social life in the country. Joseph Stalin and Adolf Hitler were totalitarian dictators. Both ruled through a secret police that terrorized people to keep them from opposing the dictators. The Communist Party in the Soviet Union had this role from 1918 to 1990. The Nazi Party in Germany supported Hitler from 1933 until the Allied victory in World War II ended his rule.

At the present time, many developing countries are dictatorships, particularly in Africa and Asia. Iraq's Saddam Hussein is a dictator. North Korea is one of the last communist dictatorships. Although countries with dictators often have constitutions and legislative bodies, the wishes of the dictators are always carried out.

EXERCISE 1

Directions: Match the type of government on the left with its description on the right. Write the correct letter on the line.

_____ 1. direct democracy   (a) has checks on the ruler

_____ 2. representative democracy   (b) people select delegates to represent them

_____ 3. absolute monarchy   (c) people vote on government issues

_____ 4. constitutional monarchy   (d) the king or queen's word is law

_____ 5. oligarchy   (e) an extreme form of dictatorship

_____ 6. totalitarianism   (f) a small group of people rule

Answers are on page 331.

The American Political Process

> ## Key Words
>
> **plurality**—the greatest number of votes in an election
>
> **simple majority**—50 percent of the votes plus a minimum of one vote
>
> **electoral college**—a special group of voters from each state that elects the president and vice president

At the heart of democracy are the concepts of consent and majority rule. Majority rule is the only practical way of achieving consensus, or group agreement. A unanimous vote (100 percent) is unlikely, and minority rule does not truly represent a consensus.

In a representative democracy such as the United States, a candidate for public office needs to win a majority of the votes cast. Sometimes a candidate needs to win only a plurality, the greatest number of votes cast, to win.

Candidate Bill Clinton won only 43 percent of the popular (people's) vote for president in 1992, but he won 370 electoral votes. It is the electoral college that elects the president. Each state has its own number of electors, depending on the size of each state. The candidate who gets the most votes from the people of a particular state also wins all the electoral votes from that state. Clinton got well over the majority of electoral votes needed to win the election.

Most bills submitted to Congress need a simple majority (50 percent plus a minimum of one vote) to become law. In special cases, majorities of two-thirds or three-fifths may be required.

The importance of a majority in American politics does not mean that the minority viewpoint is totally ignored. Compromise is often needed to get a simple majority of votes to pass legislation in Congress. Senators and representatives also take public opinion into consideration.

EXERCISE 2

Question 1 is based on the vote totals shown below.

In the election for mayor in Metropolis, Alfred Johnson was elected. The vote totals for the three candidates were:

Johnson	101,700
Alvarez	93,201
Lee	45,718

1. What term best describes Johnson's vote total?

    (1) plurality
    (2) majority
    (3) simple majority
    (4) consensus
    (5) three-fifths majority

Questions 2–4 are based on the passage on page 203.

2. In a council vote, 30 of the 50 members voted to ban smoking in all the city's restaurants. What is this vote an example of?

    (1) compromise
    (2) simple majority
    (3) three-fifths majority
    (4) consensus
    (5) two-thirds majority

3. The owners of a condominium high-rise meet each month to discuss and decide on the business of their building. This meeting closely resembles a direct democracy. Which of the following is required to reach a consensus?

    (1) The condominium board president makes decisions.
    (2) All owners must agree for consensus to be reached.
    (3) A majority of owners must approve any actions.
    (4) The five richest owners decide for the others.
    (5) The elected officers of the board make all decisions.

4. The owners of another condominium building have an elected board of five members. Which of the following would make the decisions?

    (1) The condominium board president makes decisions.
    (2) All owners must agree for a decision to be binding.
    (3) A majority of owners must approve a decision.
    (4) The five richest owners decide for the others.
    (5) The elected officers of the board make all the decisions.

Answers are on page 331.

Interest Groups and Political Parties

> ## Key Words
>
> **third party**—any U.S. political party that is independent of the two major parties
>
> **interest group**—a group of people who organize for a specific reason

Elected representatives play an important role in the American political system. As soon as these representatives take office, people try to influence their decisions. Individuals, groups, and organizations have interests that can be aided by government decisions. There are many stages of political activity between the desires and needs of citizens and final government decisions.

Interest Groups

Organized interest groups, such as labor unions and business groups, usually have active political programs. Single-issue groups, such as antismoking supporters, have become increasingly important. U.S. history has a long record of single-issue movements from Shay's rebellious debtor farmers in Massachusetts in the 1780s to today's environmental movement. Individuals believe they can be more effective if they join others with similar interests.

Interest groups have more power than individuals acting alone. They bring their numbers and influence into politics. They may raise campaign funds to aid a candidate who supports their position and provide volunteers for the candidate's election campaign. They may also put pressure on officials by writing letters, making visits, and demonstrating as a group.

Political Parties

The U.S. Constitution did not provide for political parties. However, the leaders of the young nation had many conflicts over national policy. Various organizations channeled the efforts of different interest groups into political action.

Two major parties, the Republicans and Democrats, have dominated the U.S. political system since the 1860s. They have effectively organized into interest groups. Compromise programs have united broad coalitions that campaign for the party's candidates.

Political parties select presidential candidates at national conventions. The chart at left outlines the process by which political parties choose a presidential candidate.

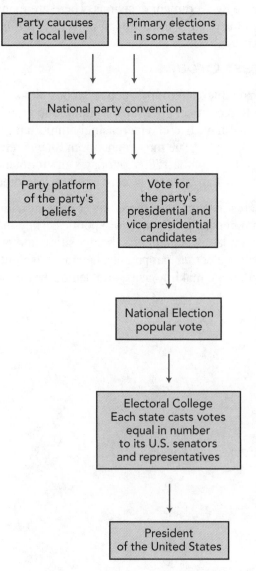

In a complex society such as the United States, the individual citizen cannot have much influence on the direction of politics without becoming part of an organized political group. Citizens should exercise their right to vote. Only through group participation in defining issues can citizens meaningfully affect the choices they will have at election time.

Politicians play an important role in the political process. They build the coalitions needed to get things done. They are not always liked by the public, but they are necessary in the American political process.

Many people usually vote for the same political party at each election. Others consider themselves "independents" and switch from one and major party to the next depending on the issues or candidates. Sometimes they support third parties.

Besides the two major parties, a wide variety of third parties have appeared from time to time in U.S. history. They include the Libertarian, Communist, American Independent, Prohibitionist, Socialist, and Populist parties. Nevertheless, the two major parties have managed to dominate politics and also have a far broader appeal to voters than the third parties with their narrower interests.

The activities of political parties, single-issue movements, and interest groups have expanded the limits of American democracy to allow more people to participate. In the process, they have formed election coalitions capable of winning power and acting on those interests.

EXERCISE 3

Directions: Write *P* for political party, *T* for third party, or *I* for interest group to identify the groups listed below.

_____ 1. antismoking lobby

_____ 2. political caucus

_____ 3. Republicans

_____ 4. Populists

_____ 5. Libertarians

_____ 6. Save the Whales

_____ 7. Americans for Democratic Action

_____ 8. isolationists

Answers are on page 331.

EXERCISE 4

Directions: Read the passage below and then put a check in front of the correct answer to the questions that follow.

Voter Turnout

The low voter turnout in this country is due to the relatively small number of voters who control elections. Most close congressional races are decided by fewer than 7,000 votes. Primary elections and state and local races are often decided by much smaller margins.

Senior citizens have protested every hint of cuts in Social Security. Elected officials know this, and Social Security is untouched because senior citizens vote.

On the other hand, surveys show that only 25 to 35 percent of eligible low-income people vote. This figure would be even lower if people with low incomes but substantial assets were counted separately. The voter turnout rate stands in sharp contrast to the 70 to 75 percent turnout among people making more than $25,000 a year. When low-income people fail to vote in numbers that match their total population, their interests are ignored.

1. As a result of voter turnout patterns, what does the writer believe?

_____ (1) The elderly do not have much influence.

_____ (2) The poor have too much influence on elections.

_____ (3) Poor people do not have much influence on elections.

2. Based on this passage, if lower-income people voted in large numbers, what could you conclude?

_____ (1) Social welfare programs would probably be expanded.

_____ (2) Social welfare programs would probably be decreased.

_____ (3) Social Security payments would be decreased.

Answers are on page 331.

Writing Activity 12

Think of a special interest group you would like to join. The group can be for or against any cause that interests you or that you think is important. In one sentence, state clearly the focus of your interest group. Then write four or five suggestions about how your group might accomplish its goal.

Answers will vary.

The U.S. Constitution

> ### Key Words
>
> **federal system**—the sharing of power between the states and the central government
>
> **checks and balances**—a system among the branches of the federal government that prevents any one branch from dominating the other two
>
> **Bill of Rights**—the first ten amendments to the U.S. Constitution that state the freedoms and rights of individuals

The years after the Revolutionary War (1783–1789) are often called the "time of troubles." The American economy was in a serious economic depression. The Articles of Confederation were adopted in 1781. They did not provide for an executive branch or a court system. The national government had no power to tax or regulate commerce between the states. Interstate commerce was carried on with the greatest difficulty because each state could issue its own currency, or paper money, and often charged their own taxes on goods.

In Massachusetts, armed farmers who were heavily in debt took part in Shay's Rebellion (1786). They seized courtrooms to prevent mortgage foreclosures. The rebellion was finally put down with little bloodshed. However, it pointed to the need for a strong central government that could put down such internal uprisings. The problems facing the new American nation made it clear that the Articles of Confederation needed to be changed drastically or dropped altogether.

Some aspects of the economic crisis—especially problems of interstate commerce—had to be dealt with. Meetings were held among some states in 1785 and 1786. These meetings led to a call for a Constitutional Convention. Its purpose was to amend the Articles of Confederation. The convention call was endorsed by the Confederation Congress. The Constitutional Convention opened in Philadelphia in May 1787.

A main issue in the Constitutional Convention concerned the division of power between the central government and the states. The final Constitution represented a victory of centralized power over states' rights. The government in Washington increased its powers and gained the right to tax, create an army and navy, control foreign trade, make treaties, and control currency. The states, however, still maintained substantial responsibilities. The kind of arrangement that divides power between a central government and the states is called a federal system.

The convention attempted to protect against overcentralization of power by basing the new government on the separation of powers. A legislative branch, made up of a House of Representatives and the Senate, was to enact laws. An executive branch, headed by the president, was to administer the government. A federal judicial (court) system was created to settle disputes and legal matters. Thus, a system of checks and balances was created in order to prevent any single branch of government from dominating the others.

Another important issue at the convention was the fair distribution of power between large and small states. This was resolved by giving each state equal representation in the Senate and basing representation in the House of Representatives on the size of the state's population. In this way, the House protected the rights of large states and the Senate protected the rights of small states.

The question of whether slaves should be counted in population totals was another issue at the convention. If slaves were counted, the Southern states, which had fewer people, would have greater representation in the House. Southern delegates argued that slaves should be counted. Northern delegates said that if slaves were counted for representation, they should be counted for taxation and taxed the same as free people.

They agreed that for both representation and taxation all free people would be counted along with three-fifths of all slaves (known as the Three-fifths Compromise). It strengthened the power of slave states in the House of Representatives. The Constitution also protected the slave trade for at least 20 years. Runaway slaves would also have to be returned to their owners.

The Constitution addressed other areas of government. There were sections on choosing the president, structuring the federal court system, and amending the Constitution. The finished Constitution was sent to conventions in each of the 13 states. In order to become law, it needed to be ratified by nine states.

There was some opposition to the document. Many Americans believed that it gave too much power to the national government. Many people also opposed the Constitution because it did not guarantee the rights of individual citizens—an objection that resulted in the Bill of Rights, the first ten amendments to the Constitution. The supporters of the Constitution, known as the Federalists, were led by Alexander Hamilton, James Madison, and John Jay. They wrote a series of articles, *The Federalist Papers,* arguing for ratification. A majority of the leaders of the Revolution, including George Washington and Benjamin Franklin, also supported the Constitution. Eleven states finally ratified the Constitution. It became effective in March of 1789.

EXERCISE 5

Directions: Match the item on the left with its description on the right. Write the correct letter on the line.

_____ 1. checks and balances

(a) the first ten amendments to the Constitution

_____ 2. federal system

(b) gave slave states a greater representation in the House of Representatives

_____ 3. *The Federalist Papers*

(c) prevents one branch of government from dominating the others

_____ 4. Three-fifths Compromise

(d) sharing of power between the states and the central government

_____ 5. Bill of Rights

(e) a series of articles that argued for ratification of the Constitution

Answers are on page 332.

Amendments to the Constitution

The protection of individual citizens' rights dominated the first session of the new Congress in 1789. During the drive for ratification, the Federalists had been forced by popular pressure to support a Bill of Rights in the form of amendments to the Constitution. Congress submitted the first ten constitutional amendments to the states for ratification. They were approved by 1791.

These first ten amendments, known as the Bill of Rights, form the basis of individual rights and liberties. These amendments guarantee the following:

- freedom of speech and the press
- the right to assemble and petition the government
- the right to keep and bear arms
- protection against unreasonable search and seizure
- the right to trial by jury
- the right to due process and protection against self-incrimination
- the right to a public trial
- the right to have an attorney
- protection against excessive bail or cruel or unusual punishment
- separation of church and state

Since the Bill of Rights, 17 more amendments have been added to the Constitution. Only one amendment has been repealed. The Eighteenth Amendment (1919), prohibition, which prohibited the drinking and sale of alcohol, was repealed by the Twenty-first Amendment (1933). The procedure for changing the Constitution was purposely made difficult. Amendments must be proposed by a two-thirds majority vote of both houses of Congress. Otherwise, two-thirds of the state legislatures can ask Congress to call a convention for proposing amendments. Any amendment must be approved by either the legislatures or special conventions in three-fourths of the states. Many proposed amendments have never been ratified because of this difficult procedure. For instance, the Equal Rights Amendment was defeated in 1982 because it fell several states short of the required 38 states needed for ratification.

All amendments that have been adopted have originated in Congress and have been ratified by the state legislatures. Among the more important are the Thirteenth (1865), abolishing slavery; the Fourteenth (1868), granting citizenship to the former slaves; the Fifteenth (1870), guaranteeing black males the right to vote; the Sixteenth (1913), establishing the federal income tax; the Nineteenth (1920), giving women the right to vote; and the Twenty-sixth (1971), lowering the voting age to 18.

The Constitution, even with amendments, is a short document, probably shorter than the bylaws of many organizations. It has vague guidelines concerning the powers and functions of the different levels of government. However, its flexibility has allowed it to survive as a symbol of national unity. The concrete meanings of its various paragraphs have constantly evolved as the country has grown and changed.

EXERCISE 6

Part I

Directions: Answer the questions below in the space provided.

1. All adopted amendments to the U.S. Constitution have originated in
   _____ .

2. The first ten amendments to the Constitution that list individual
   rights and freedoms are called the _____ .

3. The _____ of the Constitution makes the
   document as effective today as it was more than 200 years ago.

4. A new amendment must be approved by _____
   _____ of the states.

5. After the Bill of Rights, _____ more amendments
   have been added to the Constitution.

6. The _____ Amendment, prohibition, was
   repealed by the _____ Amendment in 1933.

7. Any new amendment that is proposed must receive a _____
   _____ vote from both houses of Congress.

8. The Thirteenth Amendment abolished _____ .

Part II

Directions: Read the following amendment to the Constitution and answer the question.

Amendment II

A well regulated Militia, being necessary to the security of a free State, the right of the people to keep and bear Arms, shall not be infringed.

1. Some people think that no citizen should be allowed to own a gun. How are these people able to use Amendment II as support for their cause?

   (1) The amendment refers only to a militia, or army.

   (2) The Bill of Rights were ratified in 1791, a long time ago.

   (3) Amendment II is a part of the Bill of Rights.

   (4) When the Amendment was written it referred only to men, not slaves or women.

   (5) Not every state agreed on this amendment.

Directions: Read the following amendment to the Constitution and answer the question.

Amendment V states (1) "nor shall any person be subject for the same offense to be twice put in jeopardy of life or limb; (2) nor shall be compelled in any criminal case to be a witness against himself, (3) nor be deprived of life, liberty, or property, without due process of law; (4) nor shall private property be taken for public use without just compensation."

2. When a police officer makes an arrest, the criminal suspect, by law, must be read their Miranda Rights. The Miranda Rights tell the suspect that they have the right to remain silent and warns them that anything they say can be used against them in a court of law.

   Put a check next to the number of the clause that is the basis for the Miranda Rights.

   _____ (1)

   _____ (2)

   _____ (3)

   _____ (4)

Answers are on page 332.

EXERCISE 7

Questions 1 and 2 are based on the passage below.

Many Supreme Court decisions have upheld the freedoms in the Bill of Rights. The Supreme Court has defined, limited, or expanded upon the meanings of the amendments. Below are some brief examples from the court battles over the amendments in the Bill of Rights. The examples are from the First Amendment.

". . . Congress shall make no law abridging . . . the right of the people peaceably to assemble, and to petition the government for redress of grievances."

In 1937, in the DeJonge v. Oregon case, the Supreme Court ruled that freedom of assembly was not limited only to those who wished to petition the government.

". . . Congress shall make no law . . . abridging the freedom of speech or of the press."

This amendment has become the central issue in the debate over what some perceive as obscene or pornographic materials. In 1946, the Supreme Court prevented the Postmaster General from denying second-class postal rates to Esquire magazine. In 1962, the court overturned a government practice of treating gay magazines as obscene matter and barring them from the mails. However, the Supreme Court has left the issue of what constitutes pornography up to what are called "community standards."

1. What is the main idea of this passage?

    (1) Supreme Court decisions have upheld the constitutional rights of people with controversial opinions or preferences.
    (2) Freedom of speech has always been upheld by governmental bodies.
    (3) Freedom of assembly was not clearly defined in the Bill of Rights.
    (4) The Bill of Rights should have clearly spelled out individual rights and freedoms.
    (5) The courts have always ruled in favor of the Bill of Rights.

2. The Supreme Court's decisions on obscene materials have been based on its interpretation of which type of freedom?

    (1) assembly
    (2) religion
    (3) political beliefs
    (4) sexual preference
    (5) speech and the press

Answers are on page 332.

Branches of Government

The new Constitution set up a national government with three different branches. To prevent an excess of power, the Constitution divided power and functions among the executive, legislative, and judicial branches. The Constitution also instituted a sophisticated system of checks and balances. This would prevent one branch of government from dominating any other branch.

The chart below shows the branches of government in the United States.

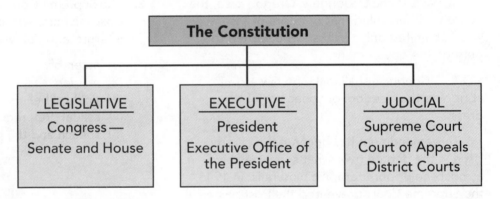

The Constitution		
LEGISLATIVE	**EXECUTIVE**	**JUDICIAL**
Congress— Senate and House	President Executive Office of the President	Supreme Court Court of Appeals District Courts

The Executive Branch

The executive branch administers the day-to-day activities of the government. The president, who is the head of the executive branch, must be at least 35 years old and a natural born citizen of the United States. The presidential term is four years. An individual is limited to two terms by the Twenty-second Amendment (1951). Another amendment allows the vice president to become president if the president dies or resigns while in office.

With the advice and consent of the Senate, the president appoints all of the major executive positions. He also appoints his own Cabinet officers, called secretaries, who are the heads of major government agencies. Some of these are State, Defense, Justice, Agriculture, Labor, and Education. The executive branch also includes federal agencies, such as the Environmental Protection Agency (EPA).

Article II of the Constitution gives the president the power to see that "the laws be faithfully executed." The executive branch is responsible for enforcing acts of Congress, court decisions, and treaties. The president can also issue proclamations and executive orders. These are legislative or lawmaking powers that have been delegated to the president either by law or by court decision. Lincoln's Emancipation Proclamation, which freed all slaves in Confederate states, is one of the most famous examples of this power of the presidency.

All bills passed by Congress must be sent to the president. If he signs the bill, it becomes law. However, he can refuse to sign the bill and return it to Congress; this action is called a veto. Congress may override the president's veto by a two-thirds vote of both houses of Congress. However, if the president does not return the bill within ten days, it automatically becomes a law, unless Congress adjourns during that period. If Congress adjourns during that ten-day period and the president does not sign the bill, he has effected a pocket veto, which cannot be overridden by Congress. The president's veto power shows how the executive branch checks the legislative branch. By using congressional override, the legislative branch checks the executive branch.

Both the president and the vice president are chosen by the electoral college. This body is made up of electors from each state. They have pledged to cast their votes for a certain candidate. When the voters cast a ballot for a presidential candidate and running mate, they are really choosing a slate of electors pledged to vote for the candidate in the electoral college in December. It is possible for a person to receive the most popular votes but fail to be elected president by the electoral college. This has occurred four times in American history: when John Quincy Adams became president in 1824, when Rutherford B. Hayes was elected in 1876, when Grover Cleveland became president in 1888, and when George W. Bush became president in 2000.

EXERCISE 8

Directions: Put a check in front of the correct answer to the questions that follow.

1. Which of the following is a lawmaking power of the president?

   _____ (1) judicial review

   _____ (2) joint resolution

   _____ (3) executive order

2. If the president should die in office, who is next in line to become president?

   _____ (1) senate majority leader

   _____ (2) vice president

   _____ (3) secretary of state

   "The President of the United States is to have power to return a bill, which shall have passed the two branches of the legislature for reconsideration; but the bill so returned is not to become a law unless upon reconsideration, it be approved by two-thirds of both houses."

   —Alexander Hamilton, *The Federalist Papers*

3. To which of the following processes was Hamilton referring?

   _____ (1) pocket veto

   _____ (2) presidential veto and congressional override

   _____ (3) executive order

4. A president is limited to how many years in office?

   _____ (1) four years

   _____ (2) eight years

   _____ (3) twelve years

Answers are on page 332.

The Legislative Branch

> ### Key Words
>
> **bicameral**—composed of two houses or legislative parts
>
> **subpoena**—a written order requiring someone to appear in court

The legislative branch of the federal government, the Congress, is responsible for writing the basic laws of the country. The Congress is a bicameral legislature, made up of two houses: the House of Representatives and the Senate. The Senate is made up of two senators from each state. The Senate has 100 members. The number of representatives from a state is determined by the number of people in the state. The House of Representatives has 435 members, a number that Congress has limited since 1910.

A representative in the House is elected for two years, must be at least 25 years of age, and also must have been a U.S. citizen for seven years. A senator is elected for six years, must be at least 30 years old, and must have been a U.S. citizen for nine years.

Powers

Congress is responsible for taxing people. The money is used to provide services to people, to defend the country, and to pay the government's debts. Congress has the power to coin money, to declare war, and to override a presidential veto with a two-thirds vote of both houses. Congress proposes amendments to the Constitution, has the power of impeachment, and organizes the federal court system.

Congress operates as a check on the executive branch. It defines the functions of the departments in the executive branch and controls the money set aside for those departments. Congress has the power to investigate numerous areas inside and outside of the government, including the executive branch. A congressional committee, like the court system, has the power to subpoena witnesses and can cite uncooperative witnesses for contempt of court. When Congress actually assumes a "watchdog" role over the executive branch, it can exert a great deal of influence.

Organization

The Speaker of the House presides over the meetings of the House of Representatives and is generally responsible for organizing its activities. The Speaker is a member of the majority party. The Senate is presided over by the vice president, who has little real power to direct the Senate and can cast only tie-breaking votes. The majority party elects a Senate Majority Leader, who leads the legislative activity in the Senate.

Both houses of Congress are organized into committees to carry out the tasks of researching, holding hearings, and writing legislation. All legislation must go through a committee before it can be considered for a vote. A committee chairperson can try to prevent a piece of legislation from reaching a vote or may speed the legislation through the committee and onto the floor. Two important committees are the House Ways and Means Committee, which considers revenue bills, and the Senate Committee on Foreign Relations, which reviews all treaties.

EXERCISE 9

Directions: Based on the passage, circle *T* for each true statement, or *F* for each false statement.

T F **1.** Congress is made up of the Senate and the House of Representatives.

T F **2.** Congress has the powers to make laws, impose taxes, coin money, and declare war.

T F **3.** Congress does not have the power to actually investigate the executive branch in the case of suspected wrongdoing.

T F **4.** A senator is elected for a term of six years, and a representative in the House is elected for two years.

T F **5.** The vice president presides over the meetings of the House of Representatives.

Answers are on page 332.

The Judicial Branch

> ### Key Word
>
> **judicial review**—the power of the Supreme Court to rule on the constitutionality of laws

The judicial branch of the federal government is responsible for interpreting laws. The primary responsibility of the federal court system is to hear cases involving federal law.

At the head of the federal courts is the Supreme Court in Washington, D.C. It consists of a chief justice and eight associate justices. These justices are appointed by the president with the approval of the Senate. They serve for life and can be impeached only for misconduct. The major function of the Supreme Court is to hear appeals of lower federal court decisions and from state courts when the questions may involve points of law or constitutionality. The Constitution gives the Supreme Court the right to hear a case first in "all cases affecting ambassadors, other public ministers, and those in which the State shall be a party."

Below the Supreme Court are the federal circuit courts of appeals. They hear appeals and review decisions of the federal district court and federal administrative bodies. At the lowest level are the federal district trial courts. All federal judges are appointed by the president.

The single most important power of the Supreme Court is its power of judicial review. The Supreme Court rules on the constitutionality of laws passed by the legislative branch or on actions taken by the executive branch. The power of judicial review was first used by the Supreme Court in 1803 in *Marbury v. Madison*. In that case, the court refused to enforce a law that it believed was unconstitutional.

The power of the Supreme Court to rule on the constitutionality of certain laws and practices has become an important part of our system of government. The judicial branch has become an equal partner in the three-way separation of powers in the federal government. American law has changed over the years as a result of various Supreme Court interpretations of the law and the Constitution.

EXERCISE 10

Directions: Underline the word or words that best complete each statement.

1. Federal judges obtain their positions by (presidential appointment, popular election).

2. The U.S. Constitution (is, is not) open to significant interpretation.

3. The Supreme Court consists of (eight, nine) justices.

4. Immediately below the Supreme Court are the federal (district trial courts, circuit courts of appeals).

5. The power of judicial review allows (the president, the Supreme Court) to rule if a law is constitutional.

6. Supreme Court justices can be impeached for (misconduct, questionable decisions).

7. The Supreme Court hears appeals from lower federal and state courts in questions of law and (interpretation, constitutionality).

8. Supreme Court justices are approved by the (House, Senate).

Answers are on page 332.

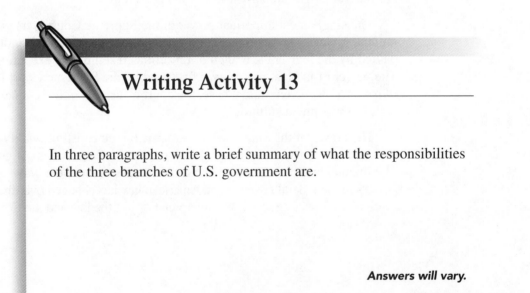

Writing Activity 13

In three paragraphs, write a brief summary of what the responsibilities of the three branches of U.S. government are.

Answers will vary.

EXERCISE 11

Directions: Read the passage below and then put a check in front of the correct answer to the questions that follow.

The Supreme Court Reverses Itself

People make the laws and interpret them according to their own beliefs and those of society. Laws are always affected by changing conditions. What the Constitution "really means" is affected by those beliefs and is subject to judicial review at any given time. The political and historical character of court decisions has led to some stunning reversals of earlier Supreme Court rulings.

The influence of surrounding conditions has figured prominently in the Supreme Court's decisions on racial segregation. Consider the two cases below:

(1) In 1896, in the midst of a period marked by extreme expressions of white supremacy, the Supreme Court ruled, in *Plessy* v. *Ferguson*, that segregation in public facilities, including public schools, was constitutional so long as the facilities were "separate but equal." At this time, many social scientists promoted theories about the superiority of whites and the inferiority of nonwhites.

(2) In 1954, the Supreme Court reversed the *Plessy* v. *Ferguson*, decision in its new decision arising from the *Brown* v. *the Board of Education* case. In the Brown decision, the Supreme Court declared that "separate but equal" schools were unconstitutional and violated provisions granting equal protection under the law. The written Constitution had not substantially changed since 1896. The political situation in the United States and in the world, however, had changed.

1. According to this passage, which best defines the decisions of the Supreme Court?

_____ (1) influenced by politics and by historical developments

_____ (2) based entirely on the written Constitution

_____ (3) not subject to major revisions

2. The passage argues that the *Plessy* v. *Ferguson* decision was very heavily influenced by which of the following?

_____ (1) politicians

_____ (2) white supremacist beliefs

_____ (3) the civil rights movement

Answers are on page 332.

State and Local Government

The central government and the states share political power under the American federal system. The central federal government has the power to tax, make war, and regulate interstate and foreign commerce. In addition, it has the right to "make all laws which shall be necessary and proper for" carrying out the powers granted to it under the Constitution. Those powers not specifically granted to the federal government are reserved for the states.

While the Constitution set a general framework, the actual relations between local governments and the central government have evolved over time. The general trend has been toward increasing power for the central government. The rise of a national economy, several major wars, the trauma of the Depression, complicated international relations, and serious urban problems have all helped to create a strong federal government.

State Governments

State governments are organized in a way that is similar to the federal government. Each state has a written constitution and a governor, the chief executive officer. States have a bicameral (two-house) legislature, except Nebraska, which has a unicameral (one-house) legislature. All states have court systems, but there are wide variations in how state governments operate. One common trend is toward increased power in the hands of governors.

States provide a wide range of public services. They maintain highways and regulate intrastate (within the state) commerce. States also provide for both education and public welfare.

One of the most important powers of the state is the creation of laws that govern the formation and powers of local governments. Counties, towns, and cities are the legal creations of the states. Many states have strong home rule laws that provide the local governments with a great deal of freedom.

Many states also provide for initiative and referendum voting. The direct initiative allows citizens to draft proposed laws. If citizens can obtain the required number of signatures on a petition, they can have the law decided on directly by the state's voters. The referendum allows voters to repeal legislation that has already been passed by voting on it in general elections. Several states also provide for recall, a special election that permits citizens to vote an official out of office before his or her term is over.

Local Governments

Local governments include counties, municipalities (cities, towns, villages), and special districts. County governments enforce state law and perform whatever other duties the state may assign. In county governments, power is usually vested in an elected board of supervisors or commissioners. County governments collect taxes, maintain roads, and manage county property such as jails, hospitals, parks, and forest preserves. County governments also protect the public health by helping to stop the spread of disease or by passing public health ordinances. Counties record documents such as deeds, mortgages, and marriage licenses. Some counties provide water and sewage service, operate airports, and maintain recreational facilities.

Counties are divided into smaller units of local government. These can include cities, towns, villages, and boroughs. Cities provide services that include police and fire protection, schools, public utilities, libraries, street and sidewalk repairs, and garbage collection.

A city is governed under a charter that is granted by the state legislature. There are three forms of city government. The first is strong mayor/weak city council (the mayor has wide authority to run the local government and to veto council actions). The second form is weak mayor/strong city council (the mayor is usually reduced to a figurehead). The third is city manager/city council (an elected council appoints a city manager and retains the power to make all policy).

The governing bodies in towns, villages, and boroughs provide some of the services that cities do but only on a smaller scale. Local government also includes special districts that serve schools, public transportation, and housing and maintain parks, bridges, and airports.

EXERCISE 12

Directions: Underline the word or words that best complete each statement.

1. Conditions such as major wars, complicated international affairs, and serious problems in major cities have led to a strong (state, federal) government.

2. Nebraska is the only state that has a unicameral, or (one-house, two-house), legislature.

3. States regulate intrastate (between states, within the state) commerce.

4. Citizens can draft proposed laws through a process known as (referendum, direct initiative).

Answers are on page 333.

EXERCISE 13

Questions 1–6 are based on the passage on pages 224 and 225.

1. Local governments are established by home rule laws enacted by which of the following?

   (1) state governments
   (2) the U.S. Congress
   (3) the U.S. Constitution
   (4) federal courts
   (5) the president

2. A group of citizens became angered by a law that the state legislature passed. They circulated a petition to have the law put to a vote by the people of the state. This is an example of what?

   (1) direct initiative
   (2) recall
   (3) referendum
   (4) home rule
   (5) local autonomy

3. A state legislator with one year left in her term goes against overwhelming public opinion in her district and votes for a state income tax. Voters who wish to remove the legislator before the next general election could set in motion the process for which action?

   (1) petition
   (2) referendum
   (3) impeachment
   (4) initiative
   (5) recall

4. The mayor of a city tries to start a project to build a new sports stadium, and the city council overrules him. The form of local government is probably which of the following?

   (1) city manager/city council
   (2) strong city council/weak mayor
   (3) strong mayor/weak city council
   (4) bicameral
   (5) federal

5. The federal government does NOT regulate which of the following?

   (1) interstate commerce
   (2) war
   (3) taxes
   (4) public utilities
   (5) foreign commerce

6. The duties of county governments include all except which of the following?

   (1) passing public health laws
   (2) recording deeds and licenses
   (3) regulating intrastate commerce
   (4) repairing sidewalks
   (5) collecting garbage

Answers are on page 333.

International Relations

> ## Key Words
>
> **treaties**—formal agreements among nations
>
> **diplomatic recognition**—a government's formal recognition of another country's government, including the exchange of ambassadors

Today's turbulent world has made the entire field of international relations more important than in any previous time. Different branches of the federal government have important roles to play in making and implementing foreign policy.

The Constitution grants the president three important foreign policy responsibilities: to act as commander-in-chief of the armed forces, to make treaties, and to appoint ambassadors. Over the years, many presidents have expanded the powers of the presidency in foreign affairs.

The president can negotiate treaties, but they require the approval of the Senate. The president can also make use of executive agreements with other nations that do not require Senate approval. Such agreements pledge the word of a particular president, but do not bind his successors to follow any earlier agreements.

Presidents can also extend diplomatic recognition to new governments or nations. In some cases, U.S. presidents have withheld diplomatic recognition in order to show disapproval of a particular nation's system of government. For example, the U.S. government withheld recognition of the former Soviet Union for sixteen years.

The chief executive's position as commander-in-chief of the armed forces has been used by presidents to order military intervention without a formal declaration of war by Congress. Without congressional authorization, President Truman sent troops into Korea in 1950. During the 1960s, Presidents Kennedy and Johnson sent troops to Vietnam. In 1983, President Reagan sent troops to Grenada. President Bush sent troops to Saudi Arabia in 1990, and President Clinton sent troops to Haiti in 1994. To restrain presidential activities that could involve the country in an undeclared war, Congress passed the War Powers Act in 1973.

The Department of State is the section of the executive branch directly responsible for foreign affairs. The State Department is also responsible for the U.S. diplomatic service. Strong-willed secretaries of state can play an influential role in foreign affairs. At times they have competed with the head of the National Security Council for influence with the president.

In foreign policy matters, Congress exerts its influence through its ability to approve or disapprove appropriations, treaties, and ambassadors and by exercising its sole right to declare war. Many of the domestic bills that Congress reviews, including tariffs, immigration, and import quotas, can have far-reaching international effects.

EXERCISE 14

Directions: Match each term on the left with its description on the right. Write the correct letter on the line.

_____ 1. treaty

_____ 2. diplomatic recognition

_____ 3. War Powers Act

_____ 4. executive agreement

_____ 5. Department of State

_____ 6. executive power of commander-in-chief

(a) allows president to intervene militarily without the approval of Congress

(b) a president's pledge to other nations, which does not need Senate approval

(c) the part of the executive branch that is responsible for foreign affairs

(d) a formal agreement with another nation, which requires Senate approval

(e) protects the United States from becoming involved in an undeclared war

(f) a formal acceptance of another country's government

Answers are on page 333.

International Organizations

International organizations have played an increasingly important role in the foreign policy of nations. One of their most important roles is the prevention of global conflict. International organizations fall into three different categories: diplomatic, economic, and military.

Diplomatic Organizations

Diplomatic international organizations have emphasized the promotion of better understanding among nations and the prevention of serious conflicts. Two important organizations have been the League of Nations (1919–1939) and the United Nations (1945–present). The League of Nations was formed after World War I as an organization of 65 countries. The United States never joined the league because of a political policy of favoring isolationism. The organization lacked any power to enforce its decisions. It finally collapsed with the onset of World War II.

The United Nations (UN) was formed at the end of World War II. At this time the United States changed its focus from isolationism to involvement in world affairs. The United States was the first to ratify the UN charter in 1945.

The UN was established to maintain international peace and to encourage friendly interaction among all the nations of the world. The UN helps countries cooperate to solve economic and social problems. As of 2000, the UN was composed of 189 members who worked together to help promote basic human rights throughout the world.

The General Assembly of the UN is composed of all the member nations. They vote on questions of world peace and other issues. Most of the UN's real decision-making power resides in the powerful Security Council. It consists of 15 members, five of which are permanent: the United States, the United Kingdom, China, Russia, and France. The Security Council investigates any disagreements in the world that might threaten world peace.

The United Nations has provided an international forum for nations to air their disputes and grievances and for diplomats to communicate with one another. The UN has also organized international peacekeeping forces to oversee settlements of local disputes.

The United Nations has sponsored many important international agencies. These include the World Health Organization (promotes higher levels of health); the Food and Agricultural Organization (increases food production and distribution); the Educational, Scientific, and Cultural Organization (provides education about people and cultures); and the United Nations Children's Fund (provides assistance to programs for children in developing countries).

Economic Organizations

The Organization of Petroleum Exporting Countries (OPEC) attempts to control the production of oil by setting world oil prices. The European Union (EU) assists in economic, social, and political developments. It also tries to establish a common foreign policy for its 15 members. International economic organizations encourage world trade, find loans for economic development, and obtain better markets for exports.

Military Alliances

Countries with common interests join military alliances for mutual defense and security reasons. The North Atlantic Treaty Organization (NATO) is a military alliance made up of the United States, Canada, and allied European nations. They have agreed to settle disputes peacefully and to help one another in the event of attack from another country.

Writing Activity 14

Do you think the United Nations is an effective organization? Remember that its purpose is to promote international peace. Also, since the UN began in 1945, there have been many wars and conflicts all over the world, including some in which the United States was involved. Write a few paragraphs explaining why you think the UN is or is not effective in what it is doing.

Answers will vary.

EXERCISE 15

Directions: Answer the following questions in the space provided.

1. What are the three categories of international organizations?

   _____

2. Why was the United Nations established?

   _____

3. What does the Security Council of the United Nations do?

   _____

4. What is one reason a nation might join an international economic organization?

   _____

5. Responding as if "an armed attack" against one or more of them in Europe or in North America were "an attack against them all" would be describing one of the functions of which organization?

   _____

6. How many members belonged to the U.N. in 1994?

   _____

7. Which country is considered a permanent member of the Security Council of the UN besides China, Russia, France, and the United States?

   _____

Answers are on page 333.

EXERCISE 16

Questions 1–3 are based on the following passage.

Metropolitan Government

Metropolitan forms of government and administration are a relatively recent development. Many metropolitan functions, such as mass transit, are too big for one town to handle. So new forms of organization have been created.

The most common of these new forms are the various special districts. These are administrative agencies set up to handle a single function, such as fire protection, health planning, or transportation.

Special districts have been criticized as undemocratic because their governing boards are often appointed instead of elected. Many critics feel that this removes the districts from direct popular control. Those holding this view want democratically elected metropolitan governing boards.

The creation of these single-function districts has helped integrate the separate services. But there has been no movement to integrate all these services into metropolitan governmental structures. Local governments are reluctant to give up power to more centralized metropolitan government. Many citizen groups feel that such a form of government would be too large to influence.

The debate over the role and form of metropolitan-wide government is sure to continue as a part of the ongoing debate over centralization versus decentralization.

1. What is the result of the growth of special districts?

   (1) Metropolitan governments have been integrated into state governments.
   (2) Government functions have been kept on a local level.
   (3) The problem of centralization has been solved.
   (4) There has been a strong trend toward metropolitan government.
   (5) City mayors have established power over suburban areas.

2. What does the author seem to believe about the debate over centralization versus decentralization?

   (1) It has been settled.
   (2) It will be settled soon.
   (3) It will probably always be with us.
   (4) It is not an important debate in this country.
   (5) It is a new development in American politics.

3. Which of the following beliefs is a major reason given by people opposing special districts?

   (1) They are inefficient.
   (2) They are too costly.
   (3) They are too large.
   (4) They are undemocratic.
   (5) They are too centralized.

Answers are on page 333.

READING EFFICIENCY E

Directions: This activity will help you to improve your reading efficiency. Before you start to read, write the present time at the top of the page. When you have completed the reading and all 5 questions, write your finishing time. Subtract to find how long you took. Score your answers. Then turn to page 340 to find your E-Factor and graph your progress.

Finishing Time	
Starting Time −	
Reading Time =	
Number of Answers Correct	

Washington, D.C., is the capital of the United States, but it is not part of any state. The federal government owns the land that Washington is on. It also controls the city. The city council of Washington can pass laws. But the U.S. Congress must approve them. Congress also approves money that the city wants to spend. If the city council makes a decision that Congress does not agree with, Congress can change the decision.

Many people in Washington do not like things the way they are. In 1982, the voters tried to make Washington a state. They chose the name New Columbia for their new state. In the early 1990s, other bills were introduced in Congress to make Washington, D.C., a state. None of the bills passed.

Puerto Rico is about 1,000 miles southeast of Florida. It belonged to Spain for over 400 years. Now it is a commonwealth. A commonwealth is an area protected by the United States. The U.S. government governs Puerto Rico. The island government makes local rules. Puerto Ricans are U.S. citizens. However, if they do not live in the United States, they cannot vote for the president. People in Puerto Rico do not pay federal income taxes. Puerto Rico has a representative in Congress. However, the representative cannot vote on final laws.

People in Puerto Rico must obey most national laws. Some voters in Puerto Rico want to join the United States as a state. Others want to break free. They want to become their own country. People in Puerto Rico have been voting

on statehood since the late 1960s. In 1993, the people in Puerto Rico voted to remain a commonwealth.

1. What is the purpose of this passage?

    (1) to convince the reader that Washington, D.C., and Puerto Rico should become states
    (2) to compare and contrast the rights of citizens of Washington, D.C., and Puerto Rico
    (3) to persuade the reader that a commonwealth is better than a state
    (4) to tell the reader about the history of Puerto Rico
    (5) to make the reader proud that he or she can vote in elections for the president

2. If Washington, D.C., became a state

    (1) the people would not have to obey national laws
    (2) the people would have representation in Congress
    (3) the mayor could veto laws passed by the federal government
    (4) the people would have lower taxes
    (5) more people would live there

3. Why do the people of Puerto Rico speak Spanish?

   (1) Spain ruled Puerto Rico for over 400 years.
   (2) Many people from Spain go to Puerto Rico for vacation.
   (3) Many people in the United States speak Spanish.
   (4) Countries where people speak Spanish are near Puerto Rico.
   (5) Spanish is easier to speak than English.

4. What conclusion can you draw from reading this passage?

   (1) Most members of Congress want Washington, D.C., to become a state.
   (2) The people of Washington, D.C., have no say in their local government.
   (3) Citizens of Puerto Rico have the same rights as people born in the United States.
   (4) The commonwealth of Puerto Rico gets no help from the U.S. government.
   (5) The people of Washington, D.C., want the same rights to govern themselves that Americans in other cities have.

5. What do the people of Washington, D.C., and Puerto Rico have in common?

   (1) They each have two senators.
   (2) They cannot vote in presidential elections.
   (3) They must obey national laws that they have no say in making.
   (4) They have the same official language.
   (5) They do not pay any kind of taxes.

   Answers are on page 333.

READING EFFICIENCY F

Directions: This activity will help you to improve your reading efficiency. Before you start to read, write the present time at the top of the page. When you have completed the reading and all 5 questions, write your finishing time. Subtract to find how long you took. Score your answers. Then turn to page 340 to find your E-Factor and graph your progress.

Finishing Time

Starting Time −

Reading Time =

Number of Answers Correct

The American colonies won their freedom from England in 1776. Each colony elected leaders. The leaders wrote a plan for their new country. Their plan was a strong, flexible framework. Their plan was the constitution. The leaders wanted to make the country peaceful and safe. They wanted to provide justice for the people.

The Constitution explains the powers the government has. It divides the power between the national and state governments. It sets up a federal system of government. The national government has the power to collect taxes. It regulates trade. It acts on matters that affect the whole country. Other powers belong to the states. States make laws about the health and welfare of their people. No state can make laws that disagree with the Constitution.

The Constitution also describes the parts of the government. The national government is divided into three branches. Each branch has a different job. This is called the separation of powers. The legislative branch has two houses. The two houses make up the Congress. The legislative branch makes the laws. The president is the head of the executive branch. The executive branch signs laws. It sees that laws are observed. The Supreme Court is the head of the judicial branch. The judicial branch interprets the laws. It decides whether the laws are being obeyed.

1. Why did the framers of the Constitution separate the federal government into three branches?

   (1) to make the U.S. government similar to the English government
   (2) to make the states strong
   (3) to make it harder to make laws
   (4) to make the government easier to run
   (5) to prevent any group from becoming too powerful

2. The states have power over all except which of the following?

   (1) operating public schools
   (2) building roads and highways
   (3) declaring war
   (4) making laws about marriage and divorce
   (5) providing health care

3. What is a federal system of government?

   (1) a government in which the national government holds all of the power
   (2) a government in which the states have more power than the national government
   (3) a government based in Washington, D.C.
   (4) a government in which the national and state governments share power
   (5) a government that is headed by one person

4. Why does the national government, rather than the individual states, print money?

   (1) The national government can control the economy if it prints money.
   (2) Trade and business would be difficult if each state had its own money.
   (3) It would be too costly for each state to print its own money.
   (4) States do not know how to print money.
   (5) The national government controls all banks in the United States.

5. Why were Americans afraid to make the national government too powerful?

   (1) They thought the national government would not meet the needs of people.
   (2) They did not trust national leaders.
   (3) They were used to only dealing with local governments.
   (4) They had just won their freedom from the too-powerful English government and didn't want another one to take its place.
   (5) They did not want to be ruled by a president.

   Answers are on page 333.

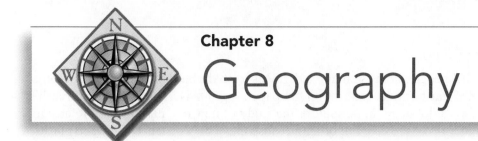

Chapter 8

Geography

This chapter introduces you to *geography*—the study of Earth and the places on it. Geography is concerned with the physical structure of Earth—its climate, soil, natural resources, waterways, and other important features. Geography is also a social science because of the very important relationship between Earth, on which people live, and the society they create.

For example, it is not likely that the people who live on the dry desert will become expert shipbuilders. You might guess that people who live along rivers and large lakes will learn shipbuilding and navigation skills. The food we grow and the livestock we raise depend on the climate and soil.

People are thus clearly influenced by their environment. But they also can change it. Engineers level hills to build highways and dam rivers to generate power. You know that industrial wastes can pollute the land, water, and air. The interactions of people and their environment make up geography.

Elements of Geography

Key Words

latitude—line that measures distance north and south of the equator

longitude—line that measures distance east and west of the prime meridian

equator—0° of latitude that divides Earth into Northern and Southern Hemispheres

prime meridian—0° of longitude that divides Earth into Eastern and Western Hemispheres

All geographers use maps and globes to study Earth. A *map* presents some part of Earth and its features on flat paper. A *globe* is a round model of Earth's surface. Globes are important for the study of how one part of Earth relates to another. They are also important because they show distances between places accurately. The following map shows half of Earth. On it are a series of lines that form a grid pattern. This grid is based on the 360° of a circle.

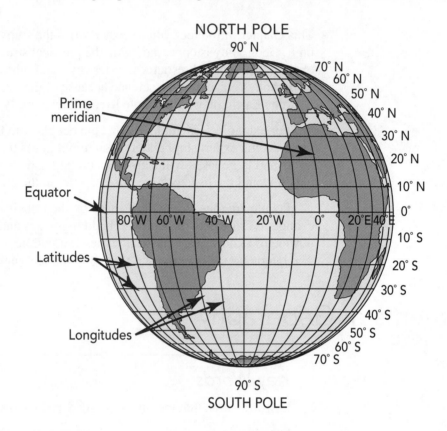

Latitude and Longitude

The lines on the globe are called lines of latitude and longitude. These imaginary lines divide Earth into the Northern Hemisphere, the Southern Hemisphere, the Eastern Hemisphere, and the Western Hemisphere. Lines that run parallel around the globe are called lines of latitude. The equator is in the middle. Latitude is measured north and south of the equator, which is the 0° line. The North Pole is 90° north, while the South Pole is 90° south.

Lines of longitude circle the globe from the North Pole to the South Pole. The 0° line of longitude is called the prime meridian. It runs through Greenwich, England. Locations east and west of the prime meridian are measured by degrees between 0° and 180° east and west. If you followed the circle of the 0° line from Greenwich over the North Pole, you would come to the 180° line in the Pacific Ocean. These measurements allow geographers to find the exact location of any place on Earth.

Hemispheres

The lines of latitude and longitude divide Earth into four hemispheres: Northern, Southern, Eastern, and Western. The United States lies in both the Northern Hemisphere and the Western Hemisphere. That's because it lies west of the prime meridian, or 0° of longitude, and north of the equator, or 0° of latitude.

EXERCISE 1

Directions: Complete the statements below in the space provided.

1. The line marking 0° of latitude is called the

   _____

2. The line marking 0° of longitude is called the

   _____

3. The lines of latitude and longitude divide Earth into four

   _____

4. What place would you find at 90° north latitude?

   _____

5. The United States lies in both the Northern Hemisphere and the

   Western Hemisphere because it lies north of the _____

   and west of the _____

Answers are on page 334.

Map Directions

Most maps tell you directions with a *compass rose,* or *direction arrow,* that points north. A compass rose is shown below. It uses the abbreviations N, S, E, and W for the four main directions north, south, east, and west. It also uses the abbreviations NE, NW, SE, and SW for the intermediate directions northeast, northwest, southeast, and southwest.

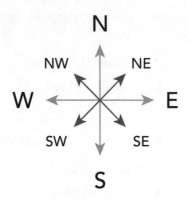

Types of Maps

> ### Key Words
>
> **topography**—the physical features of a land surface, including mountain ranges, plateaus, and lowlands
>
> **contour map**—shows changes in elevation of a land surface by a series of lines representing different heights

Maps come in many varieties. They can show natural resources, political boundaries, and cities. You have probably seen the weather map in your daily newspaper or studied a road map to find the direction and distance from one town to the next. This section examines physical, contour, and information, or thematic, maps.

Physical Maps

The physical map of South America below shows rivers and elevations of the continent. The map also labels the countries and some major cities of South America. Notice the key on the lower right. It shows four different elevations and the symbol for rivers.

SOUTH AMERICA

Contour Maps

Geographers use the term *topography* to define a region's land features such as mountain ranges, plateaus, and lowlands. Contour maps are a type of physical map. They can show topography with a series of lines representing different heights from sea level. When the lines are far apart, the rise in the land is gradual. When the lines are close together, the rise is steep.

On the left below is a contour map of a fictional island. On the right is a vertical view—or elevation—of the same island. The map shows that each interval between contour lines is 10 feet. Counting from the bottom, you can see that the island rises from sea level to 60 feet at the top. If you were a hiker on this island, a contour map would be very useful.

CONTOUR MAP

Information or Thematic Maps

Some maps give the geographer information such as population distribution, battle sites, areas where certain diseases are common, climate patterns, or types of farming. It is important that you study the title and the key on an information map. The key tells you what the symbols stand for. The time zone map below is an example of an information map.

TIME ZONES ACROSS NORTH AMERICA

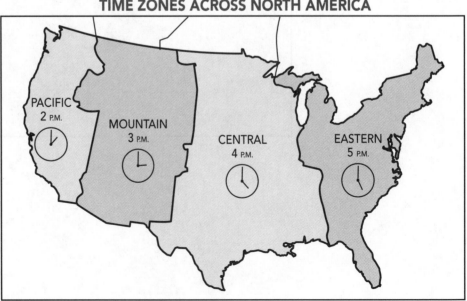

Regions

> ## Key Word
>
> **region**—an area of land having characteristics that make it different from another area of land

There are seven *continents* in the world. Each continent is a large continuous landmass that makes up part of Earth's surface. These large land areas are Asia (29.9 percent of the land area), Africa (20.6 percent), North America (14.8 percent), South America (12 percent), Antarctica (5.2 percent), Europe (7 percent), and Australia (5.2 percent).

The continents are distributed unevenly over Earth's surface. More than 65 percent of the land area, for example, lies in the Northern Hemisphere. This portion of Earth is sometimes referred to as the "land hemisphere." The Southern Hemisphere is an oceanic realm. Only about 11 percent of the Southern Hemisphere is above water.

The seven continents are large. Some of them, such as Asia and Africa, are populated by many people with widely differing cultures. To make the study of geography easier, geographers often write about areas called regions. A region usually has a number of common elements. These may be physical elements such as climate or soil. Or they may be related to the people, such as language, religion, or population—*cultural geography*.

Regions have no uniform size. Some are small, and others are quite large. Their boundaries do not have to be strictly defined by any physical features such as mountains or rivers. They can be defined by the kind of people who live there. This kind of region is called a *cultural region*.

Examples of regions include the Midwest and the South in the United States, and Central America, Scandinavia, and the Middle East elsewhere in the world. What region do you live in?

EXERCISE 2

Directions: Study the map of Central America shown below. It uses a key showing three levels of land elevation. Fill in the correct answers to the questions that follow in the space provided.

CENTRAL AMERICA

1. Which country has no land above 1,000 feet—Honduras, Nicaragua, or Belize?

   _____

2. Where would you find the highest mountains in the Central American nations—along the Pacific Ocean? along the Caribbean Sea? or toward the center of each nation?

   _____

3. Which direction would you travel to fly in a straight line from San Jose, Costa Rica, to Panama City, Panama?

   _____

4. Which country in the region has a large lake?

   _____

Answers are on page 334.

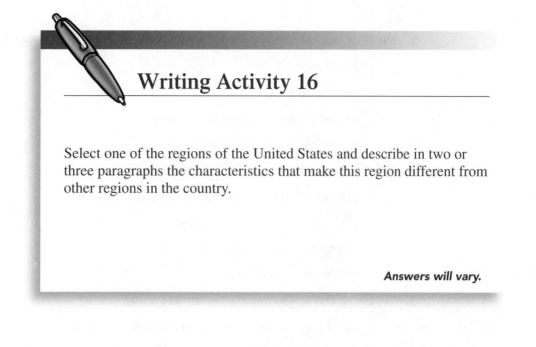

Writing Activity 16

Select one of the regions of the United States and describe in two or three paragraphs the characteristics that make this region different from other regions in the country.

Answers will vary.

EXERCISE 3

Directions: Study the map of East Asia shown below. Then put a check in front of the correct answer to the questions that follow.

EAST ASIA

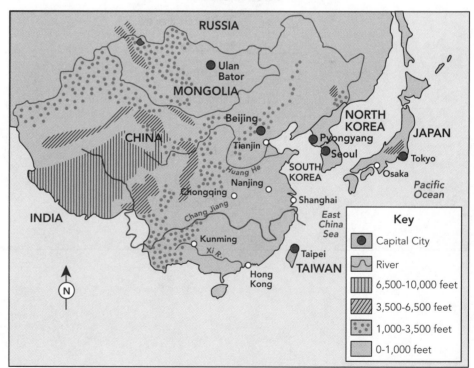

1. Most of the land in Mongolia is at what elevation above sea level?

_____ (1) 0 feet

_____ (2) 3,500 feet

_____ (3) between 350 and 3,500 feet

_____ (4) between 0 and 1,000 feet

2. The highest mountains in China are located where?

_____ (1) toward the western part of the country

_____ (2) just west of Hong Kong

_____ (3) to the east of Beijing

_____ (4) in eastern China

3. Which of the following statements is true?

_____ (1) Taiwan is an island off the coast of Korea.

_____ (2) Most of East Asia is more than 3,000 feet above sea level.

_____ (3) Beijing is located directly to the south of the East China Sea.

_____ (4) Russia borders China on the north.

4. Which location is not a part of the region of East Asia?

_____ (1) India

_____ (2) North Korea

_____ (3) Japan

_____ (4) China

5. What is the capital city of China?

_____ (1) Tianjin

_____ (2) Nanjing

_____ (3) Beijing

_____ (4) Chongqing

Answers are on page 334.

Population and Migration

> ## Key Words
>
> **demography**—the statistical study of the size, growth, movement, and distribution of human population
>
> **ecological system**—the relationships between living things and their environment
>
> **mortality rate**—the rate of deaths in a particular time and place
>
> **fertility rate**—the rate of births in a particular time and place
>
> **migration**—the movement of people from one location to another

The field of geography includes demography, which is the statistical study of the size, growth, movement, and distribution of people in various parts of the world. Geographers find the study of demography important because it shows how people relate to the land they inhabit.

In Central America, for example, the physical environment of highlands and lowlands can decide which areas of land will support more people and which will not. Any population puts pressure on its environment, including its physical features, natural resources, and the other living things that inhabit the same environment.

The ordered relationship between living things and their environment is called the ecological system. Any change in one part of this ecological system can affect changes in other parts. If farmers till the soil harder to produce more crops (intensive farming), many small animals and birds that live in the area may be destroyed. Intensive farming may also lead to soil erosion, a lowering of the water table, and the end of farming in that area.

Population Growth

The human species has been very successful in reproducing itself. In 1750, the estimated world population was 725 million. In this century, the population has grown greatly, from 1.6 billion in 1900 to 5.6 billion in 1994. The population projected for the year 2020 is 7.9 billion. This rapid growth is called the *population explosion*.

Great increases in population growth usually come about from a reduction in mortality rates (death rates), particularly of women and infants, while high fertility rates (birth rates) are maintained. The decline in infant mortality affects population growth in two ways. More people live to become adults and more women reach childbearing age. However, family planning (birth control), famine, or war may check population growth.

The Western industrial countries no longer have a population explosion because of lower birth rates. Population grows more slowly. In countries with developing economies, mortality rates have fallen but fertility rates have not. This has created a population explosion in the developing countries.

Migration

Population migration has been a constant feature of human life. People have migrated to all parts of the globe for a number of reasons, including poor economic conditions at home, the attraction of better conditions elsewhere, and the need for political and religious freedom. Since 1820, 60 million people have emigrated to the United States for all of these reasons.

Most people have been free to migrate as they please. But sometimes people have been forced to move. Millions of African Americans were forced to come to North America and South America, where they were sold as slaves. When Pakistan and India became separate nations in 1947, millions of Muslims feared for their safety in India and fled to Pakistan. At the same time, millions of Hindus in Pakistan left for India. Refugees have been an enormous problem in the twentieth century. Not only were there millions of people displaced by the changes in Europe after World War II, but more recent political strife has created huge numbers of refugees in Rwanda and the former Yugoslavia.

Whatever the cause, migration creates *cultural diffusion,* or the spread of cultural traits from one part of the world to another. The United States has absorbed the customs of many people who have settled in the country.

Those who study demography gather statistics on births, deaths, marriages, divorces, immigration, occupations, and family income. The U.S. census is conducted every ten years by the federal government. State and local agencies also gather vital statistics. Demographers frequently use maps and graphs to illustrate, for example, population distribution according to age, sex, and racial background.

EXERCISE 4

Directions: Circle T for each true statement, or F for each false statement.

T F 1. Migration is the movement of people from one country or location to another.

T F 2. The mortality rate is the number of births in a particular time and place.

T F 3. The fertility rate is the increase or decline in crop production per acre.

T F 4. Economic conditions, the search for political and religious freedom, wars, and famine are reasons for human migration.

T F 5. A change in one part of the ecological system will have no effect on any other part.

T F 6. The decline in infant mortality is a cause of the population explosion because it enables more people to live to become adults and more women to reach childbearing age.

Answers are on page 334.

EXERCISE 5

Directions: Read the passage below and study the map and graph. Then underline the correct answer to the questions that follow.

Geographers can reconstruct the demography of a region during a historical period. The map shown on the next page is based on the U.S. census of 1860. Symbols representing four population ranges show where blacks lived in the slaveholding states on the eve of the Civil War. The graph (lower right corner) shows the total population of slaves and free blacks in each state.

THE BLACK POPULATION, 1860

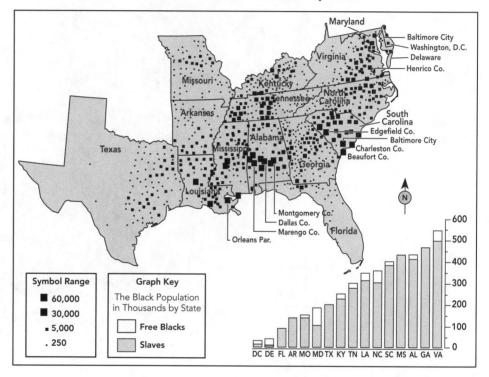

1. Most blacks in Texas lived in the (eastern, western) part of the state.

2. South Carolina had a (larger, smaller) black population than Texas in 1860.

3. A greater number of free blacks lived in (Maryland, Virginia).

4. There were more black slaves living in (Alabama, Mississippi) in 1860.

5. There were no free blacks living in Texas, Mississippi, Arkansas, Florida, and (Missouri, Georgia).

6. More blacks lived in Alabama than in (Virginia, Florida).

Answers are on page 334.

EXERCISE 6

Directions: Based on the passage and map below, circle T for each true statement or F for each false statement.

South of Egypt and west of the Arabian Peninsula lies a region whose 100 million people suffered greatly during the 1980s and 1990s. This region is called the Horn of Africa because of its shape. Five nations make up this region: Djibouti, Eritrea, Ethiopia, Somalia, and Sudan.

THE HORN OF AFRICA

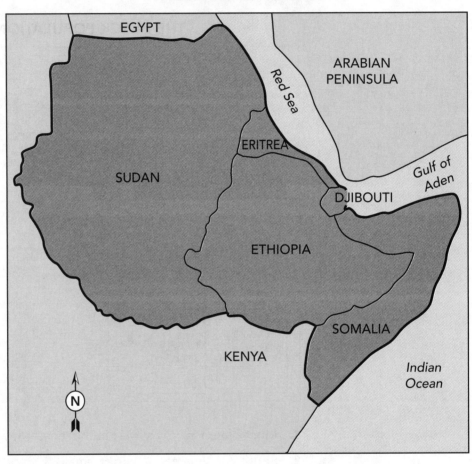

Geography has had a great impact on the lives of the people in this region. Drought, floods, and wars have killed millions of people. Many people became refugees, displaced from their homes. The United States intervened in Somalia in December 1992 to end mass starvation. It ended the famine but got caught up in the internal strife. U.S. troops were pulled out in 1994.

For many years, the region received even less rainfall than usual. Food supplies dwindled to nothing. Heat and sun burned the crops. Farm animals had neither grazing land nor enough water and wasted away or died.

The agony of this situation was heightened by skyrocketing birth rates. The population grew faster than food production. Feeding thousands of refugees increased the problems of already overburdened countries.

T F   1. The Horn of Africa has suffered from war, drought, and floods.

T F   2. The United States sent forces to Somalia to help feed the people.

T F   3. Famine took place in the region only because of greatly reduced rainfall.

T F   4. The growth in population has been greater than the production of food in the Horn of Africa.

T F   5. The five nations in the Horn of Africa are Egypt, Eritrea, Somalia, Saudi Arabia, and Sudan.

T F   6. Through U.S. intervention, Somalia's civil wars were brought to an end.

T F   7. The Horn of Africa is located east of the Arabian Peninsula.

T F   8. Many farm animals in the region died due to insufficient grazing land.

Answers are on pages 334–335.

Urban Growth

Key Words

location—the exact point on Earth where a place is found; can be expressed in degrees of latitude and longitude

suburb—a settlement that lies outside a city but within commuting distance to it

A city is an inhabited place of greater size, population, or importance than a town or a village. People in a city work in a variety of jobs. In contrast, rural settlers live in farming areas outside the city. Many rural residents work in agriculture and grow crops or raise livestock. In the twentieth century, cities have become larger and more numerous as people moved from the countryside.

A city's location explains its importance, growth, and, sometimes, decline. Access to water routes—rivers, large lakes, and oceans—has been of prime importance. For example, Chicago originally grew up where boats or goods had to be carried overland between the Great Lakes and the rivers that drain into the Mississippi. Later, Chicago's location made it an ideal center for rail transportation.

Cities grow at locations like Chicago's because travelers have to change types of transportation, either from land to water or from rivers to oceans. These changes require warehouses, laborers, merchants, banks, repair shops, and all the other businesses associated with trade. Access to transportation also means access to raw materials. The steel-making city of Pittsburgh is located near Pennsylvania's rich coal fields. Pittsburgh's location is ideal for the growth of manufacturing and industry.

Location also influences the choice of cities as political centers, such as state capitals and county seats. Once these cities became political centers, governmental activities caused them to grow. The nation's capital of Washington, D.C., is an excellent example of how location determined its selection and growth. Washington was midway between the thirteen Northern and Southern states and also close to George Washington's home at nearby Mount Vernon.

Climate can also affect city growth. Without air-conditioning and a sure supply of water, the desert city of Phoenix, Arizona, probably would not have become the ninth largest city in the United States.

Suburbs

Before the development of railroads, the growth of cities was limited by how far people could travel on foot or on animals. Modern transportation changed that. Trains, trolleys, and the automobile allowed people to work in one place and live in another. Suburbs are smaller towns that grew up within commuting distance of cities. Trucking further speeded up the growth of suburbs. Industry could move to the suburbs, bringing workers and their families from the cities.

Many cities are working hard to bring businesses back from the suburbs to restore the life of central city areas. Cities have many attractions, such as art galleries, symphony orchestras, theaters, sports events, zoos, and shopping, that draw residents and visitors. On the other hand, poverty, crime, pollution, overcrowding, and the aging of highways, bridges, schools, and other public works also demand bold solutions.

EXERCISE 7

Directions: Fill in the blanks with the correct answers from the passage in the space provided.

1. The city of _____ is a good example of how location

   influences the choice of cities as political centers.

2. In the twentieth century, more cities have grown up and become

   larger as people moved there from_____.

3. The city of _____ grew larger because technology

   helped it overcome harsh desert conditions.

4. Smaller towns that grow up around a large city are called

   _____.

5. The revolution in _____ allowed people to live

   in one place and work in another.

Answers are on page 335.

EXERCISE 8

Questions 1–7 are based on the passage below.

Denver, Colorado

You may picture Denver, Colorado, as a spotlessly clean city built high in the clear mountain air of the Rocky Mountains. This was true in the past. But today the influence of people on their environment is shown by Denver's having become one of America's most polluted cities.

The brown cloud that cloaks the city of Denver for an average of 100 days each year is made up primarily of carbon monoxide—the poisonous gas given off by industrial smokestacks and automobiles. Because Denver has not developed a good public transportation system, automobiles are a major cause of air pollution. This cloud poses a critical health risk for Denver's inhabitants. The rate of lung cancer may be anywhere from 10 to 21 percent higher than in other cities.

Geography plays a role, too. Denver is located one mile above sea level and has considerably less oxygen in its atmosphere than cities at lower altitudes. Automobiles work less efficiently and produce increased levels of carbon monoxide. People are breathing in this poisonous gas. Many people with respiratory diseases have been forced to move out of Denver to suburbs at lower altitudes.

1. What is the problem of air pollution in Denver caused by?

   (1) the city's high altitude
   (2) both natural factors and those caused by people
   (3) the brown cloud that cloaks the city
   (4) its transportation system
   (5) the mountain air of the Rocky Mountains

2. What can you infer from the passage?

   (1) If Denver had a better location, pollution would not be a problem.
   (2) Denver is the worst city in America in which to live.
   (3) Industry does not affect air pollution in Denver.
   (4) Improvements in Denver's public transportation system might help ease air pollution.
   (5) Denver's public transportation system is adequate.

3. According to the passage, which of the following is true?

   (1) There are two automobiles for every citizen of Denver.
   (2) The cloud of carbon monoxide cloaks the city of Denver an average of 100 days out of the year.
   (3) The cloud of carbon monoxide over Denver has existed for a total of 100 days.
   (4) The rate of lung cancer in Denver is at least 33 percent higher than in any other city.
   (5) Denver is located two miles above sea level.

4. What causes the high level of carbon monoxide in Denver?

   (1) its low altitude
   (2) gas from cars and smokestacks
   (3) lack of car emissions testing
   (4) brown clouds that cover the city
   (5) lack of concern about pollution

5. Because Denver is located one mile above sea level, which of the following is true?

   (1) There is less oxygen in the air.
   (2) The level of poisonous gas is lower.
   (3) More respiratory problems occur.
   (4) Fewer inhabitants should live in this area.
   (5) It is easier to breathe in this city.

6. According to the passage, which of the following best describes Denver today?

   (1) a terrible place to live
   (2) filled with clear mountain air
   (3) beautiful because of its lake vistas
   (4) ski capital of the world
   (5) more polluted than most other cities

7. Why does the writer believe that many of Denver's residents moved to the suburbs?

   (1) The suburbs are less crowded.
   (2) The suburbs have fewer industries.
   (3) The suburbs are at lower altitudes.
   (4) The suburbs have better transportation systems.
   (5) The suburbs have lower rates of lung cancer.

Answers are on page 335.

Writing Activity 17

Do you live in a city, a suburb, or in a rural area? Has your area grown or stayed about the same in the past ten years? In a few paragraphs explain why.

Answers will vary.

EXERCISE 9

Questions 1–6 are based on the information and the graphics shown below.

Colorado River Basin

The Colorado River Basin covers 244,000 square miles (about one-twelfth the area of the mainland United States) and is the only reliable source of surface water for nearly 25 million people and more than one million acres of farmland in the Southwest. The river is the most regulated in the nation, with its average flow of 15 million acre-feet* per year divided among seven states, several Indian tribes, and Mexico.**

Current populations and projections

population and projected increases among basin states; in millions.

Calif. 31.4 (48)
Ariz. 3.9 (5.7)
Colo. 3.5 (4.9)
Utah 1.8 (2.7)
N.M. 1.6 (2.3)
Nev. 1.4 (2.1)
Wyo. 0.473 (0.658)

Key: 1993 / 2000 projection

Rainfall July 1, 1993 through June 30, 1994; in inches	Actual	Normal
Calif.	14.6	22.1
Ariz.	14.1	15.8
Colo.	13.1	13.4
Utah	9.9	13.0
N.M.	10.7	12.8
Nev.	8.9	11.3
Wyo.	5.5	8.7

Key:
▸ **Colorado River water use and allotments**

Preliminary 1992 reported water use; in percent

Yearly allotment; in millions of acre-feet

Agricultural / Domestic/Industrial/Environmental

= 1 million acre-feet

*One acre-foot is 326,000 gallons of water. An average household uses between one-half and one acre-foot of water per year.
**Mexico receives 1.5 million acre-feet per year.

Sources: Census Bureau, Colorado Basin River Forecast Center, National Climatic Data Center, NOAA, U.S. Bureau of Reclamation, Water Education

1. Which three of the seven states have the largest yearly allotments of Colorado River water?

   (1) Nevada, New Mexico, Wyoming
   (2) Arizona, California, Colorado
   (3) Arizona, Colorado, Utah
   (4) California, Nevada, Utah
   (5) California, Colorado, New Mexico

2. Which state's rainfall fell below normal by the greatest amount from July 1, 1993, through June 30, 1994?

   (1) New Mexico
   (2) Utah
   (3) Colorado
   (4) Nevada
   (5) California

3. Which two states use the greatest amount of Colorado River water for agriculture?

   (1) Arizona and California
   (2) California and Wyoming
   (3) Nevada and New Mexico
   (4) Arizona and Utah
   (5) Utah and Wyoming

4. Based on the map, which of the following statements is true?

   (1) Las Vegas, Phoenix, and Tucson are all in the Lower Basin.
   (2) Colorado, Wyoming, and Mexico are all in the Upper Basin.
   (3) San Francisco, Los Angeles, and Las Vegas are all in the Lower Basin.
   (4) Las Vegas is in the Upper Basin while Phoenix and Tucson are in the Lower Basin.
   (5) Denver and Tucson are in the Upper Basin while Los Angeles is in the Lower Basin.

5. Based on population projections for the year 2020, what is the most likely effect that continued below-normal rainfall will have on the states in the Colorado River Basin?

   (1) The river will provide enough water to handle the population increase.
   (2) Strict cutbacks in both agriculture and domestic, industrial, and environmental water will be likely.
   (3) More dams will have to be built on the Colorado River to save water for years of low rainfall.
   (4) The government will have to persuade New Mexico to give up more of its share of water.
   (5) California will have to get its water from the Pacific Ocean so there is enough water remaining for the other six states.

6. Based on population increases, which state is the least likely to be affected by the need for Colorado River water in the year 2020?

   (1) California
   (2) Utah
   (3) Wyoming
   (4) Colorado
   (5) New Mexico

Questions 7–13 are based on the following passage.

El Niño is an occasional warming in the tropical Pacific that develops every four to seven years. Scientists have learned that El Niño and its cool counterpart, La Niña, exert influences far beyond their local neighborhood. Like a rock dropped into a pond, the Pacific's hot and cold spells send ripples spreading through the world's atmosphere, altering weather around much of the globe. For instance, the El Niño that simmered [in early 1993] inundated southern California with unusually heavy winter rains but dried out northeastern Brazil. The warming even contributed to the summer floods in the Midwest.

In strength, this El Niño pales in comparison to the biggest of the century, which struck in 1982 and 1983. The record warmth in the equatorial Pacific those years redirected normal jet stream patterns, generating floods and droughts that left thousands dead worldwide and caused more than $13 billion in damages.

Spurred by that event [El Niño] . . . scientists have developed computer models for predicting when the tropical Pacific will swing toward warm or cool temperatures. Nature still has the upper hand, however, . . . but major warmings and coolings advertise themselves much more openly, and the computer models have started to exhibit skill at detecting such events as many as twelve to eighteen months ahead of their actual arrival.

—Excerpted from "The Long View of Weather"
by Richard Monastersky

7. What is the main idea of this passage?

   (1) El Niño is a temporary occurrence and is unlikely to take place again.
   (2) Computer models have had some success in predicting weather 12 to 18 months ahead of time.
   (3) Computer models now can accurately predict El Niño one year in advance with 100 percent accuracy.
   (4) Computer models are useless in predicting long-range weather patterns.
   (5) El Niño has a cool counterpart named La Niña.

8. According to the passage, when do the waters of the tropical Pacific warm up?

   (1) every summer
   (2) every 12 to 18 months
   (3) every four to seven months
   (4) every four to seven years
   (5) every year

9. What do scientists know about the hot and cold spells in the Pacific?

   (1) they occur around much of the world
   (2) they occur only along the Pacific coast of North America and South America
   (3) they occur during the winter months only
   (4) they occur during the summer months only
   (5) they occur only when the winds reach sixty miles per hour

10. Which of the following is true about the great El Niño of 1982–1983?

    (1) It proved useless for scientific measurement.
    (2) It made major changes in the weather but caused little loss of life or damage.
    (3) It was caused by record warmth in the Pacific Ocean.
    (4) It had no effect on jet stream patterns.
    (5) It caused scientists to believe it marked a permanent change in climate.

11. If 1992–1993 were years of El Niño, when would you expect the next one to begin?

    (1) 1994 to 1997
    (2) 1997 to 2000
    (3) 1999 to 2003
    (4) in 10 years from those dates
    (5) There is no pattern upon which to predict when the next El Niño will occur.

12. Why was the El Niño of 1993 unusual?

    (1) It caused temperatures to drop rapidly throughout the Pacific.
    (2) It sent heavy winter rains to southern California and caused a dry period in Brazil.
    (3) It caused a hot spell in the Pacific.
    (4) It ended the floods in the Midwest.
    (5) It caused heavy rains in northern California.

13. According to the passage, what was the cost of damages due to the El Niño of 1982 and 1983?

    (1) under $20 million
    (2) about $50 million
    (3) around $10 billion
    (4) more than $13 billion
    (5) more than $20 billion

Answers are on pages 335–336.

READING EFFICIENCY G

Directions: This activity will help you to improve your reading efficiency. Before you start to study the graph, write the present time at the top of the page. When you have completed all 5 questions, write your finishing time. Subtract to find how long you took. Score your answers. Then turn to page 340 to find your E-Factor and graph your progress.

Finishing Time

Starting Time –

Reading Time =

Number of Answers Correct

UNITED STATES IMMIGRATION: 1996

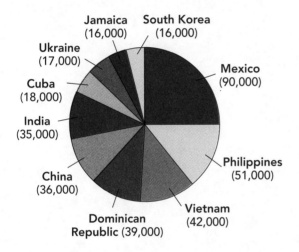

Jamaica (16,000)
South Korea (16,000)
Ukraine (17,000)
Mexico (90,000)
Cuba (18,000)
India (35,000)
Philippines (51,000)
China (36,000)
Dominican Republic (39,000)
Vietnam (42,000)

Source: U.S. Immigration and Naturalization Service

Questions 1–5 refer to the following circle graph.

1. How many legal immigrants arrived in the United States in 1996?

(1) 90,000
(2) 42,000
(3) 200,000
(4) 360,000
(5) 36,000

2. Immigrants from which country made up the largest number of immigrants to the United States in 1996?

(1) Vietnam
(2) Mexico
(3) Cuba
(4) Philippines
(5) China

3. Which of the following does this graph show?

(1) the increase in immigration between 1840 and 1996
(2) the 10 largest ancestry groups in the United States
(3) the number of legal immigrants to the United States in 1996
(4) the effects of immigration
(5) the number of people who speak a language other than English

4. Which of the following is an effect of the high number of Mexican immigrants to the United States?

(1) All U.S. citizens share the same cultural background.
(2) The cost of labor in the United States has increased.
(3) Working conditions in Mexico have improved.
(4) The number of imports from Mexico has decreased.
(5) Spanish is the second most widely spoken language in the United States.

5. Based on the graph, what conclusion can you draw?

(1) Poverty and unemployment in their native countries in recent years have caused many people to immigrate to the United States.

(2) Most immigrants in 1996 were from northern and western Europe.

(3) About 15% of immigrants return to their native country.

(4) Most immigration took place between 1800 and 1930.

(5) Many Philippine doctors and nurses have immigrated to the United States.

Answers are on page 336.

READING EFFICIENCY H

Directions: This activity will help you to improve your reading efficiency. Before you start to read, write the present time at the top of the page. When you have completed the reading and all 5 questions, write your finishing time. Subtract to find how long you took. Score your answers. Then turn to page 340 to find your E-Factor and graph your progress.

Finishing Time	
Starting Time –	
Reading Time =	
Number of Answers Correct	

A river is a large, natural stream of water that flows into a lake or ocean. The place where a river begins is called its *source*. Most rivers begin high in the mountains, where rainfall, melting ice, and snow form streams. The streams that flow from the source are called *headwaters*. The headwaters flow downhill in narrow channels. These channels, or *rills*, grow larger and wider and form brooks. The brooks turn into streams, and streams join to form rivers. The streams that carry water to a river are called *tributaries*.

The river keeps flowing until it reaches low land, where it empties into a larger body of water. The place where the river ends is called its mouth. As the water in the river reaches the mouth, its flow slows. Sometimes a river leaves rock and soil near its *mouth*. This rock and soil slowly build up to form new land, called a *delta*. Deltas are where rivers often split into several branches. Deltas have rich soil. Fruits, vegetables, and other crops grow in the Mississippi Delta in Louisiana. The Nile Delta in Northern Africa has been rich farmland since ancient times.

Some rivers have deep, broad mouths where the tide flows in. This inlet is called an *estuary*. An estuary has a mixture of fresh water and salt water. The fresh water comes from the river. The salt water comes from the ocean. The Amazon River in South American flows into the Atlantic Ocean. It is an estuary for several hundred miles.

1. Where does a river have its highest elevation?

   (1) at its delta
   (2) at its mouth
   (3) at its headwaters
   (4) at its rills
   (5) at its brooks

2. Which of the following is *not* a characteristics of a delta?

   (1) They are made of bits of rock and soil.
   (2) They were first formed in Greece.
   (3) They form near the mouths of rivers.
   (4) They have rich soil.
   (5) Many crops grow there.

3. What two parts does every river have?

   (1) mouth and delta
   (2) estuary and headwaters
   (3) source and delta
   (4) source and mouth
   (5) tributary and estuary

4. What makes the land near a delta green?

   (1) rocks and bits of soil
   (2) rich soil and abundant water
   (3) a mix of fresh water and salt water
   (4) melting ice
   (5) chemicals from nearby factories

5. People and industries sometimes dump harmful wastes into rivers. Based on what you have read, how does this affect other bodies of water?

(1) Wastes cause sediment to build up in the lake or ocean that the river empties into.

(2) Rivers carry pollution into lakes and oceans.

(3) Waterfalls occur where wastes build up in a river.

(4) The temperature of a river's tributaries decreases.

(5) Other bodies of water become desirable habitats for plants and animals.

Answers are on page 336.

Chapter 9

Economics

An *economy* is the organized way in which a society produces, distributes, and consumes goods and services. In other words, the economy is the way people make things, ship them, sell them, and use them. *Economics* is the study of how these systems work.

There are various kinds of economies. Different countries may manufacture and distribute goods, or products, in slightly different ways. A small, primitive society will have a different kind of economy than a large, industrial society. Economists study how these different systems work.

What Economists Study

Economists often specialize in one area. For example, some economists study how a whole economic system, like the U.S. economy, works. Other economists may study one small part of the economy, such as how the trucking industry in Utah works.

Economists today have an important role in guiding government policy. Economists work in such organizations as the president's Council of Economic Advisors, the General Accounting Office, and the Bureau of the Budget.

Government economists predict what will happen if different economic decisions are made. For example, if interest rates are increased, will companies lay off workers? If inflation increases, will people stop buying new cars? The advice economists give Congress and the president can have long-lasting effects on citizens.

Economists also work in private business. They make long-range economic plans for companies. They analyze how businesses operate and advise them on how to become more profitable. Economists advise labor unions on contracts and on trends in the economy.

EXERCISE 1

Directions: Put a check in front of the best answer to the questions that follow.

1. How can *economy* best be defined?

_____ (1) as a system for exchanging goods and services

_____ (2) as a system for producing goods and services

_____ (3) as a system of producing, distributing, and consuming goods and services

_____ (4) as a system for producing goods and guiding government policy

2. What might Congress ask an economist to advise them on?

_____ (1) the effects of increasing trade with Mexico

_____ (2) how to reduce the Internal Revenue Service's paperwork

_____ (3) how to improve safety in interstate trucking

_____ (4) how to reduce the chance of war in the Middle East

3. How might an economist help an electric power company?

_____ (1) by analyzing the safety of a nuclear reactor

_____ (2) by explaining why nuclear energy is too costly

_____ (3) by hiring staff to bill for electric service

_____ (4) by studying health claims against the company

Answers are on page 336.

Early Economic Systems

Economists study the history of economics as well as the economies of today. Knowing how economies formed and changed over time helps them better predict the effects of current events.

The earliest economies developed in primitive hunting and gathering societies. Nearly everything produced was immediately consumed. This simple economy began to change with the development of agriculture. Because people raised crops and animals, they often had surplus, or extra, food. This surplus was stored, traded, or sold. These extra activities created new jobs and services. Stores were opened to sell the surplus. Ships were built to move the surplus. Cities grew up around the trade centers. Governments began taxing and protecting the new economies.

In medieval Europe (600–1500 A.D.), the economy was based on agriculture. This economy was known as a feudal economy. Peasants didn't own land, yet they were tied to it. They farmed land that belonged to nobles and to the Catholic Church. The little economic activity that did not involve farming was carried out by craftsmen in the towns. Throughout this period, all economic activity was strictly controlled by tradition. People lived as they always had. Few people thought of trying to do anything different.

Economic conditions began to change with the colonizing of the New World during the sixteenth century. Gold and silver flooded into Europe and financed economic expansion. World trade began to grow. This great wealth led to developments in science and technology. By the late eighteenth century, the way people lived and worked began to change. This was the start of the period known as the Industrial Revolution.

The Industrial Revolution

The Industrial Revolution brought large numbers of people together in towns. They worked in businesses and manufacturing plants. In this new society, there were many buyers and sellers who competed for commodities, which are goods and services for which ownership can be traded or exchanged. This new economic system became known as a market economy. This term refers to the competition for goods, services, land, labor, and other resources.

The market now regulated economic life. Workers were no longer tied to a piece of land. In fact, they could now own land or businesses. They could move from job to job, selling their labor to the highest bidders.

From the 1600s through the 1900s, industrialization and the accumulation of wealth changed industry, agriculture, and society in general. Many people enjoyed great prosperity. However, other people remained in extreme poverty. Many people and governments have tried to change the system to correct what was wrong. Sometimes they tried to change it completely. Sometimes laws were passed to correct abuses without getting rid of the system.

Types of Economic Systems

Key Words

capitalism—an economic system based on private ownership of property

commodities—goods and services for which ownership can be traded or exchanged

market economy—a system of free enterprise where buyers and sellers, not the government, determine prices and output

socialism—an economic system that is based on government control of the market

---

Today, there are three main types of economic systems: capitalism, socialism, and mixed. Capitalist, or market, economies are based on private ownership and market competition.

Socialism is based on government control of the market. The government controls production, distribution, and profit. The goal of socialism is to ensure that all members of society benefit from economic activity, not just those who compete the most successfully.

Mixed economies combine capitalism and socialism. Certain industries, like transportation or mining, may be controlled by the government. Other industries may be allowed to operate in a market economy.

No country's economy is purely of one type. The United States is capitalist, but many controls have been placed on the market. Sweden is a mixed economy. Once there were many socialist economies, such as those of the former Soviet Union and of China. Now most of these socialist economies have been changed to market or mixed economies.

EXERCISE 2

Directions: Circle *T* if the statement is true, or *F* if it is false.

T F **1.** Under capitalism, labor is controlled by the government.

T F **2.** The U.S. economy will probably not change much but will remain a pure capitalist economy.

T F **3.** If the U.S. economy changed, it would probably lead to changes in the political system as well.

T F **4.** A socialist economy gives private business owners an unfair advantage.

T F **5.** In a market economy, workers can take a job with a new company whenever they think they will be better off.

Answers are on page 336.

How the Economy Works

> ## Key Words
>
> **demand**—the desire and ability of consumers to buy a product or service
>
> **equilibrium**—the price at which supply equals demand
>
> **supply**—the quantity of goods and services available for sale at all possible prices

Supply and demand is the basis for the U.S. economy. Businesses must know that there is a demand for the goods or services they want to provide. At the same time, consumers must not only want something, they must also be able to purchase it. Price is what makes this system work.

You see supply and demand working every day. If the price for a certain item goes up, demand usually goes down. If the prices go down, demand usually goes up. For example, when airline tickets are too expensive, fewer people travel, and the demand goes down. When airline ticket prices are reduced, more people travel, and the demand goes up. If airline ticket prices are reduced for too long a period, however, the supply becomes greater than the demand, and some flights have empty seats.

Producers try to control price; they also try to control supply. If there is too much of an item available, the extra product sits in warehouses, or the producer has to reduce the price so that more items can be sold. If there is too little of an item, the price may become too high, and then consumers may stop buying it altogether. Producers, however, have only limited control of either price or supply.

Prices are mainly controlled by the marketplace. Each company tries to sell its products at a lower price than its competitors so that consumers will buy from it. At the same time, the company must keep the price high enough so that it can earn a profit. The continual competition and need for profit keeps prices from getting out of control. The graph on the next page shows the relationship between supply and demand.

The curve labeled *demand* shows that there is low demand when prices are high. The demand increases as the price goes down. The curve labeled *supply* moves in the opposite direction. Supply is low when prices are low, but supply increases as prices increase. The more income a producer gets from a product, the more he or she is encouraged to produce it.

Price works to bring supply and demand into balance, or equilibrium. On the graph, the point of equilibrium is labeled *e*. Equilibrium is the point at which supply and demand match exactly. If the producer charges too much, demand decreases. If the producer charges less than the equilibrium price, demand will increase and a shortage will occur.

Every product or service has a supply-and-demand relationship. The market for the product is constantly at work to keep supply and demand in balance. If prices go too high, demand is reduced, so producers lower prices again. If demand is high and the supply is low, prices will go up. However, other producers may see that there is a high demand and high prices for this item, so they begin producing it. Eventually, the prices go down again.

EXERCISE 3

Directions: Answer the questions below in the space provided.

1. Which of the graphs above shows the relationship between price and demand? Explain why.

_____

_____

_____

_____

2. Every holiday season, some toy almost always becomes especially popular. As quickly as a shipment arrives in the store, it's sold out. Many customers are willing to pay much more than the regular price in order to get one. What would an economist say about this situation?

_____ (1) A surplus of toys caused prices to increase.

_____ (2) A shortage of toys caused prices to decline.

_____ (3) A shortage of toys caused prices to increase.

Answers are on page 336.

Total Value, Spending, and Investment

> ## *Key Words*
>
> **capital goods**—goods and services companies buy to use in producing other goods or services
>
> **consumer goods**—goods and services that people buy for their own use
>
> **gross domestic product (GDP)**—the amount of all goods and services produced within a country in one year
>
> **gross national product (GNP)**—the amount of all goods and services produced by a country in one year

The total value of all goods and services produced by a country in one year is called its gross national product (GNP). This figure includes products produced by companies with headquarters in that country that are actually made in other countries. For example, Ford Motor Company produces cars in Canada and Mexico as well as in the United States. Because it is an American company, the United States counts Ford's production in Canada and Mexico as part of the U.S. GNP. Gross domestic product (GDP) is the total of all products and services actually produced within a country. In 1993, the U.S. GNP was more than $6 trillion.

Spending by consumers makes up about 70 percent of GNP. Consumer spending, however, is not the most important force that makes the economy run. When companies buy capital goods, this has a multiplying effect. Each dollar spent on new machinery or power plants creates jobs, more investments, and eventually produces more consumer spending.

When the economy is struggling with a recession or depression, it's the result of slow spending on capital goods. Reduced production results in unemployment, which means fewer people have money to spend. Because fewer consumer goods are bought, fewer goods need to be produced and more people are laid off. A cycle of economic decline results. In our economic system, the government tries to control this cycle in order to prevent a depression or recession.

EXERCISE 4

Match each term on the left with its correct description on the right. Write the correct letter on the line.

_____ **1.** gross national product	(a) an example of a capital good
_____ **2.** employment	(b) the largest part of the GDP
_____ **3.** consumer spending	(c) a drastic decrease in investment in capital goods would increase this
_____ **4.** machine shop tools	(d) the amount of all goods and services produced by a country in one year
_____ **5.** capital goods	(e) an increase in consumer spending would result in an increase in this
_____ **6.** television	(f) during a recession, the government might encourage companies to invest in this
_____ **7.** unemployment	(g) an example of a consumer good
_____ **8.** gross domestic product	(h) the amount of all goods and services produced within a country in one year

Answers are on page 337.

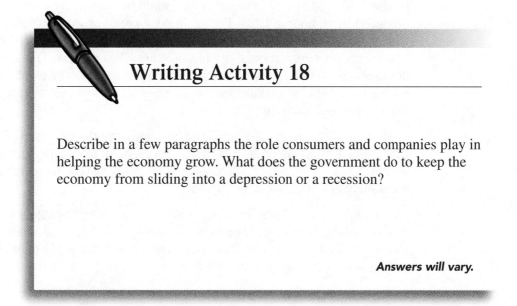

Writing Activity 18

Describe in a few paragraphs the role consumers and companies play in helping the economy grow. What does the government do to keep the economy from sliding into a depression or a recession?

Answers will vary.

How Businesses Behave

> ## Key Words
>
> **factors of production**—the things needed to make a product
>
> **marketing**—the part of business that deals with sales
>
> **monopoly**—a marketing situation in which one person or company sells all of a product or accounts for a large part of the total sales of the product
>
> **oligopoly**—a market situation in which very few sellers account for a large part of the total sales of a product
>
> **productivity**—the efficient use of the factors of production to produce goods

In a capitalist economy, businesses exist to make a profit. Businesses make a profit by managing the factors of production. These are the land, labor, and capital that are needed to produce goods. In a capitalist economy, all of these factors are for sale in the market.

In order to make a profit, businesses must keep the cost of buying the factors of production lower than the income received from selling the goods produced.

One way to keep the cost of the factors of production low is to increase productivity. Productivity is usually measured by how many goods are produced by an hour of labor. For example, a group of workers produces 60 cars per hour and together are paid $1,000 per hour. If production increases to 120 cars per hour, productivity has increased 100 percent. The workers, however, are still being paid the same amount of money. The owner has reduced one factor of production—the cost of labor—by paying less for the labor to produce each car.

Productivity can also be increased by improving the factors of production. Improving the training of the work force, investing in more efficient equipment, improving planning, and organizing the manufacturing process more efficiently are some ways to improve productivity.

In addition to making the product more cheaply, a company can increase profits by increasing sales. The part of business that deals with sales is called marketing. Companies invest heavily in marketing. They study their customers and create advertising that appeals to them.

Competition Versus Monopoly

In a market economy, businesses must compete with other businesses. Certain parts of the economy have many businesses so there is a great deal of competition. There are lots of fast-food restaurants, for example, so competition is intense.

Other areas of the economy include only a few businesses. The aluminum industry, for example, is made up of only a few very large corporations. A market in which there are few sellers of a product is called an oligopoly. Usually, there is little price competition among the sellers. Instead, they compete by advertising and offering special customer service.

A monopoly is a market situation in which there is only one seller of a product. Actually, a pure monopoly has never existed. The word has come to mean a situation in which one seller controls most of the market. American Telephone and Telegraph (AT&T), for example, is said to have had a monopoly prior to its breakup in 1984. Although a few other companies offered telephone services, AT&T was by far the dominant company. It controlled prices and services throughout the country.

EXERCISE 5

Directions: Underline the correct word or words that complete each statement below.

1. If a company increases productivity, its profits will (increase, decrease).

2. A marketing department (plans sales campaigns, manages employee morale).

3. A monopoly exists when there is only one (buyer for a product, seller that dominates the market).

4. To increase profits, it is best to (lay off employees, lower production factors).

5. In business, you sometimes hear that "the bottom line determines everything." The bottom line means (the amount of goods produced, the total profits made).

Answers are on page 337.

EXERCISE 6

Questions 1–3 are based on the following passage.

Giant corporations have long dominated American business. The top 500 industrial firms account for more that 80 percent of all industrial sales. The 800 largest corporations employ as many people as the remaining 14,000,000 businesses.

A new trend has emerged in recent decades: the growth of large corporations into multinational corporations with businesses located throughout the world. Ford, for example, has 40 subsidiary corporations around the globe. They account for one-third of Ford's invested capital and 30 percent of its work force. The foreign growth of companies like Ford has caused direct U.S. foreign investment to grow from $11 billion in 1950 to more than $486 billion in 1992. More than 25 percent of the *assets*, or total resources, of our largest corporations are invested abroad.

This growth of foreign investment has caused a number of problems for U.S. domestic industry. Production in labor-intensive industries, like electronic assembly, has been moved out of the United States to areas where labor costs are lower. Much of the work has gone to Asian countries, but there has also been substantial investment in new plants and equipment in Western Europe.

The growth of multinationals has also made it more difficult for the federal government to manage the national economy. Government plans either to slow inflation or stimulate the economy can be offset by the multinationals' ability to move money around the world to escape government control.

1. Based on the passage, what would be the result of the growth of multinationals?

   (1) an increase in the power of labor unions because workers would be part of bigger corporations
   (2) a reduction in the power of unions because companies can use nonunion labor abroad
   (3) it would not have any influence on U.S. labor-management relations
   (4) an increase in the power of unions by reducing the number of plants in the United States
   (5) an increase in the labor costs of bigger corporations

2. The largest American corporations have invested what percentage of their assets in other countries?

   (1) less than 10 percent
   (2) 20 percent
   (3) more than 25 percent
   (4) more than 30 percent
   (5) 80 percent

3. How much have direct U.S. foreign investments increased in the past 40 years?

   (1) about $100 billion
   (2) less than $150 billion
   (3) less than $225 billion
   (4) about $475 billion
   (5) more than $500 billion

Answers are on page 337.

Financial Institutions

> ## Key Words
>
> **money**—cash and all other assets that can be used to purchase goods and services or to pay debts
>
> **multiplier effect**—the growth in the value of a deposit in a bank when it is, in turn, loaned out to a succession of other banks

In economics, money is anything that is widely accepted as a means of buying goods or paying debts. It includes cash (coins and bills), but it also includes other assets, such as checks and credit cards. In fact, today most money exists only as figures in bank accounts, loan statements, and other financial statements.

The most important form of money in the economy is checking accounts. This makes sense if you remember that most workers are paid by check. In addition, most money that is spent—for rent, mortgage payments, utilities, credit payments—is paid in the form of checks. All of these checks are drawn on banks and later deposited in banks.

When a bank takes in money from depositors, it loans out some of it. The loaned money is then deposited in another bank. The second bank uses the new deposit to make its loans, which are then deposited in a third bank. This pattern continues indefinitely. Each loan creates new money. The original deposit is multiplied many times. This is called the multiplier effect. It provides money to finance the growth of the economy.

To keep the economy growing, money must circulate. If everyone were paid in cash and then kept it in a shoe box under the bed, the economy would grind to a halt. As long as people and businesses spend money and borrow money, the economy prospers.

EXERCISE 7

Directions: Circle *T* if the statement is true, or *F* if it is false.

T F **1.** If people, businesses, and the government spent only what money was on hand rather than borrowing money, the economy would become weak.

T F **2.** The multiplier effect describes the way the money supply increases when banks make loans.

T F **3.** A gasoline credit card is both an asset and money.

T F **4.** The most important form of money in the economy is cash.

Answers are on page 337.

The Federal Reserve System

Key Word

monetary policy—the regulation of the nation's supply of money and credit by the Federal Reserve Board

The money supply is controlled by the Federal Reserve System, a central bank operated by the federal government. The "Fed," as it is sometimes called, controls the amount of money available. It does this in many ways. One way is by telling banks how much money they must keep on deposit in the form of cash. When the Fed increases the amount from 20 percent to 25 percent, for example, the banks have less money to use for loans. This reduces the money supply.

The Fed controls the money supply in order to control the economy. When inflation becomes too high, the Fed may require banks to keep more money on hand as cash. This is called increasing the reserve requirement. This policy reduces the supply of money that can be loaned out. Interest rates rise because more borrowers compete for a limited supply of loanable funds. As a result, inflation is reduced since there is less money in circulation.

If the economy is weak, unemployment is high, and business is slow, the Fed may reduce the amount of cash a bank must hold. More money becomes available for loans, and the interest rate on the loans goes down. People and businesses borrow more and buy more, so the economy grows. The way in which the Fed controls the money in the economy is called the monetary policy.

Money is what makes the economy work. Monetary policy is the way the supply of money is controlled. The Fed uses this control carefully to keep the economy running smoothly.

EXERCISE 8

Directions: Put a check in front of the correct answer to the questions that follow.

1. If the country were in a recession and the Federal Reserve wanted to help the economy grow, what would it probably do?

_____ (1) increase the money supply

_____ (2) reduce the money supply

_____ (3) require banks to keep more cash on deposit

_____ (4) increase interest rates

2. Monetary policy refers to which of the following?

_____ (1) the policy of keeping all your money in cash

_____ (2) government spending

_____ (3) the Federal Reserve's ways of controlling the money supply

_____ (4) the process of multiplying the effect of money in the economy

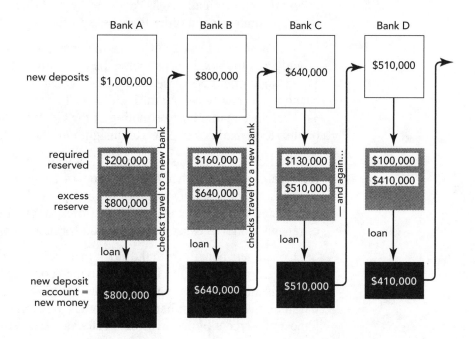

3. The diagram above illustrates which of the following?

_____ (1) the multiplier effect

_____ (2) how economies can stop growing

_____ (3) the monetary policy

_____ (4) inflation

4. Which bank has the smallest amount of excess reserve?

_____ (1) Bank A

_____ (2) Bank B

_____ (3) Bank C

_____ (4) Bank D

Answers are on page 337.

The Stock Market

The *stock market* is a market where stocks and bonds of corporations are bought and sold. It is a form of saving and investment, so it is important to the economy.

Stocks are shares of ownership in a company. The owner of a share receives **dividends,** which are payments made from the company's profits. The value of a share of stock changes over time, so it may be sold for more or less than it originally cost. People try to buy stocks at a low price and sell them at a high price in order to make a profit.

When prices of stocks increase, the market is said to be a bull market. Usually a bull market occurs when the economy as a whole is growing. When stock prices decrease, this signals a bear market. In a bear market, the economy is usually having difficulties. In 1929, stock prices fell drastically. This collapse marked the beginning of the Great Depression. Keeping an eye on the stock market can give you insight into the health of the economy.

Selling stock on the stock market is a way that businesses raise money for expansion. When owners or directors of the company sell stock in their business, they are selling a part of the company. The money they receive can be invested in new machinery, plants, stores, or other capital goods. This way of raising money is especially important for new companies and for utilities.

Consumers benefit from the stock market in several ways. First, when the market grows, new wealth is created so the economy improves. Second, the market is an effective way for individuals to save money. Most investors in the stock market are not banks, companies, or even mutual funds. In 1993, almost 46 percent of the investors in stocks were individuals.

EXERCISE 9

Directions: Underline the correct answer that completes each of the statements that follow.

1. If the value of stocks increased by 35 percent over a period of six months, this would be termed a (bull market, bear market).

2. If the value of stocks has steadily decreased in value for several months, this tells you that the general economy is probably in (good shape, bad shape).

3. When owners of stock are paid a share of the company's profits, they are receiving (investments, dividends).

Answers are on page 337.

Government in the Economy

Although the United States has a market economy, it does not operate entirely according to market forces. The federal and state governments manage the economy in various ways.

At the most basic level, the government sets up rules for doing business. For example, laws define business contracts and what they can and cannot include. Courts enforce these contracts.

At another level, the government provides public goods. The components of national defense—the army and navy, war planes, tanks, and ships—are public goods. Highways and bridges, education, public health, fire protection, and air traffic control are other important government services. These are goods that private companies will not or should not provide.

The government also regulates the market. Laws prevent monopolies from controlling the market. Agencies, such as the Food and Drug Administration (FDA) and the Federal Trade Commission (FTC), control how some kinds of businesses operate and the products they sell.

Government laws also affect the costs and uses of some factors of production. Zoning ordinances and housing codes, for instance, affect the real estate market and where businesses can locate, Labor laws and minimum wage laws affect the cost of labor. The government also deals with by-products of production. Such things as industrial wastes and air pollution result from businesses in the market. The government must control these effects of the economy before they affect the quality of people's lives.

Demand management, also called fiscal policy, is another way the government influences the economy. Demand management refers to how the government budget and taxes are used to influence demand in the economy. Before the Great Depression, the government did little to control the level of demand. Since then, the government has tried to create more demand for goods and services in order to avoid another depression.

One way the government uses demand management is by increasing its own spending when private sector spending slows down and workers are unemployed. By increasing government spending, more money is put into the economy. For example, the government might extend unemployment benefits. This puts more money in the hands of unemployed people. When they spend it, demand is created and the economy benefits. When the economy picks up again, the government will reduce unemployment benefits or other spending in order to slow inflation.

EXERCISE 10

Directions: Circle *T* if the statement is true, or *F* if it is false.

T F **1.** The government provides public goods because it can make a profit.

T F **2.** Demand management is used by the government to keep the economy healthy.

T F **3.** If the economy were booming and inflation was becoming a problem, the government might reduce spending on public goods.

T F **4.** Privately owned businesses regulate the market.

T F **5.** Decreasing unemployment benefits causes inflation rates to increase.

T F **6.** Another term for demand management is fiscal policy.

T F **7.** The United States does not operate entirely according to market forces.

T F **8.** The passage says that fire protection and air traffic control should be provided by private companies.

T F **9.** Zoning ordinances and housing codes are controlled by government laws.

Answers are on page 338.

Government and Finances

> ## Key Words
>
> **national debt**—the total amount of money owed by the federal government of the United States to its creditors
>
> **progressive tax**—a tax that takes a larger portion of income as that income increases
>
> **regressive tax**—a tax that takes a smaller portion of income as that income increases
>
> **transfer payments**—payments that transfer income from one group of people to another through the tax system

One of the most rapidly growing government expenses is welfare programs. These include Aid to Dependent Children and other forms of public aid. Welfare payments are called transfer payments because they transfer income from one group of people to another. Taxes are used to make the transfer.

Taxation is the main source of government funding. The federal government relies on income taxes. State and local governments use income, property, and sales taxes. The federal income tax is a progressive tax. This means that as people make more money, they pay a higher percentage of their income in taxes. The opposite of a progressive tax is a regressive tax. A sales tax on food is a regressive tax. It is a tax that is the same for everyone. People have to buy a certain amount of food. The less they earn, the larger the percentage of their income goes toward food and, therefore, toward taxes on food.

Governments often finance their activities by borrowing. Savings bonds, treasury bills, and municipal bonds are examples of government borrowing. This type of borrowing has added greatly to our national debt.

There is a great debate going on about the growth of government spending. In 1900, the federal budget was $400 million. In 1990, it was $1.4 trillion. In addition, state and local governments spent an additional $976 billion. Together, this represents more than 40 percent of the gross national product. Is this too much? The question is the focus of public debate.

EXERCISE 11

Directions: Answer the questions below in the space provided.

1. Federal, state, and local government spending account for what percentage of the GNP?

    _____

2. What is the main source of government funds?

    _____

3. A city government adds a one percent tax to movie tickets. Is this a progressive or regressive tax? Why?

    _____

    _____

4. How are welfare payments funded?

    _____

    _____

5. What are transfer payments?

    _____

    _____

6. Did the amount spent by the federal, state, and local governments in 1990 add up to about $2.4 trillion or about $9.7 trillion?

    _____

7. Name three ways the government finances its borrowing.

    _____

    _____

    _____

Answers are on page 338.

Taxes

Federal, state, and local governments get the money they need to operate by collecting taxes. There are different kinds of taxes that are collected by different governing bodies. Following is a table of the main types of taxes and how they are collected.

TYPE OF TAX	WHAT THE TAX IS	WHO COLLECTS THE TAX
Income tax	a percentage of wages	federal, state and local governments
Social Security tax	a percentage of wages that goes into a public insurance fund for later collection upon retirement	federal government
Capital Gains tax	a percentage of money paid out of profits from the sale of land, buildings, stocks, or other capital assets	federal government
Property tax	a percentage of money paid for owning property that is based on its value	usually local governments
Sales tax	a percentage of money paid on the purchase of goods and services	federal, state, and local governments

EXERCISE 12

Directions: In the blank, write the kind of tax the following people are paying.

_____ 1. Samantha buys party supplies for a birthday party.

_____ 2. Ms. Lopez sold her condominium in order to buy a bigger home.

_____ 3. When Pascal receives his paycheck, a percentage has been deducted by the state government.

_____ 4. Maria sells some stocks she inherited from her grandmother and receives $1000 from the sale.

_____ 5. A landlord receives a bill from the city based on the value of the apartment building he owns.

Answers are on page 338.

Consumers in the Economy

> ### Key Words
>
> **compound interest**—the interest that is figured for a period of time based on the total of the principal plus any interest that has been earned over a period of time
>
> **discretionary income**—the difference in a budget between fixed costs and income
>
> **equity**—the value in property after debt and other liabilities are paid

---

Consumers are the target of intense advertising and marketing efforts. In order to keep your own budget balanced, you should decide on specific economic goals. Do you want to buy a house or a car, go on a vacation, or just get by from day to day? In order to reach your goal, you need a plan and a budget.

A budget is a plan for spending your income. It involves figuring out how much money you have and how you will use it. The first step is to figure out your fixed costs. These are expenses you must pay each month. Examples include rent, food, utilities, and car payments. The difference between what you must spend and your total income is called discretionary income. This is income you can spend as you choose.

If you are not happy with the amount of your discretionary income, you can do three things: (1) increase your income, (2) decrease your fixed costs, or (3) change your goals.

When you set aside discretionary income to pay for your long-term goals, you can put it in a savings account. The bank will pay you interest in return for using your money. Savings accounts are safe and are usually insured by the federal government. You will receive compound interest on your savings. In other words, you will receive interest on the original amount you put in savings. In addition, each time interest is paid it will go into your account and interest will then be paid on that interest. In this way, the deposit will grow.

The most important economic decision most people make is to buy a home. When you buy a home, you develop equity in it. Equity is what you would get out of the property if you sold it and paid off the mortgage. You develop equity in two ways. By paying the mortgage each month, the amount you own slowly increases. Second, during times of inflation, the value of a house rises and equity increases.

There are several kinds of home mortgages. Traditionally, they are long-term (25 to 30 years) and have a fixed interest rate. In other words, the amount paid remains the same over the life of the loan. Today, other types of loans are also available, some with adjustable interest rates. These mortgages give home buyers more choices in how much they want to pay. They can buy a house now, for example, knowing their income will grow in the future.

Part of your economic plan should also include insurance. Health insurance is vital because of the high costs of medical care. Homeowner's insurance is necessary to protect the value of your home against burglary, fire, and other disasters. Renter's insurance can protect your possessions if you rent an apartment.

PRE-GED PRACTICE

EXERCISE 13

Choose the best answer to the questions that follow.

1. Which of the following is true about purchasing a home as an investment?

   (1) It pays compound interest.
   (2) It keeps up with inflation.
   (3) It loses equity during times of inflation.
   (4) It is insured by the federal government.
   (5) It is generally paid off with a fixed interest rate.

2. The Garcia family has an income of $2,000 per month. Their expenses (including rent, food, car payment, insurance, clothes, and miscellaneous) total $1,550. What is the Garcias' discretionary income?

   (1) $200
   (2) $450
   (3) $800
   (4) $1,000
   (5) $1,500

3. An old fable tells about an ant who works all summer to store extra food. A grasshopper, meanwhile, sings and dances and fiddles away his time, not saving anything for the future. When winter comes, the ant has plenty to eat, but the grasshopper starves. Why did the grasshopper starve?

   (1) It had failed to budget its resources.
   (2) It had fallen victim to inflation.
   (3) It had too little discretionary income.
   (4) It had not received compound interest.
   (5) It had too little equity.

4. Which of the following is NOT an example of a fixed cost?

   (1) rent
   (2) utilities
   (3) car payment
   (4) vacation
   (5) mortgage payment

Answers are on page 338.

Credit and Consumer Fraud

One of the biggest threats to your budget and economic plans is credit. When you use credit, you are adding to your fixed costs. Unlike a mortgage, which is a form of credit but one that is used to make an investment, most forms of credit are not investments.

There are many kinds of credit, including credit cards, charge accounts, and automobile loans. Credit does have advantages. It allows you to buy things you couldn't afford if you had to make one cash payment. However, credit is expensive. Before you agree to a loan of any kind, find out how much it will cost. Look for two kinds of costs: higher prices for the things you buy and interest on the loan.

If you pay off a loan in monthly installments, interest is charged on the remaining balance. Bank credit cards are an example of this kind of credit. Interest is usually high, often much higher than you would get if you took out a loan from the bank.

Laws help protect you from excessive interest charges and other kinds of consumer fraud. For instance, the Truth-in-Lending Act requires lenders to tell the consumer what the real rate of interest is. This is the annual percentage rate (APR). Consumers must also be informed of the total dollar cost of a loan.

Writing Activity 19

Do you have a credit card that you use frequently? Have you ever taken out a loan to purchase a car or a home, or to pay for college tuition? In a few paragraphs, either describe the advantages and disadvantages of paying for items with a credit card vs. paying in cash or by check, or explain how paying off a loan has worked for you.

Answers will vary.

EXERCISE 14

Directions: Based on the following passage and chart, circle *T* for each true statement, or *F* for each false statement.

Distribution of Family Income and Wealth

The chart below shows that income is actually distributed unevenly. For instance, in 1991, the top 5 percent of American families earned 17 percent of the total family income. Twenty percent of the families shared just 4.5 percent of income earned in the United States.

FAMILY INCOME 1970–1991		
Families Ranked by Income	**Percentage of U.S. Total Income Before Taxes**	
	1970	1991
Lowest fifth (20%)	4.8	4.5
Second fifth (20%)	12.2	10.7
Third fifth (20%)	17.6	16.6
Fourth fifth (20%)	23.8	24.1
Highest fifth (20%)	40.9	44.2
Top 5%	15.6	17.1

T F 1. In 1991, 20 percent of U.S. families earned 44.2 percent of the total income in the United States.

T F 2. The chart shows that in 1991, the top 40 percent of the population earned less than 40 percent of the total income.

T F 3. The chart shows that the percentage of total income of the poorest fifth of Americans declined from 1970 to 1991.

T F 4. The main idea of the paragraph and the chart is that the income was fairly evenly divided among people in the United States in 1991.

Answers are on page 338.

The Labor Market, Industry, and Unions

The *labor market* is a term used to describe the availability of jobs. When the economy is healthy, unemployment is low and jobs are plentiful. When the economy is weak, unemployment is high and jobs are hard to find. During the last three decades, the labor market and industry have both changed radically.

During the 1970s and 1980s, manufacturing industries, such as the steel and automobile industries, suffered serious declines in sales. Many companies closed; others remained open but employed far fewer people. Some of these changes resulted from fierce, new competition from companies in other countries. The U.S. steel industry, for example, was hit especially hard. The plants and equipment were old and inefficient. The companies could no longer compete successfully with foreign steel producers. As a result, many of them closed rather than investing in modernizing the plants that would make them competitive.

Some industries left the United States altogether. Many clothing and shoe manufacturers, for instance, moved to foreign countries where labor costs were cheaper. Thousands of workers were left jobless.

Still more changes resulted from the way in which products are manufactured. Robots and computers, for example, made American industry more competitive. However, they also replaced many workers in certain industries.

While these changes cost thousands of American workers their jobs, the service industries were growing rapidly. Service industries are those businesses not involved in the production of goods. They include restaurants, hotels, retail stores, health care, office jobs, and so on. Although many unemployed workers found jobs in these new businesses, they often had to take lower paying jobs.

In the 1990s, the character of American industry began undergoing another change. International trade barriers began disappearing, first with Canada and then Mexico. Trade barriers with Europe, South America, and Asia were reduced. The immediate effect of these changes has been improved trade and more jobs in the United States. The long-term effects on U.S. industry and the U.S. labor market remain unknown.

EXERCISE 15

Directions: Put a check in front of all the statements that accurately describe industry and the labor market during the 1970s, 1980s, and 1990s.

_____ **1.** Many industries faced strong competition from abroad.

_____ **2.** Companies that had out-dated equipment and plants often went out of business.

_____ **3.** When industrial workers lost their jobs, most found new, better-paying jobs in the service industry.

_____ **4.** Robots and computers made U.S. industry more competitive.

_____ **5.** Reducing international trade barriers cost thousands of American workers their jobs.

Answers are on page 339.

Labor Unions

Unions are associations of workers, usually in a particular occupation or at a certain workplace. The workers organize and bargain as a group for wages, benefits, and other working conditions. The process of bargaining as a group with management is called *collective bargaining*. And since workers are acting as a group, they can have great influence. The management may represent a small business, a multinational corporation, or even a state or local government.

The goal of collective bargaining is to agree to a *labor contract*. This is a legally binding agreement between management and labor. It states what the duties of labor and management will be for the term of the contract. It usually defines salaries, working conditions, benefits, and other terms of employment.

Often, issues dealt with by labor contract are also covered in part by federal and state laws. Racial and sexual discrimination, health and safety conditions, and rate of minimum wages are all issues that are covered in part by government regulation. However, labor contracts may go beyond these laws.

When labor and management are unable to reach an agreement, the labor union leaders may call for a *strike*. When this happens, workers as a group stop working. The power to strike is the ultimate weapon of labor unions.

In recent decades, the power of unions has weakened. This has happened in part because the industries that unions once dominated have declining work forces. The steel, auto, and railroad industries, for example, once had powerful labor unions. As these industries have grown weaker, so have the unions. In 1992, fewer than 16 percent of American workers belonged to unions.

EXERCISE 16

Directions: Based on the passage you just read, circle *T* for each true
statement, or *F* for each false statement.

T F 1. When a union cannot gain salary increases, benefits, or other
working conditions that workers want, union leaders may call
for a strike.

T F 2. More than 20 percent of American workers belong to unions.

T F 3. When management and union leaders discuss working issues,
they are engaging in collective bargaining.

T F 4. A labor contract may include rules that prevent unfair hiring
practices.

T F 5. Federal and state laws protect workers from unsafe working
conditions.

T F 6. *Management* refers to those who head small, local businesses.

T F 7. Labor contracts are entered into for an unspecified period of
time.

T F 8. The passage states that as work forces decline, the power of
unions decreases.

Answers are on page 339.

EXERCISE 17

Questions 1–3 are based on the chart below.

U.S. GROSS AND NET NATIONAL PRODUCTS (in billions/trillions of dollars)				
Gross National Product	1960 515.3	1970 1,015.5	1980 2,732.0	1990 5,524.5
Less Capital Consumption Allowance	-46.4	-88.8	-303.0	-594.8
Equals Net National Product	468.9	926.7	2,429.0	4,929.7

Source: *U.S. Department of Commerce*

1. By 1990, which of the following describes the U.S. GNP?

(1) It was more than $5 1/2 trillion.
(2) It was less than $2 1/2 billion.
(3) It was less than the GNP in 1980.
(4) It was double the GNP in 1960.
(5) It was on the decline.

2. What do you do to find the Net National Product?

(1) add the GNPs for the 30-year period
(2) add the Capital Consumption Allowance to the GNP
(3) subtract the Capital Consumption Allowance from the GNP
(4) divide the GNP by the Capital Consumption Allowance
(5) average the GNP for the 30-year period

3. If the GNP continued to grow at the same rate, what would it have been by the year 2000?

(1) about $8 million
(2) about $8 trillion
(3) about $20 billion
(4) more than $20 trillion
(5) more than $11 trillion

Questions 4–8 are based on the following passage and the graph on the next page.

In 1990, the total national debt of the United States was $3 trillion, 206.3 billion. This comes to about $13,000 for every man, woman, and child in the country.

The national debt is money the U.S. government has borrowed to pay for government expenses. This is in addition to funds raised by taxation. World Wars I and II were major causes for increases in the national debt. Deep recessions in 1974–1975 and 1979–1982 reduced tax revenues and greatly increased debt. Additional tax cuts along with increased military spending added billions more to the debt.

The federal government borrows money by selling financial instruments such as Treasury certificates, notes, and U.S. Savings Bonds. These are sold to investors. Most of these investors are U.S. citizens or financial institutions. About 80 percent of the debt is owed to American citizens.

PERCENTAGE CHANGE IN U.S. NATIONAL DEBT, 1900–1990

percentage change

2,100 — 1920 (2,100%)

2,000
500 — 1950 (495%)
400
300 — 1990 (253%)
200 — 1940 (165%) — 1980 (170%)
100 — 1910 (–8%) — 1930 (–33%) — 1960 (10%) — 1970 (30.2%)
0

national debt (in billions): 1.1   24.3   16.2   43.1   256   284   370   908   3,206

4. The greatest percentage of increase in national debt occurred during what ten-year period?

   (1) 1900–1910
   (2) 1910–1920
   (3) 1920–1930
   (4) 1940–1950
   (5) 1980–1990

5. During what two ten-year periods did the total amount of the national debt decrease?

   (1) 1900–1910 and 1920–1930
   (2) 1910–1920 and 1940–1950
   (3) 1940–1950 and 1980–1990
   (4) 1960–1970 and 1970–1980
   (5) 1970–1980 and 1980–1990

6. During what ten-year period did the actual amount of the national debt increase by the greatest number of dollars?

   (1) 1910–1920
   (2) 1940–1950
   (3) 1950–1960
   (4) 1970–1980
   (5) 1980–1990

7. According to the passage, what is the greatest cause of increased national debt?

   (1) consumer spending
   (2) selling financial instruments
   (3) capital spending on domestic programs
   (4) financing wars and military spending
   (5) welfare programs during the Great Depression

8. Another severe recession, such as the one in 1979–1982, would probably have what effect?

   (1) raise the national debt
   (2) lower the national debt
   (3) not affect the national debt
   (4) lower the interest on the debt
   (5) lower the debt ceiling

Answers are on page 339.

READING EFFICIENCY I

Directions: This activity will help you to improve your reading efficiency. Before you start to read, write the present time at the top of the page. When you have completed the reading and all 5 questions, write your finishing time. Subtract to find how long you took. Score your answers. Then turn to page 340 to find your E-Factor and graph your progress.

Finishing Time	
Starting Time –	
Reading Time =	
Number of Answers Correct	

There are many ways to invest money. The most common ways are to invest in a savings account at a bank or a credit union, in stocks, in bonds, or in mutual funds.

Banks and credit unions pay you for keeping your money in a savings account. They use your money to make loans to other people. You receive interest, or extra money, for letting the bank use your money. Interest rates at banks or credit unions are usually low. Savings accounts are a safe investment because the government guarantees your deposits up to $100,000. A CD, or a certificate of deposit, is a special kind of savings account. When you agree to leave your money in a CD for a certain amount of time, the bank pays you a higher rate of interest.

Stocks are small pieces of companies. When you buy stock in a company, you become a part owner of the company. Companies do not make any promise to pay back your money or to pay interest. You share in the company's financial success or failure. Stocks change in price daily as they are bought and sold on the stock market. There are two ways to make money in the stock market. One way is to receive dividends, or a share of the company's profits. The other way is to sell your stock to someone else at a higher price than what you paid for it.

Bonds are different than stocks. When you buy a bond, you are not buying a part of a company. Bonds are loans to companies or governments. The company or government promises to pay back the face value, or amount written on the bond. They also pay you interest at regular times. All bonds have a maturity date. The maturity date is when the company or government must pay the face value of the bond. If you sell your bond before the maturity date, you may pay a penalty.

Mutual funds are collections of money in different stocks or bonds. A mutual fund company uses the investors' money to buy stocks. Mutual funds hire professional money managers to buy and sell stocks. When you buy a piece of a mutual fund, you share in the profits or losses of the fund as a whole. Because your money is spread out over a number of stocks and bonds, if a single company does poorly it may not hurt the mutual fund overall.

1. Risk carries the possibility of making more money or losing more money. Which type of investment involves the most risk?

   (1) stocks
   (2) bonds
   (3) mutual funds
   (4) savings accounts
   (5) all investments have the same amount of risk

2. What is investing?

   (1) paying a price for something
   (2) withdrawing money from an account
   (3) using money to make money
   (4) depositing money into an account
   (5) paying a fee to borrow money

3. Which form of investment is most like an I.O.U.?

(1) mutual fund
(2) bond
(3) savings account
(4) stock
(5) CD

4. When do you get back the money you paid for a bond?

(1) one year after you buy it
(2) when it doubles its face value
(3) at regular intervals
(4) when it increases in value
(5) at the maturity date

5. People who want to avoid risk think that bonds are a good investment. Which of the following is NOT true about bonds?

(1) People know how long it will be until bonds mature.
(2) The value of a bond changes from day to day.
(3) Bonds pay higher interest rates than savings accounts.
(4) People know how much a bond will be worth at the maturity date.
(5) Investors know how much money they will get from interest payments.

Answers are on page 339.

READING EFFICIENCY J

Directions: This activity will help you to improve your reading efficiency. Before you start to read, write the present time at the top of the page. When you have completed the reading and all 5 questions, write your finishing time. Subtract to find how long you took. Score your answers. Then turn to page 340 to find your E-Factor and graph your progress.

Finishing Time	
Starting Time −	
Reading Time =	
Number of Answers Correct	

The economy of a country refers to how goods and services are divided among the country's people. No country can produce enough goods to satisfy the wants of all of its people. Most people want more than they can afford. They want more and better houses, schools, clothing, and services.

Some countries rely on central planning to provide goods and services for their people. With central planning, the government controls the production, pricing, and distribution of goods. Some countries have a capitalist economy. With a capitalist economy, individuals own the industrial goods and control business. They make their own decisions about using land and making products. They also decide if people or machines should perform jobs. In capitalist economies, people make goods to produce wealth.

Prices of goods are set by the law of supply and demand. Supply is how much of something is available. Demand is how much people want an item. If the demand is greater than the supply, the price of the item goes up. If the supply is greater than the demand, the price of the item goes down.

After goods are produced, a country must decide how to divide them among its people. In some countries, goods go only to people who can afford them. In other countries, they are shared equally.

A country must finally decide how fast its economy should grow. Every country has limited resources. It must decide what share of its resources should be used to build factories. It must decide how to balance the needs of its people now with future production. The growth of a country's economy depends on how that country uses its productive resources. Those resources include capital, natural resources, labor, and technology.

1. Super Computers has introduced the Generation 2001X computer. It is the fastest and most efficient computer on the market. So many people want to buy the Generation 2001X that Super Computers can't make them fast enough. What do you predict will happen?

   (1) People will stop wanting Generation 2001X.
   (2) The price of Generation 2001X will go down.
   (3) Super Computers will make stop making Generation 2001X.
   (4) Super Computers will go out of business.
   (5) The price of Generation 2001X will go up.

2. Why is competition an important part of a capitalist economy?

   (1) It helps big companies make more money than little ones.
   (2) It allows one company to control an industry.
   (3) It gives people better goods at higher prices.
   (4) It offers people a choice of goods and helps to keep prices low.
   (5) It keeps the government out of private business.

3. If a country cannot make a certain product, it must import, or bring in, that product from somewhere else. How does this affect the country's economy?

   (1) The country wastes some of its productive resources.
   (2) The country has less money to spend on other things because it is paying so much for the imported product.
   (3) The country has more wealth because imported goods are worth more than goods made at home.
   (4) Wages in the country increase.
   (5) The quality of goods made in the country will be higher.

4. Which of the following is NOT a productive resource?

   (1) labor
   (2) taxes
   (3) capital
   (4) natural energy
   (5) technology

5. Which of the following would make a country's economy grow?

   (1) having fewer people work
   (2) closing factories
   (3) using up the natural resources
   (4) training scientists and educating workers
   (5) importing goods

   Answers are on page 339.

Social Studies

The Posttest consists of 50 multiple-choice questions. It should give you a good idea of how well you have learned the skills you have studied in this book. You should take the Posttest only after you have completed all the chapters. Work as quickly and as carefully as you can. If a question seems too difficult, make an educated guess.

Record your answers on the answer grid below. Choose the best of five answer choices by filling in the corresponding circle on the answer grid.

Using the Evaluation Chart on page 316, circle the number of each question that you missed to determine which topics you might need to review before you move on to Contemporary's *GED Social Studies*.

Posttest Answer Grid

1 ① ② ③ ④ ⑤	18 ① ② ③ ④ ⑤	35 ① ② ③ ④ ⑤
2 ① ② ③ ④ ⑤	19 ① ② ③ ④ ⑤	36 ① ② ③ ④ ⑤
3 ① ② ③ ④ ⑤	20 ① ② ③ ④ ⑤	37 ① ② ③ ④ ⑤
4 ① ② ③ ④ ⑤	21 ① ② ③ ④ ⑤	38 ① ② ③ ④ ⑤
5 ① ② ③ ④ ⑤	22 ① ② ③ ④ ⑤	39 ① ② ③ ④ ⑤
6 ① ② ③ ④ ⑤	23 ① ② ③ ④ ⑤	40 ① ② ③ ④ ⑤
7 ① ② ③ ④ ⑤	24 ① ② ③ ④ ⑤	41 ① ② ③ ④ ⑤
8 ① ② ③ ④ ⑤	25 ① ② ③ ④ ⑤	42 ① ② ③ ④ ⑤
9 ① ② ③ ④ ⑤	26 ① ② ③ ④ ⑤	43 ① ② ③ ④ ⑤
10 ① ② ③ ④ ⑤	27 ① ② ③ ④ ⑤	44 ① ② ③ ④ ⑤
11 ① ② ③ ④ ⑤	28 ① ② ③ ④ ⑤	45 ① ② ③ ④ ⑤
12 ① ② ③ ④ ⑤	29 ① ② ③ ④ ⑤	46 ① ② ③ ④ ⑤
13 ① ② ③ ④ ⑤	30 ① ② ③ ④ ⑤	47 ① ② ③ ④ ⑤
14 ① ② ③ ④ ⑤	31 ① ② ③ ④ ⑤	48 ① ② ③ ④ ⑤
15 ① ② ③ ④ ⑤	32 ① ② ③ ④ ⑤	49 ① ② ③ ④ ⑤
16 ① ② ③ ④ ⑤	33 ① ② ③ ④ ⑤	50 ① ② ③ ④ ⑤
17 ① ② ③ ④ ⑤	34 ① ② ③ ④ ⑤	

POSTTEST

Question 1 is based on the following information.

1. Geographers often look at the places they study in terms of regions. A region does not have distinct boundaries or an exact population. It is simply an area of land with certain characteristics.

   Suppose a geographer studies precipitation patterns in the Pacific Northwest. Which of the following would best define this region?

   (1) changes in altitude from the coast to the mountains
   (2) a high annual rate of rainfall
   (3) the state boundaries of Washington and Oregon
   (4) the Pacific Northwest Railroad
   (5) the greatest amount of cultivated farmland

2. Joe and Ida Williams find that every month their money just seems to disappear. They can never save for any long-term goals. What should they do to correct the situation?

   (1) increase their monthly income
   (2) draw up a family budget
   (3) buy some life insurance
   (4) try a few get-rich-quick schemes
   (5) apply for a credit card

Question 3 refers to the following passage and cartoon.

Many Americans are shocked about the large number of deaths caused by guns and want strict gun control. Other Americans are equally determined to have the right to own guns. They point to the Second Amendment for constitutional support. It clearly states that "the right of the people to keep and bear arms shall not be infringed."

3. Which of the following might best sum up the cartoonist's view of the Second Amendment?

   (1) He favors it.
   (2) He wants it done away with.
   (3) He believes it no longer goes along with the Founding Fathers' intent.
   (4) He believes it has run into disfavor with the gun lobby.
   (5) He feels it causes too many Americans to lose sleep.

POSTTEST

Question 4 refers to the following passage.

Although human beings have been around for abut 300,000 years, it wasn't until about 5,000 years ago that they began to write. The ability to write marks the beginning of civilization. Before the beginning of civilization people were nomads. They spent most of their time walking from place to place in search of food. About 7,000 years ago people began to settle down and grow their own food.

4. Civilization depends on which of the following?

   (1) wandering from place to place
   (2) migrating toward warmer climates
   (3) growing one's own food
   (4) searching for food
   (5) constructing tall buildings

Question 5 refers to the following passage.

Farmers in 750 B.C. first settled the area around Rome. A group from the north, the Etruscans, soon overtook these farmers. The Etruscans drained swamp land for farming, established trade, and built roads and complex buildings. In 509 B.C. the Romans drove the Etruscans out, and their king along with them.

5. Which of the following did the Romans *not* get from the Etruscans?

   (1) new techniques in architecture
   (2) good roads
   (3) the idea of a republic
   (4) established trade routes
   (5) farm land

Question 6 refers to the following passage.

The Roman Empire lasted 500 years and at one time included 100 million people. Its success was due in part to able government officials; even evil and corrupt emperors did not affect their running of the empire. The cost of maintaining such a huge empire was great. After many years, the economy began to suffer from unemployment and inflation. Crime rose, and barbarians from Germany started to attack the Roman Empire.

6. Based on the information in the passage, why did the Roman Empire eventually fall?

   (1) because of evil and corrupt emperors
   (2) because of high unemployment and inflation
   (3) because of corrupt government administrators
   (4) because of a combination of different factors
   (5) because of barbarian attacks from Germany

POSTTEST

Questions 7–9 refer to the following definitions.

direct initiative—a process that allows citizens to draft laws and present them directly to the voters

referendum—a process by which voters in a state or community can repeal laws in a general election

recall—a process by which citizens can vote an elected government official out of office

primary election—an election held in advance of the general election allowing voters to select candidates for public office from one or more political parties

general election—the final election held on the same day throughout the United States

7. Citizens who want to write a tax reform law and present it directly to the voters would use which of the following?

   (1) referendum
   (2) general election
   (3) direct initiative
   (4) recall
   (5) primary election

8. A person who wishes to become his or her political party's candidate for governor must first be selected by what process?

   (1) referendum
   (2) general election
   (3) direct initiative
   (4) recall
   (5) primary election

9. California voters unhappy with Governor Pete Wilson's support of Proposition 187 (an initiative denying education and health care services to illegal immigrants) could have removed him from office before his term expired in 1999 by what process?

   (1) referendum
   (2) general election
   (3) direct initiative
   (4) recall
   (5) primary election

Question 10 is based on the following passage.

In the 1930s, the United States was preoccupied with the Great Depression and did not get involved in world affairs. During this time, England and France followed a policy of appeasement toward Germany, which was taking over territory that belonged to other countries. Germany seized all of Austria and Czechoslovakia and threatened Poland. England and France did nothing and kept their soldiers at home. Many experts in world affairs claim that appeasing Germany led to World War II.

10. In this passage, what does *appeasement* mean?

    (1) refusing to allow Germany to expand its territory
    (2) taking in unlimited numbers of immigrants
    (3) using land that belonged to someone else
    (4) compromising in the face of attacks on other nations
    (5) working to bring about world peace

POSTTEST

Question 11 refers to the following graph.

EQUILIBRIUM PRICE FOR COMPUTERS

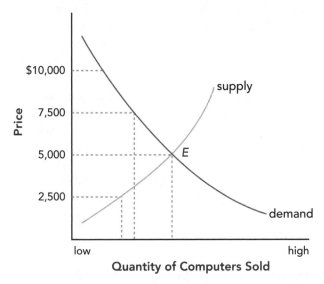

Questions 12 and 13 are based on the graph and table below.

Muslims are a growing part of the U.S. population. Their religion is called Islam. It may soon become the country's second-largest religion.

U.S. MUSLIM POPULATION

Most U.S. Muslims are immigrants

States with the highest Muslim population	
California	1,000,000
New York	800,000
Illinois	420,000
New Jersey	200,000
Indiana	180,000
Michigan	170,000
Virginia	150,000
Texas	140,000
Ohio	130,000
Maryland	70,000

11. The equilibrium price of goods or services (E) takes place at the point where supply equals demand. According to the graph, what is the equilibrium price for computers?

(1) $2,500
(2) $5,000
(3) $7,500
(4) $10,000
(5) $15,000

12. Which of the following best describes the majority of Muslims living in the United States?

(1) native-born and living in California, New York, and Ohio
(2) native-born and living in New Jersey, Texas, and Maryland
(3) immigrants and living in California, New Jersey, and Illinois
(4) immigrants and living in California, New York, and Illinois
(5) equally immigrants and native-born

13. Based on the data, you can infer which of the following about Muslims?

(1) They prefer living in rural, agricultural states.
(2) They settle in populous states that have big cities.
(3) They settle in equal numbers in all 50 states.
(4) They prefer to settle only on the East Coast.
(5) They prefer to settle only on the West Coast.

Questions 14 and 15 refer to the following passage.

In the late nineteenth century, the process of suburbanization began. This process was at work when city centers began to decentralize. Wealthy people had homes in the early suburbs. These suburbs were built near electric railroad lines. The invention of the automobile and truck furthered the growth of suburbs. These inventions meant that factories and homeowners no longer depended on being near city railroad lines.

14. According to the passage, the growth of suburbs was advanced by which of the following?

    (1) the invention of the automobile
    (2) the development of more railroad lines
    (3) the poor moving away from the city
    (4) industry moving to the country
    (5) railroads becoming obsolete

15. From this passage, you could conclude that which of the following is an important feature in shaping the physical growth of our environment?

    (1) the location of homes for wealthy people
    (2) population size
    (3) population density
    (4) transportation technology
    (5) the physical condition of the site

Question 16 refers to the following passage.

The collapse of the Roman Empire led to the period called the Middle Ages in Europe. One leader who was able to take advantage of this situation was Charlemagne. He ruled what is today France, Switzerland, Belgium, and the Netherlands as well as other parts of Europe. Pope Leo III crowned Charlemagne as the Holy Roman Emperor although the presence of the empire was long gone. Without the centralized power of the empire, trade and education declined, and not many discoveries were made in science. Charlemagne, however, was able to protect people from Viking attacks. When Charlemagne died, his empire was divided among his sons, who were not united. Unfortunately that made the people more open to Viking attacks.

16. Why are the Middle Ages often referred to as the "Dark Ages"?

    (1) Charlemagne was able to defend people from the Vikings.
    (2) Trade, education, and scientific discoveries declined.
    (3) Charlemagne did not have the support of the pope.
    (4) The Vikings took advantage of Charlemagne's divided empire.
    (5) Europe was not unified under Charlemagne's sons.

POSTTEST

Question 17 refers to the following passage.

With the invasion of the Vikings, people looked for protection wherever they could find it. This led to weaker lords pledging loyalty to stronger lords. In this way, the weaker lords became vassals. As vassals, they were allotted land from the lord to work and became knights pledged to the lord's service. One lord could have many vassals. In return they had to share some of their crops with the lord as well as serve in the lord's military, which would fight wars, guard the castle, or serve in other expeditions.

17. Based on the passage and the graphic, which of the following statements is true about the relationship between vassals and lords?

(1) There were more lords than vassals.
(2) Lords held a higher rank than vassals.
(3) Vassals and lords held similar rank.
(4) Vassals were usually poor.
(5) Lords were usually farmers.

Questions 18 and 19 refer to the following graph.

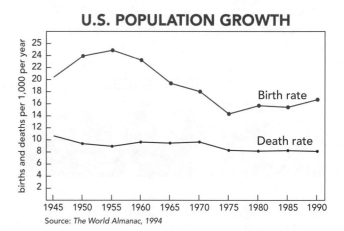

Source: *The World Almanac, 1994*

18. According to the graph, in which of the following time periods did the greatest increase in birth rate take place?

(1) 1945–1955
(2) 1955–1965
(3) 1960–1970
(4) 1970–1980
(5) 1980–1990

19. What does the graph show about current American population growth rates?

(1) They are exploding.
(2) They have remained stable since 1945.
(3) They declined during the early 1950s.
(4) They have increased dramatically since 1980.
(5) They have declined since 1955.

POSTTEST

Questions 20 and 21 refer to the following diagram.

This cross-section view shows the five Great Lakes that separate the United States and Canada.

THE GREAT LAKES

20. Which of the five Great Lakes is the deepest?

(1) Lake Ontario
(2) Lake Erie
(3) Lake Huron
(4) Lake Michigan
(5) Lake Superior

21. Which of the five Great Lakes lies above sea level?

(1) Lake Ontario
(2) Lake Erie
(3) Lake Huron
(4) Lake Michigan
(5) Lake Superior

Question 22 refers to the following two quotations:

". . . avoid the necessity of those overgrown military establishments which, under any form of government, are inauspicious [not favorable] for liberty, and which are to be regarded as particularly hostile to republican liberty."

—Farewell Address, General George Washington, 1st U.S. President, 1796

"The conjunction of an immense military establishment and a large arms industry . . . new in American experience, exercised a total influence . . . felt in every city, every state house, every office of the federal government. . . . In the councils of government, we must guard against the acquisition of unwarranted influence by the military-industrial complex."

—Farewell Address, General Dwight Eisenhower, 34th U.S. President, 1961

22. Which of the following conclusions could be drawn from both of these statements?

(1) A very large military establishment could threaten our American government.
(2) Business influence on the military has made our form of government more democratic.
(3) Only the military-industrial complex can protect our liberties.
(4) The military should be allowed more influence in government.
(5) Civilian control of the military should never be allowed.

POSTTEST

Questions 23 and 24 refer to the following poll.

Gallup polls in 1947, 1964, and 1990 surveyed Americans on whether members of the Senate and the House of Representatives should have limits on their terms in office.

CONGRESSIONAL TERM LIMITS

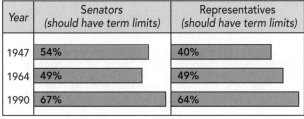

Year	Senators (should have term limits)	Representatives (should have term limits)
1947	54%	40%
1964	49%	49%
1990	67%	64%

Source: *The American Enterprise*

23. Which of the following best summarizes Americans' attitudes toward congressional term limits from 1947 to 1990?

  (1) They increasingly favored term limits for senators but not for representatives.
  (2) They increasingly favored term limits for both senators and for representatives.
  (3) They increasingly favored term limits for representatives but not for senators.
  (4) Those favoring term limits fell from 60 percent to 40 percent.
  (5) By 1990, more than 75 percent of those polled favored term limits.

24. Based on the poll, which action might you expect concerning term limits?

  (1) a constitutional amendment setting term limits for members of the House and Senate
  (2) members of Congress leaving office voluntarily after two terms
  (3) an executive order by the president setting term limits
  (4) impeachment of members of Congress who refuse to leave office
  (5) no action by members of Congress

Question 25 is based on the following cartoon.

25. Assume that the balding man stands for the American public. Which of the following best sums up the cartoonist's main point?

  (1) Doctors and mechanics, but not lawyers and politicians, must have experience to do their jobs.
  (2) The public will not allow inexperienced people to perform surgery, win a law case, or fix a car.
  (3) The public accepts inexperienced politicians in Washington but does not accept inexperienced doctors, lawyers, or mechanics.
  (4) The public believes inexperienced people can become great politicians.
  (5) The public is willing to let people try their hand at any job.

POSTTEST

Question 26 is based on the following passage.

Latin Americans made rich cultural contributions to the southwestern United States long before the twentieth century. People of Latin American background lived in the region before people migrated there from other parts of the United States. For many years, the region's ownership and boundaries were fought over by Mexico and the United States.

26. Which of the following statements is true?

   (1) Latin Americans prevented the cultural development of the Southwest.
   (2) Mexico sold Texas to the United States to end boundary disputes.
   (3) Most Mexicans left the Southwest after it became part of the United States.
   (4) The United States had completely settled the Southwest before Mexico took an interest in the region.
   (5) Latin American influence on regional culture in the Southwestern United States has a long, rich history.

Question 27 is based on the following cartoon.

27. What does this cartoon imply about American agricultural production? It has changed

   (1) from being run by large company-owned farms
   (2) as a result of government price supports
   (3) from being run by small family farms
   (4) in spite of high interest rates
   (5) toward organic farming

Question 28 is based on the following passage.

The U.S. Constitution guarantees American citizens protection against unreasonable search and seizure, trial by jury, the right to due process and protection against self-incrimination. The Constitution also guarantees the right to an attorney and a public trial and protection against an extremely large bail or unusual punishment. But what about the right of innocent citizens to be protected against criminals? Our judges go too easy on dangerous criminals. They often let criminals loose on the streets because of legal technicalities.

28. The author of this passage probably would like which of the following for suspected criminals?

   (1) to be considered innocent until proven guilty
   (2) to be guaranteed due process of law
   (3) to be kept off the streets
   (4) to be given lighter sentences
   (5) to be let out on bail

POSTTEST

Questions 29 and 30 refer to the following passage.

Prevailing winds move nitrogen and sulfur-oxide pollution from factories and automobiles in the Midwest into the eastern parts of the United States and Canada. There these pollutants become so concentrated that they give the rain a high acid content. This acid rain is killing fish and large numbers of trees in the eastern forests. The destruction of forests, if allowed to continue, will ruin watersheds, lower water tables, and cause water shortages for eastern cities.

29. What does the passage state about potential water shortages in the eastern United States and Canada?

   (1) They are unlikely.
   (2) They are the result of poor water management.
   (3) They are related to industrial activity elsewhere.
   (4) They are killing trees.
   (5) They are killing fish.

30. From this passage, what could you conclude?

   (1) Society can overcome nature.
   (2) Nature rules the development of human society.
   (3) Pollution affects only the region where it is created.
   (4) People can affect their environment, but environmental changes also can affect people.
   (5) The political effects of pollution are exaggerated.

Question 31 is based on the following passage.

The Continental Divide in North America is an imaginary boundary line. In the 48 continental United States, it straddles the Rocky Mountains. The Continental Divide separates the rivers that flow east and the rivers that flow west toward the oceans. Rivers on one side, such as the Colorado, flow west. Rivers on the other side, such as the Missouri and Mississippi, flow east from the Rockies.

31. What does the Continental Divide in the United States separate?

   (1) rivers flowing east and west
   (2) rivers flowing north and south
   (3) the Rocky Mountains and the Appalachians
   (4) Canada and the United States
   (5) North America and South America

Questions 32 and 33 refer to the following passage.

A balance sheet is a financial statement. Businesses use it to summarize their financial position at different points in time. A balance sheet has three parts: assets (everything the business has in its possession); liabilities (everything the business owes to someone else); and net worth (the difference between total assets and total liabilities). The balance sheet is based on the formula: assets – liabilities = net worth

32. How does a balance sheet describe the financial position of a business?

   (1) in terms of its debts
   (2) by counting its assets
   (3) at different points in time
   (4) by figuring out profit or loss
   (5) for a fiscal year

33. Jin Su's Chinese Restaurant has assets totaling $75,000 and liabilities totaling $53,000. What is its net worth?

   (1) $69,700
   (2) $53,000
   (3) $30,000
   (4) $22,000
   (5) $19,400

POSTTEST

Questions 34 and 35 refer to the following passage.

After the Civil War, the Radical Republicans were the strongest supporters of civil rights for blacks. Their most significant successes included the passage of three constitutional amendments guaranteeing basic civil rights and the establishment of the Freedmen's Bureau, an agency that helped former slaves to make the transition from slavery to citizenship.

34. What did the Radical Republicans support?

(1) slavery
(2) the Civil War
(3) the abolition of the Democratic Party
(4) civil rights for former slaves
(5) an end to civil rights for blacks

35. What did the Freedmen's Bureau do?

(1) helped former slaves learn to read and write
(2) helped former slaveholders find new servants
(3) moved slaves North to safety
(4) worked for constitutional amendments on civil rights
(5) established citizenship for former slaves

Question 36 refers to the following passage and chart.

Jane Benson lives in a working-class neighborhood in a small city. She wants to open a small business in her area so that she can work near her home and be her own boss. She decided to do a market survey of the area. She made up a questionnaire listing the possible products and services she could provide. Jane went from door to door asking people to answer her questions.

JANE'S RESULTS			
business	number in favor	amount they would spend per week $20/$30/$40	total amount spent
bakery	18	12 5 1	$430
drugstore	17	5 8 4	$500
fabric store	9	5 4 0	$220
restaurant	8	4 3 1	$210

36. According to the chart, which of the four businesses would be the best investment?

(1) bakery
(2) drugstore
(3) fabric store
(4) restaurant
(5) no way to tell

POSTTEST

Question 37 refers to the following dialogue.

SPEAKER A

I think people are less loyal to the major political parties today since voters tend to vote for the person rather than the party. This trend worries me. We need stability in our political system more than ever. The two-party system has worked well for us for about 200 years.

SPEAKER B

You're right about the trend, but I think it's great. The big parties will have to work to earn the independent vote. This way, they have to find out what people really want.

37. What could you say abut the two speakers?

 (1) They expect both major political parties to die soon.
 (2) They disagree on what the trend toward split-ticket voting means.
 (3) They want more than two political parties.
 (4) They disagree on whether voters are loyal to the major parties.
 (5) They are a Democrat and a Republican, respectively.

Questions 38 and 39 refer to the following passage.

The term *populism* refers to a movement to organize farmers that grew out of two economic depressions and a worldwide fall in farm prices. Farmers felt that economic policy favored industry and business. They wanted reforms to help them. In particular, they asked for an increase in the amount of money in circulation in the United States, government ownership of railroads, and laws against foreigners owning land. The Populist movement was strongest in the 1890s, then declined.

38. As a movement, what did Populism call for?

 (1) a union
 (2) economic reforms
 (3) laws against foreign immigration
 (4) political change
 (5) laws against industry and business

39. In the late nineteenth century, what were farmers hurt by?

 (1) the Populists
 (2) a worldwide fall in farm prices
 (3) an increase in the money supply
 (4) government ownership of railroads
 (5) industry and business

Questions 40 and 41 refer to the following passage.

The battle for women's suffrage lasted a hundred years. In 1920, the Nineteenth Amendment finally gave women the right to vote. One argument in favor of giving the vote to women was that women would bring more sensitivity, humanity, and commitment to fair dealings into politics. People opposed to this argument replied that women's spiritual purity and moral force would be undermined by political involvement.

40. What does *suffrage* mean?

 (1) suffering
 (2) civil rights
 (3) fair political dealings
 (4) the right to vote
 (5) emancipation

41. According to the passage, what did people fear about giving women the vote?

 They would be
 (1) less able to provide spiritual guidance
 (2) unable to do their housework
 (3) having fewer children
 (4) poor political candidates
 (5) less feminine

Questions 42 and 43 refer to the following passage.

Following World War I, many nations banded together to form the League of Nations. The league was an organization whose goal was to guarantee world peace. President Woodrow Wilson wanted the United States to take the lead in the League of Nations. However, Congress did not want the foreign policy of the United States to be tied to the articles of the league. As a result, the United States did not join the League of Nations.

42. What was the purpose of the League of Nations?

   (1) to bring an end to World War I
   (2) to let the United States take the lead in world affairs
   (3) to bring about world peace
   (4) to fight communism
   (5) to take over world affairs from President Wilson

43. Why did the United States not join the League of Nations?

   (1) President Wilson was a poor statesman
   (2) World War I was not yet over.
   (3) Congress did not want the United States to take the lead.
   (4) The league could not guarantee peace.
   (5) Some feared that U.S. foreign policy would be too closely connected with the league's articles.

Question 44 refers to the following passage.

President Franklin D. Roosevelt and British Prime Minister Winston Churchill declared the Atlantic Charter in August 1941. One of the points of this World War II document called for all nations to join together to guarantee world peace. This charter later evolved into the United Nations.

44. What could you infer from this information?

   (1) The United States was finally joining the League of Nations.
   (2) Congress still opposed the league.
   (3) The league had not guaranteed world peace.
   (4) Wilson's idea for a League of Nations to guarantee world peace was still alive.
   (5) The United States still did not want to tie its foreign policy to an international organization.

POSTTEST

Questions 45 and 46 refer to the following passage.

Many pioneers kept diaries of their incredible journeys to the American West. They wrote about their fears of hard winters, wild animals, and sickness or death. They also wrote about the loneliness of leaving behind loved ones, familiar places, and personal possessions. The pioneers described the natural beauty they came across, the friendships they established with other travelers, and the triumph of overcoming obstacles, using all the creativity they could muster.

45. What do using personal diaries in historical research gives us a sense of?

    (1) the effects of natural disasters on people
    (2) the daily experiences and feelings of people in the past
    (3) exactly what the pioneers faced
    (4) how the standard English language has changed
    (5) how the West has changed

46. What is the author's attitude toward the pioneers?

    (1) they were very courageous
    (2) they were afraid of bad weather
    (3) they were foolish to leave so much behind
    (4) they should have spent more time enjoying the natural beauty
    (5) they made lasting friendships

Question 47 is based on the following passage.

Recent scientific studies confirm that Earth's basic resources are vastly greater than what are needed to feed even the 10 billion people who are almost certain to inhabit the planet by the middle of the century. The real threat is not that Earth will run out of land, topsoil, or water, but that nations will fail to pursue the economic, trade, and research policies that can increase the production of food, limit environmental damage, and ensure that resources reach the people who need them.

47. According to the passage, what will the real problem in the year 2050 be?

    (1) Earth will run out of water.
    (2) Earth will run out of land.
    (3) Earth will no longer have good topsoil.
    (4) People will not follow the right economic and research policies.
    (5) Earth will not have the basic resources to feed 10 billion people.

Question 48 is based on the following passage.

Personal computers (PCs) are no longer simple production machines. Some computer manufacturers are calling PCs the ultimate home appliance. They say that some day people will use PCs as telephones, answering machines, and stereos. Advertisers say PCs will become as much a part of daily life as the microwave oven.

48. Based on the passage, what could you infer about PCs?

    (1) They will soon be as common as radios and TVs.
    (2) They will soon be a substitute for books.
    (3) They will soon be only a passing fad.
    (4) They will soon be used only by editors and writers.
    (5) They will soon be replaced by other gadgets.

POSTTEST

Question 49 is based on the following graph.

U.S. FARMS, 1940–1992

Source: *World Almanac, 1994; U.S. Dept. of Agriculture*

49. Which of the following trends can you infer from the data shown on the graph?

(1) More people now live and work on larger farms.

(2) More people now live and work on smaller farms.

(3) Fewer people now live and work on farms.

(4) Fewer people now live and work on smaller farms.

(5) More Americans are farmers than ever before.

Question 50 is based on the following passage.

No cure has been found for the AIDS epidemic. AIDS (acquired immunodeficiency syndrome) is a virus-caused (HIV) disease that destroys the infection-fighting blood cells. The body thus cannot fight infections or cancers.

In the 1870s, the French scientist Louis Pasteur discovered that the human body builds up antibodies to weak germs that enter it. This explains why Edward Jenner's smallpox vaccine and Jonas Salk's polio vaccine were successful.

50. What does this passage imply that scientists must do to fight AIDS?

(1) use antibiotics to kill the germs

(2) replace the body's blood cells by transfusions

(3) find a vaccine that will help antibodies kill the virus

(4) discover a vaccine that kills the antibodies

(5) move on to other diseases because AIDS is incurable

Answer Key

1. (2) The annual rate of rainfall most closely defines the region of the geographer's study: rainfall (precipitation) patterns.

2. (2) Joe and Ida Williams need to set up a budget to have control over where their money goes. The budget will give them some guidelines. None of the other choices are sure to help them save money.

3. (3) The man in bed says that the Second Amendment has backfired. This probably represents the cartoonist's viewpoint that the right to bear arms no longer is in keeping with the views of the men who wrote the Bill of Rights to the Constitution and who believed citizens had the right to have guns to protect themselves from the tyranny of the British government.

4. (3) The passage states that civilization started when people began to write. In order to have the time to learn to develop a writing system, people had to start growing their own food and give up a nomadic lifestyle.

5. (3) The Romans inherited many characteristics from the Etruscans, including techniques in architecture good roads, established trade routes, and farm land (1), (2), (4), and (5). However, the Etruscans had a king, not a republican government. The idea of a republic came from the Romans.

6. (4) The Roman Empire fell as a result of a combination of factors, including high unemployment and inflation (2), and attacks from barbarians (5). According to the passage, government administrators were not corrupt but were actually very capable (3). The corrupt emperors (1) did not affect the running of the empire.

7. (3) The definition of direct initiative tells you that it is appropriate for citizens to draft and present laws themselves.

8. (5) A political party's candidate for public office, including governor, must be first selected from a list of candidates in that party in a primary election.

9. (4) Voters can remove an elected public official from office before his or her term expires through the recall process. In this case, a majority of voters in an election would have had to approve of Governor Wilson's removal.

10. (4) Germany was able to gain territory in Europe in the 1930s. England and France were not willing to fight Germany on this issue. You can infer that England and France must have compromised in disputes over territory that Germany wanted.

11. (2) One curve is labeled supply, and the other is labeled demand. They are equal at the point of intersection (E), which represents equilibrium. The price at that point is $5,000.

12. (4) The circle graph indicates that more than half of Muslims (56 percent) are immigrants. The table lists California, New York, and Illinois as having a combined total Muslim population of 2.22 million, more than the combined total of the other states.

13. (2) The three states with the largest Muslim population also have the nation's three largest cities: New York, Los Angeles, and Chicago. None of the other answers can be verified from the data.

14. (1) The passage says, "The invention of the automobile and truck furthered the growth of suburbs."

15. (4) Because the passage describes the effects of new means of transportation on the growth of cities and their surrounding areas, choice (4) is the best answer.

16. (2) While (1), (4), and (5) are true, the Middle Ages are referred to as the Dark Ages because of the decline in education, trade, and scientific discoveries.

17. (2) This triangle indicates that there were fewer lords than vassals, and they were "on top," or had power over the vassals.

18. (1) The birth rate rose significantly from 1945 to 1955.

19. (5) The graph shows a stable death rate and a falling birthrate. Therefore, there is an overall decline in population.

20. (5) Lake Superior, at 1,330 feet, is the deepest of the Great Lakes.

21. (2) The sea level line on the cross-section passes through all the Great Lakes except Lake Erie.

22. (1) Both Washington and Eisenhower warn against allowing the military establishment to have too much influence on government. Washington says the military establishment is "hostile to republican liberty." Eisenhower says that the military-industrial complex must not be allowed to acquire too much power.

23. (2) Although the poll on senatorial term limits dropped from 54 percent in 1947 to 49 percent in 1964, the overall trend was up.

24. (1) The large number of Americans in favor of some kind of term limits for U.S. senators and representatives seems likely to bring about a constitutional amendment.

25. (3) The public is willing to accept people who are not experienced politicians to represent them in Washington. But the public would not hire doctors, lawyers, or mechanics with no experience.

26. (5) Latin American influence in the Southwest was evident long before the twentieth century. A history of interaction with Mexico goes back over a hundred years.

27. (3) The main idea of the cartoon is expressed in the last statement: small farmers have become as out of date as mules. The bill on the farmer's cap is labeled "small farmer."

28. (3) The author complains that criminals are too often let back on the streets because of legal technicalities.

29. (3) The passage tells you that pollution from factories in the Midwest contributes to the acid rain problem in the East. The killing of forests by acid rain could lead to water shortages in eastern cities.

30. (4) The passage describes a relationship in which an action of people (pollution) affects nature, creating a result that in turn affects other people (creates water shortages).

31. (1) The passage states that the Continental Divide in the United States separates rivers flowing east and west.

32. (3) The first sentence says, "A balance sheet is a financial statement. Businesses use it to summarize their financial position at different points in time." The other choices only mention individual pieces of information that can be found on a balance sheet.

33. (4) The passage gives you the formula: assets – liabilities = net worth. Using the formula, $75,000 – $53,000 = $22,000.

POSTTEST

34. (4) The passage tells you that the Radical Republicans were the strongest supporters of civil rights for blacks.

35. (1) You are told that the Freedmen's Bureau was an agency that helped blacks to make the transition from slavery to citizenship. You can guess that helping them learn to read and write would serve this purpose.

36. (2) Although the bakery has the highest score in the "number in favor" column, people said they would spend more money per week at the drugstore.

37. (2) Speakers A and B agree that people are less loyal to the major political parties than they used to be, but they interpret the trend differently. Speaker A is worried that the result will be a lack of political stability, and Speaker B is pleased at the possibility that the major parties will become more responsive.

38. (2) The reforms the Populists wanted were economic: an increase in the amount of money in circulation, government ownership of railroads, and laws against foreigners owning land.

39. (2) The first sentence states that there was a worldwide fall in farm prices.

40. (4) This paragraph is about voting rights for women, so you can infer, that *suffrage* means "the right to vote."

41. (1) The last sentence tells you that some people opposed women's suffrage because they thought political activity would interfere with women's spiritual purity. The other answers are not supported by the information in the passage.

42. (3) The second sentence says that the goal of the organization was to guarantee world peace.

43. (5) The passage states that "Congress did not want the foreign policy of the United States to be tied to the articles of the league."

44. (4) The Atlantic Charter's call for collective security later became the basis for the United Nations, founded at the end of World War II. The UN was modeled after the League of Nations, an indication that Wilson's idea was not dead.

45. (2) The passage describes how pioneers' use of personal diaries provide a sense of their feelings and experiences.

46. (1) Words such as *incredible, triumph,* and *creativity* let you know of the author's respect for the bravery the pioneers needed for those journeys.

47. (4) The passage clearly states that the real problem could be the failure of nations to pursue the necessary economic, trade, and research policies to ensure that resources reach the people who need them.

48. (1) A process of elimination leaves only choice (1), that PCs will be as common as radios and TVs. None of the other choices follow the line of thought in the passage.

49. (3) The graph shows that with the number of farms declining from 1940 to 1992, there are fewer farm families.

50. (3) The implication of the second paragraph of the passage is that a vaccine such as that discovered by Salk for polio and Jenner for smallpox must also be discovered to kill the HIV virus that causes AIDS.

Evaluation Chart

On the following chart, circle the number of any item you got wrong. Next to each item, you will see the pages you can review for items that gave you trouble. Pay special attention to skills on which you missed half or more of the questions.

Skill Area/ Content Area/	Comprehension (pages 17–32)	Application (pages 33–47)	Analysis (pages 49–66)	Evaluation (pages 67–76)
U.S. History (pages 79–149)	34, 38, 49,	35	26, 46	45
World History (pages 151–197)	5, 10, 42, 43		4, 17, 44, 50	6, 16
Civics & Government (pages 199–236)	7, 23, 40, 41	9	8, 22, 28, 37	3, 24, 25
Geography (pages 237–262)	12, 14, 18, 20, 21, 29, 31, 47		13, 19	15, 30
Economics (pages 263–296)	11, 27, 32		2, 33, 36, 49	48

Answer Key

Chapter 1

COMPREHENDING SOCIAL STUDIES MATERIALS

Exercise 1, Page 18

1. (1) The passage speaks of the alarming rate of increase in teenage suicide—now the third highest cause of death among youths 15 to 19 years old—while attention has been focused on drug abuse and pregnancy. These clues indicate that this is a new trend.
2. (4) The topic in answer (4) is the most logical follow-up story.

Exercise 2, Page 21

1. about 550,000
2. 1955
3. 1960, 1965, 1970
4. 1990

Exercise 3, Page 23

1. T
2. F   They settled in Florida and the Southwest.
3. T
4. T
5. F   They came from Italy, Greece, and Russia.
6. T
7. T
8. F   They came after the United States became an independent nation.
9. T
10. T

Exercise 4, Page 24

1. 1861
2. victories
3. Missouri Compromise
4. Kansas-Nebraska
5. Dred Scott
6. territories

PRE-GED Practice
Exercise 5, Page 26

1. (1) The overall figures show more immigrants coming from Europe, about 63 percent.
2. (3) Nearly half (47%) came from Latin America and the Caribbean.
3. (3) The percentage of persons coming to the United States from Latin America and the Caribbean during 1981–1990 was 47 percent, a 29 percent increase over the broad period 1820–1992.
4. (1) The graph on the left gives you this information.

PRE-GED Practice
Exercise 6, Page 28

1. (5) The number of persons described as strong Democrats fell from 20 percent to 15 percent in the 1970s but went back up to 20 percent by 1990.
2. (3) The number of persons defined as strong Republicans dropped from 14 percent in 1988 to 10 percent in 1990.
3. (1) The figures in the passage indicate that although the number of people who call themselves strong Democrats and strong Republicans tends to rise and fall, it does not break up the two parties. The number of people who call themselves independents rises and falls too.

Exercise 7, Page 30

1. (3) The word *nondenominational* in the passage refers to prayer. This kind of prayer does not refer to God in a specific way nor does it mention figures pertaining to any of the major religions. You could infer that nondenominational means not belonging to any particular religious group.
2. (3) Nomadic peoples are defined as those who migrate back and forth from one area to another.

PRE-GED Practice
Exercise 8 , Pages 31–32

1. (4) All the other choices either are inaccurate according to the graph or cannot be supported by the information in the graph.
2. (4) Only this answer choice covers the main idea of the graph. Choices (1), (2), and (5) make assumptions or include information not given on the graph. Choice (3), while a true statement, identifies only one piece of information, not the main idea.
3. (2) None of the other choices is supported by the graph.
4. (4) According to the graph, these two categories combined add up to 18 percent.
5. (3) The words *stretches over* in the passage give you the sense of a connected or continuous area. Since the megalopolis includes many cities, it would have to include suburban areas lying between the cities.
6. (3) The urban areas mentioned are New York, Philadelphia, Newark, and Baltimore. These are described as cities.

Chapter 2

APPLYING SOCIAL STUDIES IDEAS

Exercise 1, Pages 34–35

1. (4) The passage states that "The most important method [of improving productivity] has been the introduction of modern technology." You can apply this idea to the information that if Japan led the United States in the area of modern technology, the Japanese economy would grow faster because of its higher level of productivity.
2. (3) In the second paragraph, the passage tells you that "the introduction of modern technology, such as computers, is leading to increased manufacturing productivity."
3. (2) Measuring workers' output shows the amount of work per hour of labor. It does not necessarily increase productivity.

Exercise 2, Pages 38–39

1. T
2. F Gold mines are located in the northern and southern part of the country, where there are no coal mines.
3. F None of Australia's natural resources are found in the interior of the country.
4. F The map only shows the location of natural gas in Australia.
5. F Zinc mines are also located in the northern part of Australia.
6. F The symbols on the map and key show that more uranium than bauxite is produced.
7. F Very little cobalt is produced in Australia (only one symbol is shown).
8. T
9. F All of Australia's forests are located in its outer regions.
10. T
11. F This map doesn't show Australia's imports—only its natural resources.
12. F This map doesn't compare Australia's resources with those of other countries.

Exercise 3, Pages 42–43

1. China
2. United States, United Kingdom
3. Israel
4. China and Nigeria
5. Colombia, Mexico
6. 10 percent
7. United Kingdom
8. El Salvador
9. 1991
10. The percentage of people moving from rural areas to urban areas increased for most countries during this time period.

PRE-GED Practice
Exercise 4, Pages 44–47

1. (2) The bar graph shows lower figures for the Korean War (157,000) and Persian Gulf War (760).

2. (1) The Civil War was the most costly in the ratio of casualties to number serving—nearly one out of every three.

3. (5) Fewer than 500,000 soldiers served in the Persian Gulf War.

4. (3) The bar graph on the right shows that there were about 1 million, 5 thousand casualties during the Civil War and about 1 million, 110 thousand casualties during World War II.

5. (5) The bar graph on the left shows that about 8.7 million persons served during the Vietnam War.

6. (3) There were about 320,000 casualties during World War I.

7. (2) This is the only choice supported by the data on the graph. The bars for casualties are highest for the Civil War and World War II.

8. (3) The Pawnee were in the region cutting through the center of the map. The key shows that the Plains Indians lived in this region.

9. (1) The farthest northern parts of the map match the Eskimo and Aleut section of the key.

10. (5) If you check the Southwest Indians portion of the map, you will find the Hopi Indians there.

11. (1) The map key shows that the Cherokee were part of the Eastern Forest Indians.

12. (4) This answer is the only one supported by the information in the graph.

13. (2) This answer contains the regions that have the highest life expectancies.

Chapter 3

ANALYZING SOCIAL STUDIES MATERIALS

Exercise 1, Page 50

1. F
2. O
3. O
4. F
5. F
6. O
7. F

Exercise 2, Page 51

Middle Ages: rich people—inner city; working classes and the poor—outer edge

Early 20th century: wealthy people—suburbs; poor people—inner cities

Recent 20th century : rich people—central part of cities; poor people—outer edges

Exercise 3, Pages 53–54

1. (3) The table shows that consumption of poultry products rose from 33.8 pounds in 1970 to 55.9 pounds in 1990, a rise of more than 50 percent.

2. (2) The table shows that Americans are eating less meat and more fruits and vegetables.

3. (4) The table shows that from 1980 to 1990, Americans ate more fresh fruit and more fish.

4. (3) Americans decreased their consumption of red meat.

PRE-GED Practice
Exercise 4, Page 55

1. (2) The passage explains that infant mortality has dropped considerably because public health measures have reduced diseases.

2. (2) More young women will survive to child-bearing age, thus further increasing population growth.

PRE-GED Practice
Exercise 5, Page 56

1. (4) The first event in the sequence, the discovery of Soviet missile bases in Cuba, was followed by President Kennedy's naval blockade of Cuba.

2. (1) The United States ended the naval blockade of Cuba after the Soviet Union had not only withdrawn the missiles but had also dismantled the bases.

Exercise 6, Pages 59–60

1. (4) U.S. per capita income was at its highest in 1989.
2. (2) The lines in graph 2 match the figures in the table.
3. (2) It increased by about $2,000.
4. (1) Only the fact that per capita income dropped in 1990 after steady upward growth in the 1980s can be inferred from the graph.

Exercise 7, Page 61

1. 1987–1989
2. 1993–1995
3. Yes, during 1993–1995
4. 1981–1983; 1993–1995
5. The Republican membership increased.

PRE-GED Practice
Exercise 8, Page 63

1. (2) The Catholic Church was tied closely to the Spanish government, and the Catholic religion was taught in schools. From this information, you can infer that the traditional religion of the country is Catholicism.
2. (2) Because a new constitution after Franco's death did away with the special position of the Catholic Church, you can infer that the church had a special place while Franco was in power.
3. (5) This is the only sport mentioned that does not center on the abundance of lakes in the area.
4. (4) All of the other industries are mentioned in the passage except for foresting timber.

PRE-GED Practice
Exercise 9, Pages 65–66

1. (3) An implication of the passage is that when you buy something that you plan to pay off a month at a time, you should be sure you will be able to pay the amount of the monthly installment.

2. (3) You can conclude from the last sentence that charging an item may increase the final cost because you will also be paying interest.
3. (2) The passage states that the children did what they saw others do, so children who are honest are imitating people around them who are honest.
4. (5) All the other statements are true.
5. (4) This is the only statement that is clearly supported by the graph.

Chapter 4

EVALUATING SOCIAL STUDIES MATERIALS

Exercise 1, Page 68

1. No. 1. The buyer did not make a written offer.
2. Yes. This situation represents a legal contract because both parties have agreed in writing to the terms of the contract.
3. No. 1 and 2. Besides not agreeing on the price, neither the buyer or the seller put anything in writing.

Exercise 2, Page 69

1. (3) This scenario has no bearing on his theory.
2. (1) This scenario would support Erikson's theory. Because the girl misses so much school, she is not able to take full advantage of the institution to help her grow away from her family.
3. (1) This scenario would support Erikson's theory. You can deduce from the fact that the student had a decent grade point average that the teenager was successful in school, and most likely, was then successful in separating from his or her parents. Thus, he or she was able to be successful in the military.

Exercise 3, Page 71

1. (2) The passage offers two theories for the rise in crime: (1) too many rewards for the criminal and too few reasons to do honest work and (2) crime results from social and economic conditions.

2. (2) This answer is supported by information given in the first sentence of the second paragraph.

Exercise 4, Page 73

1. (2) You need to examine the writer's descriptions of the two senators. The senator from North Carolina is confident, amiable, and strides briskly (a positive description). The senator from New York darts into sight, scurries, and huddles nervously (a negative description).
2. (3) Amiably means friendly and relaxed. The other words have negative connotations.

PRE-GED Practice
Exercise 5, Pages 75–76

1. (5) Sentences 1, 5, and 6 show the writer's bias.
2. (5) The passage states that only the Democratic and the Republican parties have ever controlled Congress and every president during the past century has belonged to one of the two parties. This shows the considerable strength and support the two parties have had and continue to have in the United States.
3. (2) The author's opinions in several sentences clearly indicate the author's bias toward the two-party system.
4. (3) The sign in the cartoon and the desolate location of the smoker show the main idea of the cartoon, which is that there are now far fewer areas in which people are allowed to smoke.
5. (5) Judging from the picture of "Uncle Sam" sitting at the loan officer's desk and the worried look on the other customers' faces, you can assume that the cartoonist believes that the Social Security system is going broke.
6. (3) The best choice is that the cartoonist has little faith in the Social Security system.

Chapter 5

U.S. HISTORY

Exercise 1, Page 81

Comprehension
1. Columbus
2. gold and silver
3. to pay for their passage from Europe
4. Indentured servants bind themselves by a contract to work for a master for a certain number of years; slaves were brought to the Americas by force, and most of them were enslaved for the rest of their lives.
5. France
6. England
7. to establish religious communities
8. between 50 and 75 percent
9. Spain

Exercise 2, Page 83

Comprehension
1. (1) The English followed the policy of mercantilism, which means that the colonies exist for the good of the mother country and should buy English manufactured goods.
2. (3) The passage refers to representative bodies as centers of opposition to English policies.
3. (3) France lost most of its North American territories to England.
4. (2) Seventeenth century colonists also bought manufactured goods.

Exercise 3, Page 85

Comprehension
1. (b)
2. (d)
3. (e)
4. (a)
5. (c)

Comprehension

6. (3) The passage states clearly that the colonists dumped the tea into Boston Harbor to protest against unfair laws such as the Sugar Act, the Stamp Act, and the Tea Act.

Analysis

7. (2) The only correct answer is that Spain's colonies in Latin America also rebelled.

Exercise 4, Page 86

Comprehension

1. (3) The passage states that "unalienable rights" are provided by their Creator, and thus cannot be taken away. All the other choices deal directly with human involvement.

Application

2. (1) and (3)

The Declaration of Independence allows the people the right to change or abolish the existing government. Choice (2) is incorrect because the United States does not have a monarch, it is also false because monarchs cannot be appointed. While choices (4) and (5) may occur, they are not recommended by the Declaration of Independence.

Exercise 5, Page 88

Comprehension

1. English colonies, Africa, West Indies
2. Molasses was used to make rum, which in turn was traded in Africa for slaves.
3. They provided cheap labor.
4. They made voyages on which they profited by 100 percent to 1,000 percent.
5. The profits from slavery financed England's industrial growth.
6. Slavery ended after the Civil War.

Exercise 6, Page 90

Comprehension

1. (3) British control of forts on the Great Lakes and French control of the Mississippi River posed the most serious problems.

2. (2) The last paragraph says that Americans united around national instead of regional interests after the War of 1812.

Application

3. (1) Governments facing a divided nation have used war against foreign enemies to temporarily unite the country.

Exercise 7, Page 93

Analysis

1. (3) The North was most opposed to the annexation of Texas.

Evaluation

2. (1) The Northern states were opposed to having another slave-owning Southern state in the Union.

PRE-GED Practice
Exercise 8, Page 95

Comprehension

1. (1) The passage states that the extension of voting rights was limited to white males.

Analysis

2. (1)

Exercise 9, Page 95

Comprehension

1. (c)
2. (b)
3. (e)
4. (a)
5. (d)

Exercise 10, Pages 96–97

Analysis

1. (1) The letter mentions "teams starting for several days," and that he got some information from "some distance on the prairies." You can infer that this route was well-known.

2. (2) The writer mentions that there was "little or no old grass to be had as it has been eaten and burned off." From this you can infer their need to bring along feed for the animals.

3. (1) They appear to be charging a lot for necessities. The writer mentions that some things are cheaper but "They put the screws very tight to emigrants for all small jobs and articles the emigrants are obliged to get."

4. (4) The first sentence of the second paragraph mentions these items that can be had "to some better advantage."

Exercise 11, Page 99

Comprehension

1. T
2. T
3. F It limited slavery to the land stretching west from the southern border of Missouri only.
4. T
5. T
6. T
7. F Brown failed in his attempt to arm the slaves for rebellion.
8. F Douglass was an eloquent speaker who toured the North, raising support for abolitionism.

PRE-GED Practice
Exercise 12, Page 100

Comprehension

1. (3) They believed that if they did not secede, slavery would certainly be abolished when more free states were admitted to the Union.

2. (1) The passage states that the Emancipation Proclamation helped to undermine the South.

Exercise 13, Page 102

Comprehension

1. (e)
2. (d)
3. (b)
4. (a)
5. (c)

PRE-GED Practice
Exercise 14, Page 102

Evaluation

1. (3) The table shows the largest percent of difference under iron and steel.

2. (4) The table shows that the North was clearly ahead in all areas of economic development.

Exercise 15, Pages 103–104

Comprehension

1. (4) Despite the humorous, satiric tone, the author's main point is that he knows he was exploited in the past and has no intention of letting it happen again.

Analysis

2. (2) At the end of the letter Anderson says, "there was never any pay-day for the Negroes anymore than for horses or cows."

Exercise 16, Page 105

Comprehension

1. T

Analysis

2. T

Evaluation

3. T

PRE-GED Practice
Exercise 17, Page 107

Comprehension

1. (3) The passage states that the McCormick Reaper "revolutionized . . . agriculture by mechanizing the farm."

Evaluation

2. (5) The last sentence of the fourth paragraph says that new immigrants often faced poverty and discrimination (an unexpected hardship), but they did not come to America looking for it.

Analysis

3. (2) The opposite was true. Monopolies raised prices and kept wages low.

Comprehension

4. (4) This is the main idea of the passage: how industrialization affected the economy, population distribution, social classes, and politics.
5. (2) The growth and centralization of industry hastened the growth of cities.

Evaluation

6. (2) This is an inference about how historical change takes place. Change in a major part of society, such as the economy, generally affects all other areas of society.

Exercise 18, Page 108

Comprehension

1. part of their crop
2. Jim Crow laws
3. poll taxes, literacy tests
4. South

Exercise 19, Page 110

Analysis

1. (4) The passage points out that the workers and farmers were organizing against the power of monopolies and that these groups supported the Populist Party.

Application

2. (3) The American experience showed that widespread change and social turmoil goes along with industrialization.

Comprehension

3. (3) The passage describes the use of police, militia, and federal troops.

Evaluation

4. (4) In rural areas, people protested the high cost of credit.

Exercise 20, Page 111

Comprehension

1. 1901–1910
2. 1821–1830

Evaluation

3. (2) The passage discusses urbanization in the late nineteenth and early twentieth centuries. The graph shows a high rate of immigration at the same time.

Exercise 21, Page 112

Comprehension

1. (c)
2. (d)
3. (a)
4. (b)
5. (e)

Exercise 22, Page 114

Comprehension

1. F   Industrialization and urbanization worsened social conditions.
2. T
3. F   There existed a very small class of wealthy industrialists and a large new class of poorly paid workers.
4. T
5. T
6. F   In 1900, the United States replaced Great Britain as the leading industrial producer in the world.
7. F   Henry Ford developed the first modern factory production line.
8. T
9. T
10. F   Political institutions that had been suitable for farmers and small businesses could no longer deal with the problems of a large-scale industrial society.

PRE-GED Practice
Exercise 23, Page 116

Comprehension

1. (4) The passage states that Theodore Roosevelt believed the Republicans had given up on reform, so he formed a third party, the Progressive (Bull Moose) Party.

Application

2. (5) The passage says that progressivism led to a course between private business doing as it pleased and placing large parts of the economy under government control.

Comprehension

3. (3) The essay points out that limited local resources at the local level caused the reformers to turn to the federal government for help.

4. (2) The third sentence of the third paragraph gives you this information.

Exercise 24, Page 117

Comprehension

1. (2) The speaker says, "we have no faith in man's protection. . . . Give us the ballot, and we will protect ourselves."

Evaluation

2. (3) Women often worked on production tasks at home. It was cheaper for many employers because working conditions and hours were not regulated.

Exercise 25, Page 119

Comprehension

1. Spain
2. Hawaii
3. gunboat diplomacy
4. imperialism
5. foreign trade, colonial empire
6. European colonization, interference
7. Africa, Asia
8. Spain
9. Mark Twain

Exercise 26, Page 120

Comprehension

1. arrows on the map and the map key
2. 1983
3. Puerto Rico, Virgin Islands, Guantánamo Bay

Analysis

4. (2) The number of military interventions, establishment of a military base at Guantánamo Bay in Cuba, and the building of the Panama Canal indicate great U.S. interest in the Caribbean region, as an outgrowth of the Monroe Doctrine.

PRE-GED Practice
Exercise 27, Page 122

Comprehension

1. (1) The passage discusses swings between involvement and isolationism in world affairs.

Comprehension

2. (2) The United States tried to stay out of World War I, but loss of U.S. lives from increased German submarine attacks forced it to join the war on the side of the Allies.

Exercise 28, Page 123

Comprehension

1. T   The passage refers to mass production and the eagerness of Americans to buy new products.

Analysis

2. T   President Coolidge made this remark, and the passage makes it clear that consumerism, migration, etc., all fed a booming economy—a good climate for business.

Comprehension

3. F   The passage states that women found jobs in the expanding economy.

Analysis

4. F   African Americans left the South in large numbers and their culture influenced the country as a whole.

Comprehension

5. T   The passage states that Congress passed strict immigration quotas.
6. T   Many writers became expatriates in Europe during this time.
7. T   Swing is described as a form of jazz that became popular with whites. Jazz was brought to the North by Southern blacks.

Exercise 29, Page 125

Analysis

1. (3) The passage states that the United States had no unemployment insurance and no Social Security; and that private relief agencies had difficulty caring for so many people. You can infer that private charitable organizations bore the brunt of public welfare when the Depression began.

2. (1) The first graph shows that unemployment rose, while the second graph shows that the gross national product declined.

Comprehension

3. (3) The passage states that the New Deal established the idea that government had a role to play in keeping people economically secure.

Exercise 30, Page 127

Comprehension

1. (d)
2. (a)
3. (f)
4. (b)
5. (g)
6. (c)
7. (e)
8. (k)
9. (h)
10. (i)
11. (l)
12. (j)

Exercise 31, Page 128

Analysis

1. (3) This passage describes how a complicated strike was organized and was eventually successful.

Evaluation

2. (1) The strikers had support outside the plant.

Exercise 32, Page 130

Comprehension

1. F The passage states that the two countries became hostile when the war ended.

2. F They were called satellites.

3. T The passage states that the containment policy was drawn up to limit communism to areas where it was already established.

4. F NATO was the military alliance; the Marshall Plan was economic aid to help Europe rebuild after World War II.

Analysis

5. T The passage does not say directly that the Korean War was fought to contain communism, but the entire discussion is about a Cold War to contain it.

Exercise 33, Page 131

Analysis

1. (2) The United States found containing communism of greater concern than supporting countries trying to be free of colonial powers. When the Soviet Union supported nationalism, the United States was against it.

Comprehension

2. (3) The passage states that many elements complicated Third World conflict in addition to nationalism. None of the other choices is correct.

3. (4) The last paragraph states that Fidel Castro set up a communist government in Cuba in 1959.

Exercise 34, Page 133

Comprehension

1. South Vietnam
2. South Vietnam
3. domino theory

Evaluation

4. at home

Exercise 35, Page 135

Part A

Comprehension

1. (b)
2. (e)
3. (d)
4. (c)
5. (f)
6. (a)

Part B

Comprehension

1. Nixon
2. Solidarity
3. prices, output
4. Mikhail Gorbachev

Exercise 36, Page 136

Evaluation

(4) The sign on the pile of bricks on the left in the cartoon says "Never Again." On the right, a new wall to keep out immigrants is being built. The cartoonist is implying that Germany has not learned its lesson from the past in facing current immigration problems.

PRE-GED Practice
Exercise 37, Page 139

Evaluation

1. (2) The last sentence in the first paragraph says that his colleagues condemned his actions.
2. (1) The "cost in American involvement" refers both to people's lives that were lost and to the high monetary cost of the war.

Exercise 38, Page 141

Comprehension

1. segregation, public
2. nonviolent

Evaluation

3. successful
4. widespread

Exercise 39, Page 142

Analysis

1. (2) The figure in the chair (representing the taxpayer) cannot read the bottom line after "will cost" and so does not know the cost of Clinton's health care plan.

Evaluation

2. (3) The cartoonist may or may not favor Clinton's health care plan but he is definitely concerned about its cost and implies that Clinton doesn't know how much it will cost either.

Exercise 40, Page 144

Comprehension

1. (4) The increase from 1980 to 1990 of $2,358.4 billion is larger than in any other ten-year period.

Evaluation

2. (2) World War II (1941–1945) accounted for the increase in the national debt from $42.9 billion in 1940 to $256.1 billion in 1950.

PRE-GED Practice
Exercise 41, Page 145

Comprehension

1. (3) Stoddart wanted the river cleaned up so that people could swim safely in it again.

Analysis

2. (1) Stoddart sparked the cleanup campaign, but she could not do it singlehandedly. Her solution was to build coalitions of business, labor, and the companies that caused the pollution.

Evaluation

3. (4) Environmental changes can be achieved in many ways, but you might infer that the more people work together and not against each other, the better chance they'll have of making changes.

READING EFFICIENCIES

Reading Efficiency A, Pages 146–147

1. (3)
2. (5)
3. (1)
4. (2)
5. (2)

Reading Efficiency B, Pages 148–149

1. (3)
2. (1)
3. (5)
4. (2)
5. (3)

Chapter 6

WORLD HISTORY

Exercise 1, Page 152

Comprehension
1. (2)
2. (1) The passage states that about 5,000 years ago, people created a system of letters and began to write history.
3. (3)
4. (1)
5. (3)

Exercise 2, Page 154

Comprehension
1. (3)
2. (1)

Exercise 3, Page 154

Comprehension
1. T The passage states that the fertile soil left after the Nile flooded made it possible for Egyptians to grow a wide variety of foods.
2. T
3. T
4. F The passage states that hieroglyphics was based on pictures.

Exercise 4, Page 156

Comprehension
1. d
2. a
3. c
4. e
5. b

Exercise 5, Page 158

Comprehension
1. republic
2. only the rich and powerful
3. northern Africa
4. government
5. peace
6. Roman general
7. the Ides of March

Exercise 6, Page 160

Comprehension
1. The Aryans invaded the Indus River valley and Chinese civilization began in the Hwang Ho valley of China.

Analysis
2. Buddha—he was born in 563 B.C., and Confucius was born in 551 B.C.

Comprehension
3. 200 B.C.

Exercise 7, Page 160

Answers will vary, but should include some of these points: both started in Asia, established stable settlements in river valleys, built cities, developed social classes, and created their own religious or philosophical traditions.

Exercise 8, Page 162

Comprehension
1. (3)
2. (4)
3. (1)
4. (4)

Exercise 9, Page 164

Comprehension
1. Constantinople, Cairo, Baghdad
2. north

Analysis
3. south

Exercise 10, Page 164

Comprehension
1. F
2. T
3. F
4. F
5. F

Exercise 11, Page 166

Comprehension
1. (c)
2. (g)
3. (b)
4. (f)
5. (i)
6. (d)
7. (e)
8. (h)
9. (j)
10. (a)

Exercise 12, Page 168

Comprehension
1. Middle Ages
2. this life
3. classic civilizations
4. the Catholic Church
5. was fixed and immovable
6. going over land
7. Asia

Exercise 13, Page 169

Comprehension
1. Marco Polo—20 years
2. Vasco Da Gama
3. John Cabot
4. south

Exercise 14, Page 171

Comprehension
1. Pascal
2. Galileo
3. 1676
4. the circulation of human blood
5. the astronomical telescope
6. Janssen
7. Germany

Exercise 15, Page 173

The correct order is:
  Bastille stormed by citizens
  Reign of Terror began
  Louis XVI executed
  Napoleon crowned emperor
  The Battle of Waterloo
  Napoleon sent to St. Helena

Exercise 16, Pages 173–174

Comprehension
1. T
2. T
3. F
4. T
5. T
6. T

Exercise 17, Page 175

Comprehension
1. (3) The text states that Shah Jahan had the Taj Mahal built as a tomb for his wife.
2. (1) The text states that power rested in the hands of the shogun.
3. (2)
4. (1) The text states that before Perry's visit, the Japanese cut themselves off from the rest of the world.
5. (2)

Exercise 18, Page 177

Comprehension
1. Industrialism, steam engine
2. textile
3. into cities, factories

Exercise 19, Page 179

Comprehension
1. (4)
2. (1)
3. (3)
4. (3) The passage states that Japan also became an imperial power.
5. (2)

Exercise 20, Page 181

Comprehension
1. Russia
2. France, Russia, Germany, Austria-Hungary
3. Germany
4. The United States by far. This was due mostly to its late entry into the war.

Exercise 21, Page 181

Comprehension
1. d
2. f
3. a
4. e
5. b
6. c

Exercise 22, Page 183

Comprehension
1. the execution of Nicholas
2. the death of Lenin
3. False
4. True

Exercise 23, Page 185

Comprehension
1. the Rhineland, Sudetenland, Austria, Czech lands
2. Czech lands
3. the Polish Corridor

Exercise 24, Page 187

Evaluation
1. The United States; The war was not fought on American soil.
Analysis
2. France, Great Britain, and the United States.
Comprehension
3. Soviet Union
4. Poland, Germany, and France
Evaluation
5. The United States dropped atomic bombs on two Japanese cities.

Exercise 25, Page 189

1. F
2. T
3. F
4. T
5. F
6. F
7. F
8. T
9. T
10. F

Exercise 26, Page 191

Comprehension
1. 15
2. Germany; Luxembourg
3. Luxembourg; Greece
4. Germany, Austria, and Luxembourg
5. 10

Exercise 27, Page 193

Comprehension
1. Europe
Analysis
2. Europe
3. 1.8 billion
4. Africa—its population will more than double

READING EFFICIENCIES

Reading Efficiency C, Pages 194–195

1. (5)
2. (2)
3. (4)
4. (3)
5. (2)

Reading Efficiency D, Pages 196–197

1. (1)
2. (4)
3. (3)
4. (5)
5. (4)

Chapter 7

CIVICS & GOVERNMENT

Exercise 1, Page 202

Comprehension
1. (c)
2. (b)
3. (d)
4. (a)
5. (f)
6. (e)

PRE-GED Practice
Exercise 2 , Page 204

Analysis
1. (1) A plurality is the greatest number of votes cast when there are more than two candidates, no one of which gets a simple majority.
Application
2. (3) A 30 out of 50 vote constitutes a three-fifths majority.
3. (3) The first section discussed direct democracy in which a simple majority is normally required to reach consensus.
4. (5) In a representative democracy, people select delegates to represent them.

Exercise 3, Page 207

Evaluation
1. I
2. P
3. P
4. T
5. T
6. I
7. I
8. I

Exercise 4, Page 208

Evaluation
1. (3) The writer believes that poor people do not vote in proportion to their numbers in the population. Consequently, they have much less political influence than groups that do tend to vote in proportion to their numbers.
Analysis
2. (1) If lower-income people voted in significant numbers, elected officials would have to pay more attention to their interests and there might be an expansion of programs serving the poor.

Exercise 5, Page 211
Comprehension

1. (c)
2. (d)
3. (e)
4. (b)
5. (a)

Exercise 6, Pages 213–214
Part I

Comprehension
1. Congress
2. Bill of Rights
3. flexibility
4. three-fourths
5. seventeen
6. eighteenth, twenty-first
7. two-thirds majority
8. slavery

Part II

Analysis
1. (1)
Evaluation
2. (2) Clause 2 states that no one will be forced to be a witness against himself or herself; therefore, he or she has the right to remain silent.

PRE-GED Practice
Exercise 7, Page 215

Comprehension
1. (1) The Supreme Court has used its power to define certain rights of people who have controversial ideas. There is not a unified viewpoint about what they mean.
2. (5) The cases concerning obscenity and pornography are discussed in terms of the right to free speech and a free press.

Exercise 8, Page 218

Comprehension
1. (3) Executive orders issued by the president have the effect of law.
2. (2) The vice president succeeds the president in the event of the president's death or a severe incapacity that prevents the president from functioning in office.
Application
3. (2) Hamilton described the process of a presidential veto and the procedure for override.
4. (2) Two four-year terms constitute eight years in office.

Exercise 9, Page 220

Comprehension
1. T
2. T
3. F   Congress does have the power to investigate the executive branch.
4. T
5. F   The Speaker of the House carries out this role.

Exercise 10, Page 222

Comprehension
1. presidential appointment
2. is
3. nine
4. circuit courts of appeals
5. the Supreme Court
6. misconduct
7. constitutionality
8. Senate

Exercise 11, Page 223

Comprehension
1. (1) The passage points out that some Supreme Court decisions were heavily influenced by political and historical developments.
2. (2) The passage places the court's *Plessy v. Ferguson* decision in the context of white supremacist prejudice in 1896.

Exercise 12, Page 225

Comprehension
1. federal
2. one-house
3. within the state
4. direct initiative

PRE-GED Practice
Exercise 13, Page 226

Comprehension
1. (1) Local governments are legal creations of the state.

Application
2. (3) The passage explains that legislation can be repealed by a referendum.
3. (5) The passage says that some states give their voters the right to recall unpopular elected officials.
4. (2) A city council that can overrule the mayor on key decisions describes a strong council/weak mayor form of city government.

Comprehension
5. (4) Public utilities fall within the realm of city and county governments.

Evaluation
6. (3) Intrastate commerce is a function of state governments.

Exercise 14, Page 228

Comprehension
1. (d)
2. (f)
3. (e)
4. (b)
5. (c)
6. (a)

Exercise 15 , Page 231

Comprehension
1. diplomatic, economic, and military
2. to maintain international peace and encourage friendly relations among nations
3. investigates world disagreements

4. Answers will vary. Possible answers include: to increase trade; to get help in economic development; to get a larger market for exported goods.

Analysis
5. NATO

Comprehension
6. 184
7. United Kingdom

PRE-GED Practice
Exercise 16, Page 232

Analysis
1. (2) Special districts have integrated specific functions on a local level.

Evaluation
2. (3) The author believes that this controversy has been with us for a long time and will continue.

Comprehension
3. (4) The passage mentions this in the first sentence of the third paragraph.

READING EFFICIENCIES

Reading Efficiency E, Pages 233–234

1. (2)
2. (2)
3. (1)
4. (5)
5. (3)

Reading Efficiency F, Pages 235–236

1. (5)
2. (3)
3. (4)
4. (2)
5. (4)

Chapter 8

GEOGRAPHY

Exercise 1, Page 239

Comprehension

1. equator
2. prime meridian
3. hemispheres
4. North Pole
5. equator, prime meridian

Exercise 2, Page 244

Comprehension

1. Belize. The map key confirms this.
2. toward the center. The mountains run like a spine down the center of Central America; coastal lowlands border the Pacific Ocean and the Caribbean Sea.
3. east. Panama City lies almost due east of San Jose.
4. Nicaragua. Lake Nicaragua and Lake Managua are in the southern part of the country.

Exercise 3, Pages 245–246

Comprehension

1. (4) The key uses a solid color to represent a range from 0 to 1,000 feet, which covers most of Mongolia.
2. (1) The vertical lines indicate the highest elevation. The only place these lines appear is in the western part of China.

Analysis

3. (4) The map shows that Russia touches China on the north. None of the other statements is supported by information on the map.
4. (1) While India is labeled on the map, it is clearly not part of East Asia. You can tell this by the lack of elevations in India and the fact that only a part of India is shown on the map.

Comprehension

5. (3) The large dot next to Beijing indicates that it is the capital city of China

Exercise 4 , Page 248

Evaluation

1. T
2. F The mortality rate measures deaths.
3. F The fertility rate measures the birth rate.
4. T
5. F A change in one part of the ecological system often has an effect on other parts of the system.
6. T

Exercise 5, Page 249

Comprehension

1. eastern. The map clearly indicates that most blacks lived in eastern Texas.
2. larger. The map and the map key show that South Carolina had more counties with black residents than Texas did.
3. Maryland. The graph and the key show that Maryland had a greater number of free blacks than Virginia had.

Analysis

4. Mississippi. The graph shows that there were more black slaves living in Mississippi than in Alabama in 1860.

Comprehension

5. Georgia. The solid black bar on the graph key shows that there were no free blacks living in Georgia.
6. Florida. The graph shows that very few blacks lived in Florida.

Exercise 6, Pages 250–251

Comprehension

1. T
2. T
3. F War also caused people to flee their homes. As refugees, they were a burden on countries that already had severe food shortages.
4. T
5. F Egypt and Saudi Arabia are not a part of the region described in the passage. Djibouti and Ethiopia are missing in the statement.

6. **F** The United States intervened in Somalia to end mass starvation. When the United States got involved in political strife in Somalia, the troops were pulled out.

7. **F** The first sentence of the paragraph above the map says that the Horn of Africa is west of the Arabian Peninsula. The map shows this also.

8. **T**

Exercise 7, Page 253

Comprehension

1. Washington, D.C.
2. rural areas (or the countryside)
3. Phoenix, Arizona
4. suburbs
5. transportation

PRE-GED Practice
Exercise 8, Page 254

Evaluation

1. (2) The passage describes how the altitude of Denver combines with the exhaust from automobiles to create air pollution.

Analysis

2. (4) Denver has an abundance of automobiles. Better public transportation would decrease the number of cars and thus ease pollution problems.

Comprehension

3. (2) This fact is stated in the second paragraph.
4. (2) This information is also given in the second paragraph.
5. (1) The second sentence in the last paragraph gives you this information.
6. (5) The last sentence of the first paragraph describes Denver as having become "one of America's most polluted cities."
7. (3) The last sentence of the passage says that people with respiratory problems have moved to the suburbs at lower altitudes.

PRE-GED Practice
Exercise 9, Pages 256–258

Comprehension

1. (2) The key and the pail symbols show that the three states that have the largest yearly allotment in million acre-feet of water are Arizona (2.8), California (4.4), and Colorado (3.8).

Analysis

2. (5) California. The table above the map shows that normal rainfall is 22.1 inches but the actual rainfall was 14.6 inches, or 7.5 inches below normal. This is more than any other state in the Colorado River Basin.

Comprehension

3. (4) The pie charts show that Utah uses 93.5 percent and Arizona 88.6 percent of the water allotment for agriculture.
4. (1) The boundary of the map shows that all three cities are in the Lower Basin.

Evaluation

5. (2) In years of lower rainfall, the river might not be able to handle the increased population, so strict cutbacks may have to be put into effect.

Analysis

6. (3) Wyoming has the least increase in total population, or 185,000. While New Mexico has a lower water allotment (0.8 percent) than Wyoming (1.0 percent), New Mexico also has a projected increase in population of 700,000, or 515,000 more than Wyoming by the year 2020.

Evaluation

7. (2) The first sentence of the last paragraph says that computers have been developed for predicting when El Niño will take place. It notes that computer models have begun to detect weather events 12 to 18 months ahead of their arrival.

Comprehension

8. (4) The first paragraph states that warming in the Pacific develops every four to seven years.

9. (1) The first paragraph notes that "the Pacific's hot and cold spells send ripples spreading through the world's atmosphere, altering weather around much of the globe."

10. (3) Paragraph two states that the El Niño of 1982–1983 was the biggest of the century and was caused by record warmth in the equatorial Pacific.

Analysis

11. (2) If El Niño occurs every four to seven years, then it should have occurred between 1997 and 2000.

Comprehension

12. (2) The last part of the first paragraph gives you this information.

13. (4) The last sentence of the second paragraph says that the El Niño of 1982 and 1983 caused more than $13 billion in damages.

READING EFFICIENCIES

Reading Efficiency G, Pages 259–260

1. (4)
2. (2)
3. (3)
4. (5)
5. (1)

Reading Efficiency H, Pages 261–262

1. (3)
2. (5)
3. (4)
4. (2)
5. (2)

Chapter 9

ECONOMICS

Exercise 1, Page 264

Comprehension

1. (3) The economy is the organized way in which goods and services are produced, distributed, sold, and used.

Application

2. (1) Economists would make predictions about how increased trade with Mexico would affect U.S. jobs, taxes, and other matters.

3. (2) Economists analyze the economics of different decisions. Choice (3) is incorrect because it involves day-to-day business rather than analysis and forecasting.

Exercise 2, Page 266

Comprehension

1. F Under capitalism, labor, like other commodities, is controlled by the market.

2. F Historically, economic systems have continuously changed. It's likely that change will continue. This statement is also false because the United States does not now have a pure capitalist economy.

3. T In the past, political systems were influenced by economic systems. This trend will probably continue in the future.

4. F In a socialist economy, business is controlled by the government. Business is not owned privately.

5. T In a market economy, workers are not tied to anyone or any place. They can sell their services to the highest bidder.

Exercise 3, Page 269

Analysis

1. (1) Graph 1 is the correct choice. It shows demand increasing as prices decrease. Graph 2 is incorrect because it shows demand increasing as prices increase. Graph 3 is incorrect because it shows price increasing at first then decreasing as demand increases.

2. (3) The events show that demand was high but the supply was low. A "seller's market" resulted because some people were willing to pay much higher prices for the toy.

Exercise 4, Page 271

Comprehension

1. (d)
2. (e)
3. (b)
4. (a)
5. (f)
6. (g)
7. (c)
8. (h)

Exercise 5, Page 273

Comprehension

1. increase. An increase in productivity means the business is operating more efficiently. That is, it's producing more goods with the same amount of labor or other costs. As a result, profits increase.
2. plans sales campaigns. They also work to increase sales.
3. seller that dominates the market.
4. lower production factors. This means that the employer pays less for materials, labor, or the other commodities needed to produce a product, so profits will increase. Laying off employees causes poor morale and can adversely affect productivity.
5. the total profits made. Making a profit is the purpose of business in a capitalist economy.

PRE-GED Practice
Exercise 6, Page 274

Comprehension

1. (2) Multinationals can move production abroad where labor costs are low.
2. (3) According to the essay, more than 25 percent of the assets of the largest corporations are invested abroad.
3. (4) The second paragraph says that direct U.S. foreign investments grew from $11 billion in 1950 to more than $486 billion in 1992 (an increase of $475 billion).

Exercise 7, Page 275

Comprehension

1. T   Credit and borrowing money are a source of economic growth. The multiplying effect helps expand the economy. Without it, the economy would not grow.
2. T   When a deposit is made, a bank loans the money, which is then deposited in another bank, which can then loan money, which is then deposited again, and so on.
3. T   Money is an asset that can be used to buy something. An asset is something a person has that has financial value.
4. F   The most important form of money is checks because they set up the multiplying effect.

Exercise 8, Pages 276–277

Application

1. (1) By increasing the money supply, the Fed would encourage people and businesses to borrow and spend more money. The result would be increased business activity and a growing economy.

Comprehension

2. (3) This is how the Federal Reserve controls money.

Analysis

3. (1) The diagram shows the multiplier effect that successive loans by banks increases the money supply.

Comprehension

4. (4) Bank D has the least amount of excess reserve ($410,000).

Exercise 9, Page 278

Comprehension

1. bull market. This happens when the value of stocks increases rapidly or by a large amount over a period of time.
2. bad shape. When the stock market does poorly, it usually indicates that the economy as a whole is not growing.
3. dividends. These are the profits paid by a company to investors who own stock, or shares, of the company.

Exercise 10, Page 280

Analysis

1. F The government provides public goods because they are needed by the public and either will not or should not be produced by private companies.
2. T Demand management is used to boost or limit economic growth.
3. T By removing money from the economy, the government can reduce the rate of economic growth, thereby controlling inflation.
4. F This is one of the functions of the government.
5. F No. When unemployment benefits are reduced, this slows down inflation.
6. T The second to last paragraph says that demand management is also called fiscal policy and that it's another way the government influences the economy.
7. T The first sentence of the passage says that although the United States has a market economy, it does not operate entirely according to market forces. The state and federal governments manage the economy in various ways.
8. F The third paragraph says that fire protection and air traffic control are important government services that private companies will not or should not provide.
9. T The fifth paragraph says that these are two factors of production that are controlled by government laws.

Exercise 11, Page 282

Comprehension

1. more than 40 percent
2. taxes
3. This is a regressive tax because it is the same for everyone.
4. through taxes
5. payments that transfer income from one group of people to another
6. about 2.4 trillion ($1.4 trillion by the federal government and $976 billion by state and local governments)

7. through savings bonds, treasury bills, and municipal bonds

Exercise 12, Page 283

1. sales tax
2. capital gains tax
3. income tax
4. capital gains tax
5. property tax

PRE-GED Practice
Exercise 13, Page 285

Comprehension

1. (2) The value of a house usually increases during times of inflation.

Application

2. (2) Discretionary income is the difference between fixed, or necessary, costs and total income ($2,000 − $1,550 = $450).
3. (1) The grasshopper had eaten up his discretionary income in immediate consumption and failed to budget for the long term.
4. (4) Fixed costs are expenses that you must pay on a regular basis. Money for vacations is likely to come out of discretionary income.

Exercise 14, Page 287

Comprehension

1. T According to the chart, about 44.2 percent of U.S. income was earned by the top 20 percent (highest fifth) of the population in 1991.
2. F The chart shows that in 1991, the top 40 percent of the population earned about 68.3 percent of total income.
3. T The poorest fifth of the population earned 4.8 percent of the total income in 1970 but only 4.5 percent in 1991.
4. F The main idea of the paragraph and chart is that the United States has a society made up of different economic classes. The facts demonstrate that income is not evenly distributed in the United States.

Exercise 15, Page 289

Comprehension

Choices (1), (2), and (4) are correct. Choice (3) is incorrect because many industrial workers lost their jobs, and many did find new jobs in the service industry However, jobs in the service industry rarely paid as much as jobs in manufacturing. Choice (5) is incorrect because the immediate effect of reduced international trade barriers has been an increase in the number of jobs in the United States.

Exercise 16, Page 290

Comprehension

1. T   Strikes are the most powerful tool unions have.
2. F   Fewer than 16 percent of American workers belong to unions.
3. T   Collective bargaining is the negotiating, or bargaining, process that takes place between unions and management.
4. T   Hiring practices are often included in labor agreements.
5. T   Many federal and state laws and agencies oversee the health and safety of American workers.
6. F   Management may represent a small business, a multinational corporation, or even a state or local government.
7. F   A labor contract is a legally binding agreement about the duties of labor and management that lasts for the term of the contract.
8. T   As once-powerful industries decline, so do their unions.

PRE-GED Practice
Exercise 17, Pages 291–292

1. (1) The chart indicates that by 1990, the GNP was $5,524,500,000,000, or more than $5½ trillion.
2. (3) The Net National Product is less than the GNP, and the column on the left shows that the GNP less the Capital Consumption Allowance equals the Net National Product.

3. (5) Since 1960, the GNP has approximately doubled every 10 years. By the year 2000, it should have equaled more than $11 trillion.
4. (2) From 1910 to 1920, the national debt increased by 2,100 percent.
5. (1) The chart shows that during 1900–1910 the national debt decreased by 8 percent and from 1920–1930 the national debt decreased by 33 percent.
6. (5) The national debt grew by more than $2 trillion from 1980–1990.
7. (4) World Wars I and II were major causes of the debt. Military spending during the 1980s added billions more to the debt.
8. (1) Since past recessions added to the debt, it is likely another will also increase the national debt.

READING EFFICIENCIES

Reading Efficiency I, Pages 293–294

1. (1)
2. (3)
3. (2)
4. (5)
5. (2)

Reading Efficiency J, Pages 295–296

1. (5)
2. (4)
3. (2)
4. (2)
5. (4)

Using the Reading Efficiency Activities

Contemporary's Reading Efficiency Activities will help increase your reading speed and your comprehension accuracy. The activities are similar to the reading passages and questions you will find on the GED Test.

Your goal is to complete each exercise in less than 10 minutes. You should also answer at least 4 of the questions correctly. If you can always score within this range (within the shaded areas of the Efficiency Factor Chart), you should be successful with the readings and the number of questions on each GED Test.

Once you know the amount of time it took you to complete the activity and the number of questions you answered correctly, look at the Efficiency Factor Chart. Find your time along the left side and your number of correct answers along the top. If your time falls between two of the times on this chart, round up to the higher time. Move across and down until your time and number correct meet. This is your E-Factor.

Find where your E-Factor fits on the Efficiency Factor Grid. Make a dot to the right of that number on the line below the number of the Reading Efficiency Activity you completed.

As you read other Activities, mark your E-Factor and connect the dots to create a line graph. You should see a line that moves upward as it crosses the grid. If your E-factor is not improving, ask your teacher what you can do to increase either your speed or your accuracy.

EFFICIENCY FACTOR (E-FACTOR) CHART

Number Correct

Reading Time	0	1	2	3	4	5
6.0	0	33	67	99	133	167
6.5	0	31	62	92	123	154
7.0	0	29	57	86	114	143
7.5	0	27	53	80	107	133
8.0	0	25	50	75	100	125
8.5	0	24	47	71	94	118
9.0	0	22	44	67	89	111
9.5	0	21	42	63	84	105
10.0	0	20	40	60	80	100
10.5	0	19	38	57	76	95
11.0	0	18	36	55	73	91
11.5	0	17	35	52	70	87
12.0	0	17	33	50	67	83

READING EFFICIENCY

EFFICIENCY FACTOR (E-FACTOR) GRID

Reading #: A B C D E F G H I J

170
165
160
155
150
145
140
135
130
125
120
115
110
105
100
95
90
85
80
75
70
65
60
55
50
45
40
35
30
25
20
15

E-Factor ___ ___ ___ ___ ___ ___ ___ ___ ___ ___

Glossary

A

abdicate: to give up a throne

abolitionist: member of an antislavery movement before the Civil War

absolute monarchy: a type of government in which the king or queen's word is the law

alliance: an agreement between nations to come to the aid of an ally if that ally is attacked

analyze: to break something down into its basic parts to better understand the meaning of the whole

annexation: taking over of lands not originally part of a country

apply: to use information from one situation to explain or understand information in another

armistice: a stopping of fighting between countries

arms race: a continuous buildup of large amounts of weapons and of a huge military force by one country in order to gain an advantage over another country

assets: total resources of a person or a business

B

bar graph: a graph that compares quantities by using bars of different lengths

bicameral: composed of two houses or legislative parts

Bill of Rights: the first ten amendments to the U.S. Constitution that state the freedoms and rights of individuals

Brown v. Board of Education: the unanimous Supreme Court decision in 1954 that struck down racial segregation in public schools

C

capital goods: goods and services companies buy to use in producing other goods and services

capitalism: an economic system based on private ownership of property

Cathedral: the main Christian church in a town or city

cause and effect: the process of showing how one event causes another event to happen

character: the personal values that make a person decide how to behave

checks and balances: a system among the branches of the federal government that prevents any one branch from dominating the other two

Christianity: the religion founded on the teachings of Jesus

circle graph: a graph that shows how a total amount of something is divided into parts

city-state: an independent Greek city with its own government and laws

civilization: an advanced state of human living in which people have cities and an organized government

Cold War: the period of conflict between the superpowers of the United States and the former Soviet Union and their allies after World War II

collective bargaining: a meeting between labor representatives and employers to settle disputes about hours, wages, and working conditions

collectives: Russian farms run by large groups of peasants working together

colonization: the act of one country taking over direct control of another

commodities: goads and services for which ownership can be traded or exchanged

communism: a system practiced in the former Soviet Union in which private ownership of property and the means of production was not permissible

comparison: the process of examining similarities

compass rose (direction arrow): a drawing on a map that uses abbreviations to show directions compound interest: the interest that is figured for a period of time based on the total of the principal plus any interest that has been earned over a period of time

compound interest: the interest that is figured for a period of time based on the total of the principal plus any interest that has been earned over a period of time

comprehend: to understand what something means

constitutional monarchy: a limited monarchy that has constitutional checks upon the ruler

consumer goods: goods and services that people buy for their own use

containment: U.S. foreign policy to block further expansion of communism after World War II

context: the words surrounding an unknown word that help define the word

continent: a large continuous landmass that makes up part of Earth's surface

contour map: shows changes in elevation of a land surface by a series of lines representing different heights

contrast: the process of looking at differences between people, things, or ideas

Crusades: a series of campaigns to recapture the Holy Lands from the Muslims

culture: all the beliefs, values, ideas, customs, knowledge, and traditions of a society

D

demand: the desire and ability of consumers to buy a product or service

demand management: government actions to influence how much demand there is in the economy; also called fiscal policy

democracy: a form of government in which the people rule

demography: the statistical study of the size, growth, movement, and distribution of human population

detente: a policy that called for more peaceful cooperation between the United States and the former Soviet Union

dictatorship: a form of government in which a dictator or ruler has complete control

diplomatic recognition: a government's formal recognition of another country's government, including the exchange of ambassadors

direct democracy: a democracy in which the people have a direct voice and vote in the government

direct initiative: the process. that allows citizens to draft laws by obtaining enough signatures on a petition to present the law directly to the voters

discretionary income: the difference in a budget between fixed costs and income

dividends: payments made from a company's profits

domino theory: the argument noted by President Eisenhower that if one nation faces great danger, so will its neighbor and then the next country until a whole region falls

drawing conclusions: predicting the outcome of events or determining the relationship of facts in a passage

Dred Scott case: the controversial 1857 Supreme Court decision ruling that slaves were not citizens and that slaves were the property of their masters

E

ecological system: the relationships between living things and their environment

economics: the study of how people produce, distribute, and consume goods and services

economy: the organized way in which a society produces, distributes, and consumes goods and services

editorial (political) cartoons: drawings that express an opinion and bring attention to a social or political problem

electoral college: a special group of voters from each state that elects the president and vice president

equator: 0° of latitude that divides Earth into Northern and Southern Hemispheres

equilibrium: the price at which supply equals demand

equity: the value in property after debt and other liabilities are paid

ethnic background: the racial or cultural origins of people

ethnic cleansing: widespread murder meant to eliminate certain ethnic groups

ethnocentrism: the act of judging another society by one's own standards

Euro: the new European currency meant to replace national currencies

European Union: the current European organization that promotes economic growth and free trade

evaluate: judge the value or logic of an idea

evaluation of logic: a judgment of the way writers present and use their ideas

F

fact: a statement that can be proved

factors of production: the things needed to make a product

fascism: a political system that always puts the state above the individual, and which usually has a dictator to carry out its social and economic policies

federal system: the sharing of power between the states and the central government

fertility rate: the rate of births in a particular time and place

feudalism: a complex system for organizing medieval society around shared obligations between lords and vassals

G

geography: the study of Earth; namely, its physical description and the places on it

global culture: certain customs and desires shared by many of the world's people

globe: a round model of Earth's surface

government: the body or institution that makes and administers society's laws

gross domestic product (GDP): the amount of all goods and services produced within a country in one year

gross national product (GNP): the amount of all goods and services produced by a country in one year

guerrilla: a person who carries out acts of sabotage, strike-and-run military action, or terror against the enemy

guillotine: a device used by the French to behead people

gunboat diplomacy: U.S. practice of sending troops into countries of the Western Hemisphere to protect U.S. interests

H

hieroglyphics: an ancient form of Egyptian writing that used pictures

history: the study of important events that happened in the past

home rule laws: state laws that provide local governments with a great deal of self-government

Homo sapiens: the term used to identify human beings, which means "thinking men"

I

icon: a sacred painting or sculpture used to decorate a church

impeachment: the process of charging a public officeholder with a crime or misconduct in office so that the person can be removed from office

imperialism: a policy by which a nation extends its control over other lands

indentured servant: one who worked for a specific period of time in the American colonies as payment of a debt

industrialization: the development of large-scale industries and mass-production techniques

industrial unionism: organizing of unskilled and semiskilled factory workers chiefly by the CIO

inference: going beyond the directly stated information and finding a meaning that is only suggested; reading between the lines

information map (or thematic map): a map that gives information on a specific subject

institution: a system that society uses to fill the needs of its people and to teach patterns of behavior

interest group: a group of people who organize for a specific reason

isolationism: national policy or attitude that a nation will do better if it pays more attention to domestic matters rather than to international matters

J

Jacksonian Democracy: an age of reform that roughly paralleled President Andrew Jackson's term in office

Jim Crow laws: racial segregation laws passed in the South during the late nineteenth and early twentieth centuries

judicial review: the power of the Supreme Court to rule on the constitutionality of laws

K

key (or legend): a list that explains the symbols used on a map

Koran: the holy book of Islam based on Allah's messages to Mohammad

L

labor contract: an agreement between management and labor that establishes salaries, terms of employment, working conditions, benefits, duties, responsibilities, and the rights of labor and management

labor market: a term used to describe the availability of jobs

latitude: line that measures distance north and south of the equator

line graph: graph that shows how one or more items of information have changed over time by using a series of connected points

literal understanding: understanding information that is stated directly

location: the exact point on Earth where a place is; can be expressed in degrees of latitude and longitude

logical consistency: the writer's use of sound reasoning in developing an idea

longitude: line that measures distance east and west of the prime meridian

M

main idea: a statement that tells what a whole selection is about

Manifest Destiny: American belief that it was the country's destiny to take over the entire North American continent

map: a representation of some part of Earth and its features on flat paper

market economy: another name for free enterprise where buyers and sellers, not the government, determine prices and output

marketing: the part of business that deals with sales

material culture: the level of tools and technology in a given society

McCarthyism: careless and groundless attacks on people suspected of being communists; associated with Senator McCarthy's anti-communist tactics

medieval: a term used for the Middle Ages

mercantilism: seventeenth-century practice in which the colonies supplied the mother country with raw materials and became a market for manufactured goods

migration: the movement of people from one location to another

mixed economies: an economic system that combines capitalism and socialism

Mohammad: the founder of the religion of Islam

monetary policy: the regulation of the nation's supply of money and credit by the Federal Reserve Board

money: cash and all other assets that can be used to purchase goods and services or to pay debts

monopoly: a market situation in which one person or company sells all of a product or accounts for a large part of the total sales of the product

mortality rate: the rate of deaths in a particular time and place

mosiac: art works created by piecing together colorful bits of glass, stone, or other material

motivation: reasons why a person starts, stops, or continues an activity

muckrakers: writers who exposed corruption in business and politics during the early twentieth century

multiplier effect: the growth in the value of a deposit in a bank when it is, in turn, loaned out to a succession of other banks

N

national debt: the total amount of money owed by the federal government of the United States to its creditors

nationalism: the desire of a certain group of people to have their own nation

Nazis: the political party of Adolf Hitler

neurosis: a personality disorder in which a person is unusually anxious in dealing with others

norms: the normal accepted behavior society expects of a person

O

oligarchy: a type of government in which a small group of people rule

oligopoly: a market situation in which very few sellers account for a large part of the total sales of a product

opinion: a personal belief or feeling that cannot be proved

organization: a group formed for a specific purpose or goal

P

pharaoh: a ruler of ancient Egypt

physical map: a map that shows different geographic features such as mountains, deserts, lakes, and rivers

pictograph: a graph that uses a series of symbols to show an amount or a quantity

pilgrimage: a religious journey to a holy place

plurality: the greatest number of votes in an election

pocket veto: an automatic veto of a bill not signed by the president within ten days of a congressional adjournment

political geography: the study of the relationships among people and nations

political science: the study of the institutions of government and how they work

political system: an institution that organizes power relationships in a society

prime meridian: 0° of longitude that divides Earth into Eastern and Western Hemispheres

productivity: the efficient use of the factors of production to produce goods

Progressive Era: a period of many social and political reforms largely backed by Presidents Theodore Roosevelt, Taft, and Wilson

progressive tax: a tax that takes a larger portion of income as that income increases

protectorate: a weak country controlled by a stronger one

public goods: goods and services the government provides for its citizens

pyramid: a giant stone tomb built for a pharaoh

R

recall: a procedure that permits voters to remove an elected official from office before his or her term is over

referendum: the process by which voters can approve or reject legislation

reform: a movement to improve society

region: an area of land having characteristics that make it different from another area of land

regressive tax: a tax that takes a smaller portion of income as that income increases

representative: one who stands or acts for another through delegated authority

representative democracy: a democracy in which people select delegates or substitutes to represent them

republic: a form of government in which the people elect representatives

revolution: the overthrow of a ruler or government by the governed

role: expected pattern of behavior in a group or in society

S

samurai: Japanese warriors who lived up to a strict code of conduct

scale: a line on a map that shows the relationship between the distance on the map and the actual distance on land

scanning: the practice of rapidly looking over a passage or graphic to find a specific detail

scientific method: the careful use of observation and experimentation to solve scientific problems

secession: the act of a state seceding (leaving) a country to which it belongs

sectionalism: the economic, political, and social differences among the regions of the United States

sequence-of-events: an approach that organizes a series of events in the order in which they happened

sharecropper: a tenant farmer who pays a portion of the crop as rent for the land

shogun: the supreme military ruler in Japan before 1861

simple majority: 50 percent of the votes plus a minimum of one vote

social class: a group of people who share a common economic position in society

social contract: the belief that there is an unwritten agreement between the citizens and their government to protect human rights

Social Darwinism: the theory that the development of society is based on the survival of the fittest

socialism: an economic system that is based on government control of the market

socialization: the way in which a person learns the normal behavior, habits, and beliefs of a society

social stratification: the division of society into classes

society: a group of people with shared values and organized patterns of behavior

sociology: the study of the behavior of groups of people

special-purpose map: a map that uses different colors, patterns, and symbols to give information

stock market: a market where stocks and bonds of corporations are bought and sold

stocks: shares of ownership in a company

strike: a work stoppage by members of a union to force an employer to agree to demands for salaries, terms of employment, or benefits

subpoena: a written order requiring someone to appear in court

suburb: a settlement that lies outside a city but within commuting distance to it

supply: the quantity of goods and services available for sale at all possible prices

supporting details: details that expand on the main idea or make it clearer

T

table: a list of numbers placed in columns and rows to make it easier to make comparisons

technology: methods which make production cheaper and more efficient

theory: a belief that explains an event or a behavior

third party: any U.S. political party that is independent of the two major parties

Third World: developing nations of Asia, Africa, and Latin America, many of which gained their independence after World War II, and were not allied with either superpower

tone: a writer's own bias or opinion about a subject expressed in a piece of writing

topography: the physical features of a land surface, including mountain ranges, plateaus, and lowlands

totalitarianism: an extreme type of dictatorship that controls the political, economic, and social life of a country

trade deficit: an excess of the value of imports over the value of exports; also called unfavorable balance of trade

transfer payments: payments that transfer income from one group of people to another through the tax system

treaties: formal agreements among nations

tyranny: a government in which all power is in the hands of a single ruler

U

United Nations (U.N.): an international organization created in 1945 to promote peace throughout the world

unstated main idea: an idea that is only suggested and not stated directly

urbanization: the growth of large cities, with a population shift away from rural areas

V

values: standards of behavior or beliefs set by a society

vassal: a lord who owed military service to a higher lord

veto: the presidential power to refuse to sign into law a bill that has been approved by Congress; can be overridden by Congress

W

women's suffrage: the right of women to vote

Index